THE PURSUIT OF HAPPINESS IN THE FOUNDING ERA

The Pursuit of Happiness

IN THE FOUNDING ERA

An Intellectual History

CARLI N. CONKLIN

UNIVERSITY OF MISSOURI PRESS
Columbia

Publication of this volume has been supported with a gift from the
Kinder Institute on Constitutional Democracy

Paperback ISBN: 9780826222237

Library of Congress Cataloging-in-Publication Data

Names: Conklin, Carli N., 1975- author.
Title: The pursuit of happiness in the founding era : an intellectual history
    / Carli N. Conklin.
Description: Columbia, Missouri : University of Missouri, 2019. | Series:
    Studies in constitutional democracy | Includes bibliographical references
    and index. |
Identifiers: LCCN 2018043085 (print) | LCCN 2018049476 (ebook) | ISBN
    9780826274274 (e-book) | ISBN 9780826221858 (hardback)
Subjects: LCSH: Constitutional history--United States. | Separation of
    powers--United States | United States. Declaration of Independence. |
    United States. Constitution. | Locke, John, 1632-1704. | Political
    science--Philosophy. | Blackstone, William, 1723-1780. Commentaries on the
    laws of England. | Democracy--United States--History. | BISAC: PHILOSOPHY
    / Political. | HISTORY / United States / Revolutionary Period (1775-1800).
    | LAW / Natural Law.
Classification: LCC KF4541 (ebook) | LCC KF4541 .C553 2019 (print) | DDC
    342.08/5--dc23
LC record available at https://lccn.loc.gov/2018043085

∞™ This paper meets the requirements of the
American National Standard for Permanence of Paper
for Printed Library Materials, Z39.48, 1984.

Typefaces: Bembo and Frutiger

STUDIES IN CONSTITUTIONAL DEMOCRACY

Justin B. Dyer and Jeffrey L. Pasley, Series Editors

The Studies in Constitutional Democracy Series explores the origins and development of American constitutional and democratic traditions, as well as their applications and interpretations throughout the world. The often subtle interaction between constitutionalism's commitment to the rule of law and democracy's emphasis on the rule of the many lies at the heart of this enterprise. Bringing together insights from history and political theory, the series showcases interdisciplinary scholarship that traces constitutional and democratic themes in American politics, law, society, and culture, with an eye to both the practical and theoretical implications.

Previous Titles in Studies in Constitutional Democracy

The Panic of 1819: The First Great Depression
Andrew H. Browning

Lloyd Gaines and the Fight to End Segregation
James W. Endersby and William T. Horner

Aristocracy in America: From the Sketch-Book of a German Nobleman
Francis J. Grund
Edited and with an Introduction by Armin Mattes

From Oligarchy to Republicanism: The Great Task of Reconstruction
Forrest Nabors

John Henry Wigmore and the Rules of Evidence:
The Hidden Origins of Modern Law
Andrew Porwancher

Bureaucracy in America:
The Administrative State's Challenge to Constitutional Government
Joseph Postell

The Myth of Coequal Branches:
Restoring the Constitution's Separation of Functions
David J. Siemers

For my parents, Dr. Keith R. Conklin and Cathy A. Conklin

A father's goodness is higher than the mountain,

A mother's goodness deeper than the sea.

—attributed to a Japanese proverb

CONTENTS

ACKNOWLEDGMENTS

I have had the opportunity to share the ideas at the heart of this work with so many terrific audiences over the years. I would like to thank my wonderful former colleagues at John Brown University, where interdisciplinary engagement and intellectual curiosity are on constant display. It was while teaching legal history and introductory political theory at JBU that I first began asking the key questions at the heart of this work. In a similar vein, I am deeply indebted to the outstanding past and present faculty at the University of Virginia School of Law and Corcoran Department of History, who so willingly shared with me their love for their academic disciplines. For their suggestions on this project, in particular, I would like to thank Barbara E. Armacost, Paul Halliday, and Karen Parshall. Paul Kershaw, Elizabeth Meyer, and Hunter R. Rawlings III contributed much to my understanding of Anglo-Saxon England and the classical world. I will be forever grateful to have had the opportunity to explore this topic under my PhD advisor, Charles W. McCurdy. My special thanks also go out to G. Edward White, whose comments on earlier iterations of this work have been invaluable.

This work benefited from presentations in a variety of academic settings over the years, including the Lehrman American Studies Institute at Princeton University; the Institute for Constitutional History's Summer Research Seminar at George Washington University; the Center for Christian Study in Charlottesville, Virginia; the University of Missouri School of Law; the University of Arkansas–Fayetteville School of Law; Regent University School of Law and Robertson School of Government; Washington University in St. Louis School of Law's Junior Faculty Workshop; the Shawnee Trail Regional Conference on American Politics and Constitutionalism; and the Society of Early Americanists' Religion and Politics in Early America Conference, which was co-sponsored by the John C. Danforth Center in Religion and Politics at Washington University in St. Louis and the Kinder Institute on Constitutional Democracy. Jeffrey A. Brauch, Michelle Cecil, the late Richard Chewning, Shirley Clarke Chewning, Martha Dragich, Justin B. Dyer, Alan Charles Kors, Paul Litton, Stephen M. Sheppard, Richard Skalstad, Bill Wilder, and Donna Wilson are among those who provided insightful feedback and suggestions at earlier stages of this work. I greatly appreciate the work of *Washington University Jurisprudence Review* editor in chief Krista C. McCormack and chief executive articles editor Matthew K. Suess, whose professionalism and careful editorial eye aided me in an earlier article-length exploration of this topic. Although the external reviewers for this current project remain anonymous, I would like to thank them here for the care with which they read this work and for their detailed and incisive comments. My research assistant, Taylor Tutin, proved invaluable in the latter stages of this project. Any errors remain mine, alone.

This project benefited from research leave, funding, and the support of terrific colleagues at the University of Missouri School of Law and Kinder Institute on Constitutional Democracy. Finally, I am grateful to everyone at the University of Missouri Press for their professionalism, patience, humor, and warm collegiality in shepherding the manuscript through to publication. It has been a particular honor to publish this work through the Studies in Constitutional Democracy series.

It is no accident that the names and venues above cut across a wide variety of academic fields and subfields: law, history (including early American history, American legal history, Roman history, Greek history, and Anglo-Saxon history), political theory, the classics, philosophy, theology, and mathematics. The variety is reflective of the multiple-traditions school of the founding era, which is where this work ended, but not where it began. As I began looking into the meaning of the pursuit of happiness in its historical context, I was delighted to find that Thomas Jefferson, John Adams, and Benjamin Franklin inhabited an intellectual world that was invigorating both in its breadth and in its depth. They spoke with ease across academic disciplines and subfields in ways that are, at times, disconcerting to a modern reader and, with our emphasis on specialization, seemingly impossible to emulate. This work therefore relies not only on the writings of the founders and their Enlightenment-era contemporaries, but also on the works of more recent scholars, both those who have dedicated their time and scholarly attention to exploring the depths of a specific field or subfield and those who have dedicated their time and scholarly attention to identifying the places where those fields or subfields connect or overlap. For the former, I am indebted to I. Bernard Cohen, for his illuminating work on the influence of scientific thinking on the founders, in general, and on John Adams, Benjamin Franklin, and Thomas Jefferson, in particular; to Wilfrid Prest and Carol Matthews, whose scholarship has added nuance and depth to historical accounts of the life and legal philosophy of William Blackstone; to Daniel Dreisbach and Carl J. Richard, whose recent works have added compelling detail and complexity to our understanding of how the Bible influenced the founders in their personal lives and their political thought; to Charles Barzun, for his insightful work on the impact of the Scottish Common Sense school on early American legal thought; and to Carl J. Richard (again) for his excellent work on the founders' classical heritage.

The goal of this work is to provide an intellectual history—the history of an idea—in the best sense of the term. Its purpose is, in the words of Thomas Jefferson, "not . . . to invent new ideas altogether" but, instead, to illuminate the intermingling and ultimate convergence of several old ideas at a single place of particular meaning: the pursuit of happiness. I hope you enjoy the journey as much as I have.

THE PURSUIT OF HAPPINESS IN THE FOUNDING ERA

INTRODUCTION

We hold these truths to be self-evident, that all men are created equal, that they are endowed by their Creator with certain unalienable Rights, that among these are Life, Liberty, and the pursuit of Happiness.

—Declaration of Independence (1776)

From 1823 forward, the phrase "pursuit of happiness" appeared in ninety-six United States Supreme Court cases.[1] The pursuit of happiness was used by litigants to argue for everything from the right to privacy to the right to pursue one's chosen occupation, and it was invoked by the Court to uphold the same. *Black's Law Dictionary* cites to that case law as it defines the right to the pursuit of happiness as "[t]he constitutional right to pursue any lawful business or activity that might yield the highest enjoyment, increase one's prosperity, or allow the development of one's faculties as long as it is not inconsistent with others' rights."[2] While this definition reflects how the right to the pursuit of happiness has been cited in Supreme Court case law from the 1820s forward, it does not tell us how the phrase was understood in its historical context.

Historians have long struggled to define the pursuit of happiness as an unalienable right. Most accounts begin in 1689 with John Locke's *Two Treatises of Government*. In *The Second Treatise*, Locke lists the natural rights of "life, liberty, and estate," with "estate" being what we today would call "property." Locke defined "property" in a narrower sense, as that with which man "mixed his labour . . . and thereby makes it his [own]" and, as will be discussed later, in the broader sense of man's natural right to "life, liberty, and estate."[3] Locke's work was widely popular among the founders, in general, and with Jefferson, in particular.[4] The traditional explanation for pursuit of happiness draws on these connections and holds that, when writing the Declaration, Jefferson deliberately mirrored Locke's listing of

unalienable rights, but with one exception: Jefferson omitted Locke's unalienable right of property and included the unalienable right of the pursuit
of happiness instead.

From there, the historical accounts attempt to make sense of the reasons
Jefferson would replace property with the pursuit of happiness. The most
persistent explanation offered is that Jefferson was uncomfortable enough
with slavery to want to avoid perpetuating a property ownership in slaves
by including an unalienable right to property in the Declaration.[5] Yet even
if this explanation is true, it is not complete. Jefferson's discomfort with
slavery may explain why he would omit property from Locke's original
listing. It does not explain why Jefferson would insert the pursuit of happiness in its place.

In attempting to explain the substitution, historians have taken two approaches. The first approach argues that the substitution has substantive
meaning. As discussed more fully in appendix 2, historians adopting this
approach have argued that the pursuit of happiness evokes a synonymous
right to property, the happiness to be found in the acquisition of material
comfort, the happiness to be found in family life, or the Scottish Enlightenment idea of public virtue.[6] But each of these definitions has its difficulties.
The first two definitions articulate various forms of property ownership,
but eighteenth-century rights theorists, including John Locke, articulated
property and the pursuit of happiness as distinct—not synonymous—rights.[7]
As historian Jan Lewis highlights in her work, the third definition of happiness as family life was a concept that did not develop until the nineteenth
century, which would make its application to the Declaration anachronistic.
Finally, the idea of happiness as public virtue, while more in keeping with
eighteenth-century understandings of happiness, omits the placement of
the phrase in the unalienable-rights portion of the Declaration not as a public duty but as an individual and unalienable right. It was not uncommon, at
the time of the Declaration, to view rights and duties in relationship to one
another, with any given right encompassing a corresponding duty. A full
understanding of the pursuit of happiness would need to fully consider both
the public-duty and the private-right implications of the phrase.

The second, and more common, approach to defining the pursuit of happiness has been to conclude that it is a substitution for property that has no
substantive meaning—or, at least, not one that is presently discernible. This
understanding is best articulated by Rufus Choate's 1856 description of the
phrase as one of the Declaration's "glittering . . . generalities";[8] it sounds
pretty and appealing, but it is either too general or too individualized to

have any practical, substantive meaning. This line of thinking suggests that Jefferson inserted the pursuit of happiness into the Declaration not in an attempt to list a substantive unalienable right but instead as an instrument of rhetoric, and it is as an instrument of rhetoric that the phrase does its work. It adds rhythm and beauty to Jefferson's listing of unalienable rights, and if the pursuit of happiness does anything more in the Declaration, it is only to add a sense of undefined idealism to the listing of unalienable rights the Declaration contains.

The pursuit of happiness as a glittering generality is the definition that has most recently taken hold among historians, and it makes sense within a common twenty-first-century understanding of happiness as feeling good. But this definition seems at odds with what we know of Jefferson as a meticulous and deliberate writer and proponent of the rights and duties of man. When forming his list of unalienable rights—those rights that are so important that we obtain them simply by being human and that are so essential to our humanity that we cannot alienate them from our persons—Jefferson selected only a representative three. "Life" is the precondition upon which all other rights were to be exercised. "Liberty" also carries a preconditional weightiness, since, in order to exercise one's rights, one must first be at liberty to do so. But what are we to make of the pursuit of happiness? Why would Jefferson then include a phrase as glib, and as seemingly overly generalized, as the pursuit of happiness in a document that was, in all other respects, a serious and quite particular declaration of man's natural and political rights?

This question becomes more complex when examined in connection with the introductory portion of William Blackstone's *Commentaries on the Laws of England*.[9] The *Commentaries*, published from 1765 to 1769, were a written version of lectures on English common law that Blackstone had been delivering at Oxford University for more than a decade prior. As the Vinerian Chair in Common Law, Blackstone was the first professor to lecture on English law in the English university system. Blackstone's *Commentaries* went on to provide the foundation of late-eighteenth- and nineteenth-century legal education not only in England but also in the British colonies in mainland North America and then the new United States.

In the second section of his introduction to the *Commentaries*, Blackstone argues that God has created laws of nature by which the entire natural world is to be governed. In a fascinating passage on jurisprudence, Blackstone claims that the pursuit of happiness is the primary method by which men can know and then apply the law of nature as it pertains to humans: men can readily "discover . . . what the law of nature directs in every circumstance of life; by considering, what method will tend the most effectually to our own substantial happiness."[10] As will be demonstrated, Blackstone understood happiness to be synonymous with the Greek concept of *eudaimonia*; it evoked a sense of well-being or a state of flourishing that is the result of living a fit or virtuous life. In the words of eighteenth-century dictionary author Samuel Johnson, "fit" is "[c]onvenient; meet; proper; right."[11] It is to be rightly ordered to the law of nature. Rather than being fleeting or temporal, Blackstone described such happiness as "real" and "substantial."[12] As highlighted in dictionary definitions of the time, to be real indicated that such happiness was "not fictitious; not imaginary; [but] true; genuine." In other words, it was not a mere perception of happiness or sense of feeling good but a state that reflected reality. It was substantial in that it pertained to the substance or essence of the thing—in this case, the substance or essence of what it meant to be fully human.[13] Thus, for Blackstone, to pursue happiness was to pursue a fit or rightly ordered life, one that was in harmony with what is true or real, as expressed within the law of nature as it pertains to man. In fact, when revising the *Commentaries* for the eighth edition, which was published in 1778 just prior to his death, Blackstone seems at pains to make this point even more clearly by revising the phrase to read "That man should pursue his own true and substantial happiness," a phrasing that mirrored his descriptions of happiness as "real" and "substantial" from the first edition of this portion of the *Commentaries* forward.[14]

Knowing of Jefferson's antipathy for Blackstone (Jefferson famously referred to Blackstone as a "honeyed" Tory and viewed Blackstone's *Commentaries* as overly simplistic in comparison with the works of Sir Edward Coke),[15] it does not seem, at first glance, that Jefferson would have shared Blackstone's understanding of the pursuit of happiness when Jefferson included the phrase in the Declaration. Yet the framing of the phrase in both works suggests otherwise. Blackstone's discussion of the pursuit of happiness was included in the second section of his introduction, titled "Of the Nature of Laws in General." His discussion of the pursuit of happiness was both preceded by and informed by his discussion of those laws, a contextual placement that we see mirrored in the Declaration.[16] In both texts, the authors sought to summarize their understanding of the relationship between the Creator, nature, man, and law. In both texts, pursuit of happiness played a prominent role in that discussion.

The work that follows then seeks to determine the eighteenth-century legal meaning of pursuit of happiness by undertaking two parallel investigations. The first investigation will explore William Blackstone's use of the pursuit of happiness and the work it performs in his *Commentaries on the Laws of England*. The second investigation will explore the pursuit of happiness and the work it performs in the Declaration of Independence. Each investigation sets aside twenty-first-century understandings of happiness and pursuit of happiness and, instead, adopts a methodology that focuses on understanding historical actors and ideas in their own context. This methodology is advocated for by historian G. E. White in his work "Recovering the World of the Marshall Court."[17]

According to White, early American legal historians (particularly those studying the Marshall Court) all too frequently encounter two problems: First, if modern mind-sets and philosophies include a "conscious repudiation" of previous mind-sets and philosophies, historians may fail to understand "how a sensible actor" could hold those mind-sets and philosophies with which they, themselves, disagree. Second, if the conscious repudiation is strong enough, legal historians will then look for "other 'causes' to explain the motivation or actions of these earlier legal or judicial figures," missing the actual motivations and actions of these earlier figures as a result.[18]

To remedy this problem, White urges legal historians first to reject the notion that earlier ways of thinking are necessarily inferior to later ways of thinking and then "to engage in a suspension of contemporary belief" while conducting their research. In other words, White urges legal historians to take the past on its own terms, however incomprehensible those terms may be to present-day sensibilities, and to adopt a methodology that focuses on understanding historical actors and ideas within their own context.[19]

It is this methodology I adopted as I explored the meaning of the pursuit of happiness as it was used first by Blackstone in his *Commentaries on the Laws of England* and then in the Declaration of Independence by the American founders. This exploration suggests that, instead of being a mere substitution for Locke's property or a glittering generality, the pursuit of happiness in the Declaration has a clear and distinct meaning, and it is the same meaning as outlined by Blackstone when he included a discussion and definition of the phrase in his *Commentaries on the Laws of England*.

An investigation into the historical context of each document does not reveal a specific reference proving that the founders intended to evoke Blackstone's understanding of the pursuit of happiness when they included the phrase in the Declaration. It does not reveal a reference to Blackstone's

pursuit of happiness in early drafts of the Declaration, in the edits that followed, or in Thomas Jefferson's or John Adams's later reflections on the
text. Instead, this investigation reveals something even more compelling,
given the intellectual diversity of the founders who edited and then approved the Declaration of Independence and its inclusion of the pursuit of
happiness as an unalienable right: each of four key strands of thought that
were prevalent at the American founding—English law and legal theory,
the history and philosophy of classical antiquity, Christianity, and the Scottish Enlightenment's focus on Newtonian science—had, at their core, the
same understanding of epistemology or ways of knowing that Blackstone
described when he defined the pursuit of happiness in the introductory portion of his *Commentaries*. The pursuit of happiness, as used in both works,
refers to man's ability to know the law of nature as it pertains to man and
man's unalienable right to then choose to pursue a life of virtue or, in other
words, a life lived in harmony with those natural law principles.[20] The result
would be *eudaimonia*, or man's own real and substantial happiness.

★ ★ ★

This exploration of the pursuit of happiness will unfold in three parts. Part
1 will begin with a discussion of Blackstone's definition of the pursuit of
happiness and the placement and purpose of that phrase in the *Commentaries*.
Specifically, it will describe Blackstone's inclusion of the pursuit of happiness in his *Commentaries* as a science of jurisprudence by which his students
could know and then rightly apply the first principles of the common law
in their future work as lawyers, judges, jurors, or members of Parliament
(MPs). Second, it will demonstrate that Blackstone was not alone in defining the pursuit of happiness in this way but was simply articulating an
understanding of the pursuit of happiness that was common among the latitudinarian Anglican theologians and Scottish Common Sense philosophers
of his day. Part 1 will conclude with an exploration of Blackstone's goal of
using the pursuit of happiness as a means of improving and perfecting the
English common law and the emphasis he placed on examples from history
and architecture to communicate that goal.

Part 2 will explore the pursuit of happiness as it was used in the Declaration of Independence. First, it will describe the placement of the phrase
in the Declaration, the treatment of pursuit of happiness throughout the
drafting of the document, and its context within the Declaration's larger
structure. Second, it will explore the intellectual backdrop of the Declaration, with an emphasis on four key strands of thought that were prevalent

during the founding era: English law and legal theory, the history and philosophy of classical antiquity, Christianity, and the Scottish Enlightenment's focus on Newtonian science. It will explore how Thomas Jefferson, John Adams, and Benjamin Franklin—the initial drafters of the Declaration—intermingled these strands in their own political, natural, and moral philosophies. Next, it will demonstrate that the pursuit of happiness is defined at the place where the four strands converge, which is in an understanding of the natural world governed by first principles, most frequently described in the founding era as fundamental principles or the laws of nature and of nature's God. Part 2 will conclude with a discussion of how Jefferson, Adams, and Franklin, like Blackstone, ultimately understood the pursuit of happiness within the Greek concept of *eudaimonia*, the well-being or human flourishing that results from a life lived in harmony with those laws.

While parts 1 and 2 provide evidence that Blackstone and the founders understood the pursuit of happiness to have the same Enlightenment-era meaning, part 3 will explore how that meaning had two distinct applications in the *Commentaries* and the Declaration. First, it will highlight Blackstone's and the founders' shared definition of the pursuit of happiness. Second, it will explore their dual applications of the phrase as a private right and a public duty. It will begin by describing the private-right use of the phrase, as exemplified by the founders' inclusion of the pursuit of happiness as one of the individual and unalienable rights listed in the Declaration and Blackstone's claim that the law of eternal justice is "inseparably interwoven" with the happiness of each individual. Then it will discuss the public-duty applications of the phrase. This public-duty usage was exemplified by Blackstone's belief that the pursuit of happiness as a science of jurisprudence would enable future lawyers, judges, jurors, and MPs to conduct their legal work in harmony with the first principles of the English common law—and his insistence that future lawmakers had a duty to determine and apply the law within that framework. It is also reflected in the founders' repeated statements, both before and after the Declaration of Independence, that to secure the happiness of the people is a proper end of good governance. Part 3 will then explore how the private-right and public-duty applications of the pursuit of happiness overlapped, both through the founders' discussion of virtue and through Blackstone's and the founders' belief that the public duty of the pursuit of happiness both informed and limited its private pursuit. Finally, part 3 will conclude by putting theory into practice with an exploration of how, despite their diverging political opinions, William

Blackstone and Thomas Jefferson utilized the pursuit of happiness as a science of jurisprudence in remarkably similar ways in their efforts to improve and perfect the criminal law of England and the new United States.

Readers who are interested in historians' efforts to understand Blackstone as a legal thinker and the *Commentaries* as a legal text may want to explore the historiographical overview of Blackstone and the *Commentaries* that I have included in appendix 1. Readers who would like to know more about previous histories of the pursuit of happiness in the Declaration of Independence may be interested in the historiographical discussion included in appendix 2.

In the chapters ahead, I will refer often to Blackstone's *Commentaries on the Laws of England*, Introduction, Section the Second, "Of the Nature of Laws in General." The full text of this portion of Blackstone's *Commentaries* is included in appendix 3, with Blackstone's edits in editions 2–8 of the *Commentaries* marked. Appendixes 4–6 include reconstructions of the Declaration of Independence to highlight how it was altered—and what stayed the same—throughout the drafting process.

This work preserves the punctuation, spelling, and grammar of the original sources, without the addition of [*sic*] to highlight inconsistencies with modern spelling and language usage. Any changes to the original sources have been marked.

The *Chicago Manual of Style* suggests the use of quotation marks for direct quotations and for special words or phrases. To follow these guidelines with the pursuit of happiness would make it unclear when quotation marks were used to indicate the pursuit of happiness as an idea (a special phrase) versus when quotation marks were used to indicate how the pursuit of happiness appeared in a specific text (a direct quotation). To promote clarity, this work places the pursuit of happiness in quotation marks only when necessary to draw the reader's attention to the details of how the words appeared in a specific text.

The drafts of the Declaration of Independence include "the pursuit of happiness" with no capitalization. During the final printing of the Declaration, many words were capitalized, resulting in a final reading of "the pursuit of Happiness." This variance in capitalization has been preserved in direct quotations from these documents.

PART I.

The Pursuit of Happiness in
Blackstone's *Commentaries on the Laws of England*

CHAPTER 1

Placement and Purpose:
A New Science of Jurisprudence

> For [the Creator] has so intimately connected, so inseparably interwoven the laws of eternal justice with the happiness of each individual, that the latter cannot be attained but by observing the former; and, if the former be punctually obeyed, it cannot but induce the latter. In consequence of which mutual connection of justice and human felicity, he has not perplexed the law of nature with a multitude of abstracted rules and precepts, referring merely to the fitness or unfitness of things, as some have vainly surmised; but has graciously reduced the rule of obedience to this one paternal precept, "that man should "pursue his own happiness." This is the foundation of what we call ethics, or natural law.

—William Blackstone, *Commentaries on the Laws of England* (1765–69)

On October 25, 1758, what would later become the introduction to Blackstone's *Commentaries on the Laws of England* was read aloud at the beginning of the Vinerian lectures on English law at Oxford University.[1] As was made clear in his first Vinerian lecture, Blackstone had a vision for reforming English legal education. The key question that informed his task was the question of the knowledge and structure of the law itself. Was the English law, as Blackstone contemporary Sir William Jones asked in 1781, "merely an unconnected series of decrees and ordinances," or was it "a *Science*" that should "claim an exalted rank in the empire of *reason* . . . founded on principle"?[2] If the former, the English law was suitable for study in its particulars but perhaps had no larger significance. If the latter, then the English law should be viewed as an interrelated "great system of jurisprudence, like that of the Universe," which "had to consist 'of many subordinate systems,' all 'connected by nice links and beautiful dependencies' and each 'reducible to a few plain *elements*.'"[3] In other words, if the English law was but a series of oral or written positive law pronouncements disconnected from any larger

principles or underlying foundations, then the only thing that could be
expected of English legal education was experience in the law through the
apprenticeship system, which was already occurring at the Inns of Court.[4]
If, on the other hand, the English law was "a great system of jurisprudence"
that had been built upon a natural law foundation, and if the existing positive law had been formed on the basis of these larger principles, then English legal education ought to begin with the study of law as a science and
a system or, in other words, with a study of these foundational principles.

In his *Commentaries*, Blackstone argued well for the latter:

> [Law is] a science, which distinguishes the criterions of right and wrong;
> which teaches to establish the one, and prevent, punish, or redress the other;
> which employs in it's theory the noblest faculties of the soul, and exerts in
> it's practice the cardinal virtues of the heart; a science, which is universal in
> it's use and extent, accommodated to each individual, yet comprehending
> the whole community; that a science like this should have ever been deemed
> unnecessary to be studied in an university, is matter of astonishment and
> concern. Surely, if it were not before an object of academical knowledge, it
> was high time to make it one; and to those who can doubt the propriety of
> it's reception among us (if any such there be) we may return an answer in
> their own way; that ethics are confessedly a branch of academical learning,
> and Aristotle *himself has said*, speaking of the laws of his own country, that
> jurisprudence or the knowledge of those laws is the principal and most perfect
> branch of ethics.[5]

"The best way to learn any science," stated eighteenth-century theologian and scholar Isaac Watts, "is to begin with a regular system, or a short
and plain scheme of that science well drawn up into a narrow compass."
The science of law envisioned by Blackstone was—or, as he advocated,
ought to be—governed by a system in this Latin sense of the word: a
systema, or a "scheme which unites many things in order."[6] The common
law, as it had developed over centuries, was, to Blackstone, an "ordered
assemblage of principles and doctrines." It was a single system, capable of
being "cultivated, methodized, and explained in a course of academical
lectures."[7]

In promoting an education in English law at the university level, Blackstone saw himself as following the example of Roman jurists, who had attempted "to imprint on [students'] tender minds an early knowledge of the

laws and constitutions of their country." Although Roman civil and canon law had been studied in the English universities for centuries, this was not so for the English law. Blackstone lamented that the laws and constitution of England were not included in the general course of university study at Oxford and Cambridge, as the Roman civil law was on the Continent, and sought to prompt his fellow Englishmen to obtain "a competent knowledge in that science, which is to be the guardian of his natural rights and the rule of his civil conduct." Since such study was in its "infancy" and new to mid-eighteenth-century English university students, Blackstone felt the burden of defending his position and therefore wrote the introduction to his *Commentaries* as an apologetic for the study of the English common law, the ramifications of neglecting such study, and the need to provide English law as a course of study for all English university students. He believed it was "an undeniable position, that a competent knowledge of the laws of that society, in which we live, is the proper accomplishment of every gentleman and scholar; an highly useful, I had almost said essential, part of liberal and polite education."[8]

Thus, from the beginning of his work, Blackstone viewed himself as continuing in a long tradition of university-level law teaching that had thrived on the Continent, and needed to be redirected, in England, away from the civil law and toward the English common law. Blackstone was enthusiastic about both the subject of law and the students who would sit in on his lectures. In terms of his subject, the common law of England, he argued strongly that the English system of law was superior to the civil law system of the Continent and that England was governed by a "system of laws" that made it "perhaps the only [land] in the universe, in which political or civil liberty is the very end and scope of the constitution." Blackstone believed that England's "admirable system of laws" had been "built upon the soundest foundations, and approved by the experience of the ages," and he wanted to pass those foundations on to the university student population. While affirming the "written reason" of the Roman civil law, Blackstone was most concerned with teaching the English university students about their "own immemorial customs, or the sanctions of an English Parliament."[9]

Blackstone's emphasis on both the layperson and the aspiring lawyer understanding the law was instrumental to his ultimate goal of English law reform. Blackstone believed that all university students, not only aspiring lawyers who would later train at the Inns of Court, should have an acquaintance with the law, to the extent possible given their varying conditions, fortunes, and degrees of leisure. In an attempt to make a legal education compelling to those university students who did not aspire to careers in law, Blackstone appealed to their interests. He stated that gentlemen should seek learning in the law in order to better understand the law of property (which governed their own concerns), to serve properly on a jury, and to carry out "legal and effectual justice" in the role of a magistrate. He especially emphasized such education for future MPs. Parliament had the ability to pass statutes that would affirm, disaffirm, or alter the common law. Therefore, Blackstone ascribed to MPs especially a high sense of duty in improving and preserving the laws of England, describing their role as follows: "They are the guardians of the English constitution; the makers, repealers, and interpreters of the English laws; delegated to watch, to check, and to avert every dangerous innovation, to propose, to adopt, and to cherish any solid and well-weighed improvement; bound by every tie of nature, of honour, and of religion, to transmit that constitution and those laws to their posterity, amended if possible, at least without any derogation."[10]

Blackstone also appealed to university students by laying a challenge before them. He argued that "the science of legislation" was "the noblest and most difficult of any" of the sciences and that the common law of England had suffered from "the defective education" of the English lawmakers: "[I]t's symmetry has been destroyed, it's proportions distorted, and it's majestic simplicity exchanged for specious embellishments and fantastic novelties." In fact, Blackstone agreed with Sir Edward Coke that it was Parliament's uneducated alterations to the common law that had led to "almost all the perplexed questions, almost all the niceties, intricacies, and delays" of the English law in the first place.[11] Since the majority of MPs had attended Cambridge or Oxford in the mid-eighteenth century,[12] and could be expected to continue to do so in the years to come, it would be particularly effective for future MPs to be trained in law at the university level.

If Blackstone was hard on the gentlemen who might one day serve as lawmakers in Parliament, he was even more so on the members of the nobility who might one day become judges. Blackstone believed that judges, even more than MPs, had the power to guide the development of the common law, for good or for ill. The decisions of superior judges, Blackstone argued, were "final, decisive, irrevocable: no appeal, no correction, not even a review can be had." Blackstone believed the nobility had been granted entry into the position of judge because they alone had the means to obtain the education in law necessary for proper fulfillment of the judicial role. He did not mince words in his charge to the nobility regarding their duty to obtain a legal education, which would then enable them to judge rightly: "[I]gnorance of the laws of the land hath ever been esteemed dishonourable, in those who are entrusted by their country to maintain, to administer, and to amend them."[13]

Blackstone's charge to his students shows how strongly he believed in his first means of law reform, which was the inclusion of an education in English common law at the university level. Blackstone's second means of reform was to include in that education instruction in a particularly English science of jurisprudence or theory of law. That theory of law was embodied in Blackstone's understanding of the pursuit of happiness. To understand Blackstone's push for a particularly English law and jurisprudence, we must first consider what he was pushing back against: a long tradition of teaching Roman emperor Justinian's *Corpus Juris Civilis* and Scholastic reasoning in English legal education.

Justinian's *Corpus Juris Civilis*, and the Scholastic method of jurisprudence that was taught alongside it, heavily emphasized deductive, syllogistic reasoning, which Blackstone believed to be the cause of all of the complexities and inconsistencies in human law. Blackstone attempted to depart from both Justinian and the Scholastics in his assertion that the Creator had made the path to knowledge of the law of nature open to every man through the pursuit of happiness. To more fully understand that departure, an overview of Justinian and Scholastic jurisprudence is helpful.

Emperor Justinian ruled the eastern portion of the Roman Empire from 527 to 565.[14] In addition to seeking to unify the Roman Empire under one orthodox Christian faith, Justinian also sought to unify the empire under one law. Justinian believed that, as emperor, his task was to promote justice.[15] To that end, and almost immediately after becoming emperor, Justinian appointed a commission of legal scholars to clarify the Roman law and bring it up to date. The ten-person commission worked almost as speedily as Justinian as they combed through texts, "removing needless repetitions or contradictions, bringing passages up to date," all toward their main goal of "working out an orderly arrangement" of Roman law.[16]

Within two years, Justinian appointed a second commission, whose task was to "delete, abridge, harmonize, collate, update, and clarify [legal] texts, drawn from some 2,000 books written by some thirty-nine different authorities" and then distill them into a single text.[17] The *Digest* that resulted was "an anthology of extracts from the writings of the great jurists," which included both references to the original sources and "substantive changes . . . necessary" to bring the law up to date.[18] In this way, the *Digest* not only compiled but also harmonized the law. Finally, Justinian ordered the creation of the *Institutes*, a distillation of the Roman law into "basic principles" for the beginning student of law.[19]

Justinian's undertaking harmonized and distilled the main principles of the Roman law, addressed the legal necessities of the day, and gave new authority to Justinian himself, as his work replaced prior legal texts. All three parts together (the *Code*, the *Digest*, and the *Institutes*) formed a "self-sufficient whole" and came to be known as the *Corpus Juris Civilis*, or "the body of the Civil Law," a name that distinguished Justinian's work from the church's canon law.[20]

Justinian advocated for the study of law in the Roman Empire and began the *Institutes* with a charge "to the young desirous of legal knowledge," claiming that the laws they were about to study in the *Code* were a picture of "lucid harmony" free from "that which is unnecessary or erroneous."[21] His edict for the creation of the *Digest*, although lengthy, is reproduced here, as it provides insight into the status of the Roman law at the time of Justinian's emperorship and his plans for creating a harmonized collection of that law:

> [S]ince there is nothing to be found in all things so worthy of attention as the authority of the law, which properly regulates all affairs both divine and human and expels all injustice: We have found the entire arrangement of the law which has come down to us from the foundation of the City of Rome and the times of Romulus, to be so confused that it is extended to an infinite length and is not within the grasp of human capacity; and hence We were first induced to begin by examining what had been enacted by former most venerated princes, to correct their constitutions, and make them more easily understood; to the end that being included in a single Code, and having had removed all that is superfluous in resemblance and all iniquitous discord, they may afford to all men the ready assistance of their true meaning.
>
> After having concluded this work and collected it all in a single volume under Our illustrious name, raising Ourself above small and comparatively insignificant matters, We have hastened to attempt the most complete and thorough amendment of the entire law, to collect and revise the whole body of Roman jurisprudence, and to assemble in one book the scattered treatises of so many authors; which no one else has heretofore ventured to hope for or to expect . . .
>
> Therefore We order you [Tribonian] to read and revise the books relating to the Roman law drawn up by the jurists of antiquity, upon whom the most

venerated princes conferred authority to write and interpret the same; so that from these all the substance may be collected, and, as far as may be possible, there shall remain no laws either similar to or inconsistent with one another, but that there may be compiled from them a summary which will take the place of all.[22]

Justinian believed that the content of the *Corpus Juris Civilis* was grounded in "natural laws which are followed by all nations alike, deriving from divine providence, remain[ing] always constant and immutable." He viewed the work as "a statement of universal principles of justice" and hoped that it would "be the epitome of human justice according to God's guidance" for years to come.[23] His hope was realized in part. Perhaps one of the greatest consequences of Justinian's work was how it brought together, in one set of texts, the history of Roman law and preserved it for future generations.[24] In the centuries that followed, governing authorities in the West continually looked to the ideas set forth in the Roman law and articulated in the *Corpus Juris Civilis* as both applicable and authoritative.[25] The *Corpus Juris Civilis* was then rediscovered in a piecemeal process that lasted throughout the eleventh and twelfth centuries.[26] Its rediscovery coincided with the founding of universities on the European Continent. It was this law content, along with the Roman canon law, that was taught at the university level, both on the Continent and in England, throughout the Middle Ages. The method of jurisprudence that was taught alongside the Roman law was that of the Scholastics.

Scholasticism, a system of reasoning based on deductive reasoning, was the predominant method of teaching jurisprudence (theory or philosophy of law) and epistemology (a theory of knowledge or understanding) within the medieval university system. It had prevailed in the English university system since the days of St. Thomas Aquinas, who himself drew upon the works of Aristotle.[27] Scholasticism was also the methodology adopted by the Roman Catholic clergy.

Blackstone viewed the Scholastic tradition, like he viewed the Roman Catholic version of Christianity, as unnecessarily complex and ultimately unknowable by the layperson—reliant upon trained professionals, priests, or lawyers schooled in the Scholastic tradition to identify first principles and their proper applications. He decried the complexity of the Roman Scholastic jurisprudence, not only because it took epistemology out of the hands of the layperson, but also because he believed that it was the undue complexity of the Scholastic method of jurisprudence that had led to the inconsistencies in the common law. Blackstone argued for a simpler science, emphasizing that principles of law could be discovered even without "a chain of metaphysical disquisitions" or "the due exertion of right reason." Blackstone's desire for a simpler epistemology and jurisprudence is made clear in the introduction to his *Commentaries*:

> But if the discovery of these first principles of the law of nature depended only upon the due exertion of right reason, and could not otherwise be attained than by a chain of metaphysical disquisitions, mankind would have wanted some inducement to have quickened their inquiries, and the greater part of the world would have rested content in mental indolence, and ignorance it's inseparable companion. As, therefore, the creator is a being not only of infinite *power,* and *wisdom,* but also of infinite *goodness,* he has been pleased so to contrive the constitution and frame of humanity, that we should want no other prompter to enquire after and pursue the rule of right, but only our own self-love, that universal principle of action. For he has so intimately connected, so inseparably interwoven the laws of eternal justice with the happiness of each individual, that the latter cannot be attained but by observing the former; and, if the former be punctually obeyed, it cannot but induce the latter. In consequence of which mutual connection of justice and human felicity, he has not perplexed the law of nature with a multitude of abstracted rules and precepts, referring merely to the fitness or unfitness of things, as some have vainly surmised; but has graciously reduced the rule of obedience to this one paternal precept, "that man should "pursue his own happiness." This is the foundation of what we call ethics, or natural law. For the several articles into which it is branched in our systems, amount to no more than demonstrating, that this or that action tends to man's real happiness, and therefore very justly concluding that the performance of it is a part of the law of nature; or, on the other hand, that this or that action is destructive of man's real happiness, and therefore that the law of nature forbids it.[28]

Blackstone's arguments against "a chain of metaphysical disquisitions" or "the due exertion of right reason" as the means to discerning the natural law are indicative of the anti-Aristotelian sentiment present in the English universities during his years of study.[29] Aristotle's method of scientific reasoning involved logical, syllogistic deduction of law "from first principles." The problem with syllogistic reasoning from first principles was that the first principles themselves could not be proved, since "other more fundamental principles must lie behind them to serve as the premises for that reasoning." To Blackstone's way of thinking, this led to endless abstract pursuits in attempting to define first principles and a multiplicity of complexities and incoherencies in outcome. Aristotle himself seemed to acknowledge as much when he argued for a more practical form of reasoning by induction, which drew knowledge of first principles from practical experience. Such principles would not be proved by logical syllogisms. "Instead, they are self-evident."[30]

As suggested in his discussion of the "fitness" of things, Blackstone was influenced by Aristotle's more practical form of reasoning from experience. Blackstone wanted to move away from the metaphysical form of Scholastic reasoning that had prevailed in England even after the Protestant Reformation and toward a more Anglican jurisprudence that would be accessible to the layperson and broadly applicable to English law. In addition, Blackstone thought that, in contrast to Scholasticism, this more English style of jurisprudence would be better suited to the English universities, which he wanted to see distinguished from universities on the Continent.

The university system on the European Continent had begun in 1088 with the founding of the first university at Bologne and then a university in Paris, each of which had its own model of education. Oxford was formed more than a century later. Where European universities, on the model of Bologne, "came to focus on professional training in law and medicine," the English universities of Cambridge and Oxford were founded on the model of Paris and were "devoted primarily to philosophy and theology," which involved education in "the canon law of the church [for the clergy] and [in] the civil or Roman law which trained servants for the state."[31]

Scholasticism had prevailed throughout the universities when both England and the Continent were under the authority of the Roman Catholic Church. King Henry VIII's decision to remove England from the authority of the Roman Catholic Church in 1534 had ramifications not only for English politics and the established church but also for English education and law. After the Reformation in England, university education was effectively limited to Anglicans, as Oxford required its students to affirm the Anglican Thirty-Nine Articles and Cambridge required its graduates to do the same.[32] Henry VIII eradicated the canon law, emphasizing theology as taught directly from the holy scriptures. Students began to study both Hebrew and Greek, so as to read the Old and New Testaments in their original languages, eliminating any corruption that might come by way of translation. A focus on classical authors added Latin to the curriculum as well.[33]

In spite of these curricular changes, the traditional method of teaching survived, although with significant criticism. The English university emphasis on teaching the Roman civil law, and the absence of teaching on English common law, also remained. In contrast, universities on the Continent gave their own law, the Roman civil law, a place of primary position and offered the study of Roman law not only for legal practitioners but also as part of the broader educational program for laypersons.[34]

Edward Gibbon's time at Oxford provides us with insight into mid-eighteenth-century views of the education Oxford then offered—an educational framework that Blackstone would push back against. Gibbon attended Oxford in 1752 for approximately a year, shortly before Blackstone began lecturing on English law. Gibbon claimed that "the English universities were trapped in the medieval past," unaffected by the ideas and innovations of the Enlightenment. Gibbon wanted to see something more Protestant, and more enlightened, in his studies. "The Arts," Gibbon stated, "are *supposed* to include the liberal knowledge of Philosophy and literature; but I am informed that some tattered shreds of the old Logic and Metaphysics compose the exercises for a Batchelor and Master's degree." Instead of Scholastic logic and metaphysical discourse, what Gibbon really wanted to study was the "new philosophy of Locke and Hume," but it was "altogether absent from the Oxbridge curriculum."[35]

Gibbon's comments about the outdated education he encountered at Oxford would not have surprised Blackstone, who sought to reform English-law teaching and jurisprudence at Oxford during the mid-eighteenth century. Cambridge had begun to depart from this older model—and its Scholastic foundation—when, in an eighteenth-century curricular reform, it began offering John Locke and Isaac Newton alongside the more traditional study of the classics; Oxford had been more hesitant to change. Blackstone knew that, both for aspiring lawyers and for gentlemen who wished to have a basic understanding of the law, legal education at Oxford had little to offer.[36] Roman civil law and the canon law had prevailed at Oxford since the mid-twelfth century, while training in the English common law remained available only through apprenticeship training in one of England's professional legal societies, known collectively as the Inns of Court. Thus, the path for an aspiring English lawyer was first to complete general studies at the university level and then, through apprenticeship, to begin studies in law.[37]

Blackstone began to change this outdated model in 1753, when he delivered his first lectures on English law at Oxford University. That same year,

Oxford received a bequest that led to the establishment of the Vinerian Professorship in English Law, the first university professorship created specifically for the purpose of instruction in the common law. Blackstone was named to the Vinerian Professorship and, in 1758, began delivering on a routine basis the lectures on English common law that he had first given five years prior. These lectures transformed English legal education and formed the substantive and organizational framework for his *Commentaries*.[38]

When Blackstone began his English-law lectures in 1753, future lawyers had long been gaining experience with the body of English law in the existing apprenticeship system at the Inns of Court. They had the benefit of earlier texts on English law, including Christopher St. Germain's widely popular *Doctor and Student* (1518) and Sir Matthew Hale's *Analysis of the Law* (1713), both of which seem to have significantly influenced the structure and content of the *Commentaries*.[39] But future lawyers did not yet have training in the English law at the university level. Blackstone decried the way in which this apprenticeship model urged future lawyers to place practice before theory and thus to begin "at the wrong end." He expressed great concern for the future of a lawyer trained in this manner: "[I]f he be uninstructed in the elements and first principles upon which the rule of practice is founded, the least variation from established precedents will totally distract and bewilder him: *ita lex scripta est* [so the law is written] is the utmost his knowledge will arrive at; he must never aspire to form, and seldom expect to comprehend, any arguments drawn *a priori* [from the former], from the spirit of the laws and the natural foundations of justice."[40]

To remedy this lack, Blackstone argued that a university-level education in English jurisprudence—an education in how to know and apply the first principles of the law—must precede apprenticeship at the Inns of Court. He argued, "The advantages that might result to the science of the law itself, when a little more attended to in these seats of knowledge, perhaps would be very considerable." Specifically, Blackstone believed that, as learned men turned their attention to the study of law, they would lend themselves to a type of work reminiscent of Justinian's law reforms but specifically suited to the law of England: "[I]mproving it's method, retrenching it's superfluities, and reconciling the little contrarieties, which the practice of many centuries will necessarily create in any human system: a task, which those who are deeply employed in business, and the more active scenes of the profession, can hardly condescend to engage in."[41]

Blackstone believed that the English law was a coherent system based on fundamental principles that could be known by man. The fact that the English law as it existed at the time of the *Commentaries* was, in some ways, out of sync with those fundamental principles in no way invalidated either the existence of those principles or the natural coherency of the law. Neither did it preclude future lawmakers and judges from being able to rightly discern and apply those principles in the English common-law system. Instead, the existing inconsistencies in the law provided support for Blackstone's argument that the study of English law, as a system, needed to be coupled with an English science of jurisprudence. If errors and confusion had made their way into the English law, this was to be expected, due to a long history of English reception of the Roman civil law and canon law and due to the unnecessary complexity of the Scholastic method of jurisprudence that had prevailed in the English universities. Blackstone argued for a simpler science of jurisprudence. That simpler science of jurisprudence was the pursuit of happiness.

In the introduction to his *Commentaries*, Blackstone argued strongly for the pursuit of happiness as the primary method of English jurisprudence. He began his jurisprudential discussion with this definition of law, which drew upon prominent philosophical, religious, and scientific ideas of the day: "Law, in it's most general and comprehensive sense, signifies a rule of action; and is applied indiscriminately to all kinds of action, whether animate, or inanimate, rational or irrational. Thus we say, the laws of motion, of gravitation, of optics, or mechanics, as well as the laws of nature and of nations. And it is that rule of action, which is prescribed by some superior, and which the inferior is bound to obey."[42]

As will be discussed more fully in part 2, Isaac Newton described these rules of action or principles that governed the natural world as "laws of nature," and Blackstone adopted this same phrasing in his *Commentaries*.[43] In his discussion here, Blackstone appears to be borrowing from his Anglican predecessor Richard Hooker, who himself drew upon both sixteenth-century English legal theorist Christopher St. Germain and thirteenth-century Scholastic St. Thomas Aquinas.[44] So where Newton described the laws that govern the natural world as the "laws of nature," Hooker, in *Of the Laws of Ecclesiastical Polity* (1593), described those same laws as "nature's law." Hooker then distinguished nature's law from six other types of law. The most important for our purposes are the eternal law of God, to which all other law, including nature's law, must comport; the law of reason, which is nature's law as it pertains to man; positive law, or law made by humans;

and divine law, or the holy scriptures. Blackstone described nature's law as it pertains to man not as Hooker's "law of reason" but as the "law of nature" and, later in his *Commentaries*, as "natural law."[45] He then used "divine law" or the synonymous terms "law of God," "law of revelation," and "revealed law" to refer to the divine law. Like Hooker, Blackstone used the term "positive law" for man-made law. He then used the similarly worded "laws of eternal justice" for Hooker's overarching eternal law of God, with which all other law—including the laws of nature, law of nature, law of revelation, divine law, and positive law—must comport.

What are we to make of Blackstone's discussion here? It is a fascinating mixture of Hooker and Newton, each of whom drew upon earlier legal philosophers and each of whom was influential in eighteenth-century legal thought. Furthermore, the philosophy of law that Blackstone outlines in the introduction to his *Commentaries* remarkably mirrors the legal philosophy of his eighteenth-century Genevan contemporary Jean-Jacques Burlamaqui, whose work *The Principles of Natural and Politic Law* (1747) contained not only a theory of natural law but also a theory of natural jurisprudence, which included among its methods the pursuit of happiness.

According to Blackstone, "[W]hen the supreme being formed the universe, and created matter out of nothing, he impressed certain principles upon that matter, from which it can never depart, and without which it would cease to be." These certain principles are the laws of nature. To Blackstone, the laws of nature that governed inanimate and animate but irrational creation were no different in source or in purpose from the law of nature that governed animate rational creation—mankind. In either case, law remained a "rule of action, which is prescribed by some superior, and which the inferior is bound to obey." Man, like the rest of creation, "must necessarily be subject to the laws of his creator, for he is entirely a dependent being." Because man "depends absolutely upon his maker for every thing, it is necessary that he should in all points conform to his maker's will," which Blackstone termed "the law of nature."[46]

Yet Blackstone specifically separates out mankind from the rest of creation, both in his discussion and in his alternate phrasing of the "laws of nature" and the "law of nature." Blackstone's distinction here is both incredibly important and of little consequence. It is of little consequence in that, as his discussion highlights, the law of nature is simply that portion of the laws of nature that pertains to man, a created being. Thus, the source of the law (the Creator) and the purpose of the law that "rule of action, which is prescribed by some superior, and which the inferior is bound to obey,"

remain unchanged. At the same time, this distinction is incredibly important because it is Blackstone's way of emphasizing the special status of man
as compared to the rest of creation and man's special relationship to law as a
result. Blackstone clearly distinguished man from the rest of creation based
upon man's unique, God-given ability "to think" and "to will."[47] With this
distinction, Blackstone laid the groundwork for the pursuit of happiness.

Blackstone believed God gave man the ability to think and to will because he intended man to regulate his own behavior in accordance with the
natural law; God wanted humans to use their "reason and freewill" to discern the "immutable laws of human nature, whereby [human] freewill is in
some degree regulated and restrained." Blackstone's discussion here is fascinating because, by his very definition, he acknowledged an inherent and
immutable limitation on human free will that he also saw reflected in the
laws God set in place to govern the natural world. Just as God established
"certain rules" to govern motion, so too did he establish "immutable laws
of human nature . . . and gave [man] also the faculty of reason to discover
the purport of those laws."[48]

Where the laws that governed "inactive matter [. . . and] vegetable and
animal life" are "equally fixed and invariable," "performed in a wondrous
involuntary manner, and guided by unerring rules laid down by the great
creator," the laws that govern man are of a different sort. As Blackstone
summarized, these were "laws, in their more confined sense . . . the rules,
not of action in general, but of *human* action or conduct: that is, the precepts
by which man, the noblest of all sublunary beings, a creature endowed with
both reason and freewill, is commanded to make use of those faculties in
the general regulation of his behaviour."[49]

Blackstone's view of human free will was not without limitation. Instead,
it was the bounded freedom of a life of virtue, within which he believed
man would flourish and experience, in the Greek language, *eudaimonia* or,
in the English, "well-being."[50] And here is where Blackstone comes full
circle, articulating a conception of happiness that harmonizes with Aristotle's own discussion in *The Nichomachean Ethics*. According Aristotle, "[T]he
good of man is exercise of his faculties in accordance with excellence or
virtue, or, if there be more than one, in accordance with the best and most
complete virtue."[51] Man's prompter in choosing to regulate himself in pursuit of the good life, or the life of virtue, was his own happiness. As noted
previously, Blackstone connected these ideas under the heading of "ethics,
or natural law." "For the several articles into which it is branched in our

systems, amount to no more than demonstrating, that this or that action tends to man's real happiness, and therefore very justly concluding that the performance of it is a part of the law of nature; or, on the other hand, that this or that action is destructive of man's real happiness, and therefore that the law of nature forbids it."[52]

Blackstone's discussion of man's reason and free will in relation to the natural law served as a foundation for his discussion of the English common law as a whole. Just as the laws of nature preceded the creation of plants and animals, and were intended to regulate and restrain them, so too had the law of human nature "existed in the nature of things antecedent to any positive precept."[53] The natural law laid down by the Creator not only was antecedent to positive law but also was intended to regulate and restrain it. If men or governments were to flourish, they would do so by setting rules of action for their own conduct that fell within the boundary lines of God's natural law. If man acted, in his free will, against the law of nature, he would fail to flourish as a human. Similarly, if a government passed laws through its legislators, or handed down judicial decisions through its judges, that were repugnant to the natural law principles set in place by God, that government, too, would fail to thrive.

Blackstone saw this rule of action as the key deficiency of the English common law of his day: English judges and MPs had wandered from the first principles of the English common law, and the law had become inconsistent and corrupted as a result. Therefore, English lawmakers needed to be trained, not only in the content or system of the law, but also in the science of jurisprudence, or in the skills and knowledge necessary to know and apply first principles, to bring English common law back into harmony with the law of nature and the law of God. Yet even as he sought to separate the study of English law from what he deemed as overly abstract Greek philosophy and an undue influence from the Roman civil law, Blackstone remained indebted to both. In an adaptation of Aristotle that would have been obvious to his readers, Blackstone defined the pursuit of happiness in terms that harmonized with Aristotle's conclusion that "the good of man is exercise of his faculties in accordance with excellence or virtue"—both "living well and doing well"—therein lies happiness.[54] And in a rare nod to the Roman civil law, Blackstone argued that even Justinian had recognized the importance of fundamental first principles when he structured his *Institutes* around three of the main "eternal, immutable laws of good and evil, to which the creator himself in all his dispensations conforms; and which he has enabled human reason to discover, so far as they are necessary for the conduct of human actions." "Such among others," wrote Blackstone, "are these principles: that we should live honestly, should hurt nobody, and should render to every one it's due." Blackstone wanted to see these immutable laws elucidated in the study of the English common law as well.[55]

CHAPTER 2

An Enlightenment Epistemology:
Anglican Theology and Scottish Common Sense Philosophy

Blackstone was not alone in his understanding of the English law as a science based on first principles. But in arguing for the pursuit of happiness as a science of jurisprudence, Blackstone argued for a method of jurisprudence that was particularly rooted in the Enlightenment ideas of his day, as expressed by both latitudinarian Anglicans and Scottish Common Sense philosophers.[1]

Anglican Theology: The Latitudinarian School

In the two centuries following Henry VIII's withdrawal of England from the authority of the Roman Catholic Church, England experienced ongoing turmoil in terms of its public and private religious identity, with accompanying purges—Anglican, Catholic, and dissident—of the universities.[2] The idea of an English church separate from Rome (and needing to be increasingly and continually separated from Rome) is an idea Blackstone furthers at various points within his *Commentaries*. Blackstone's discussion here is fairly polemical, but nevertheless reflective of the rhetoric of his times.

Blackstone, an orthodox Anglican, attended the public sermons of the prominent Anglican clergymen of his day, where he heard a combination of philosophy, politics, and theology that had been the hallmark of English Anglicanism since the sixteenth century.[3] That post-Reformation England saw continual transitions between rulers who were more or less friendly to Catholics, Protestants, and dissenters meant that these ideas had political consequences. Blackstone wove together theology, philosophy, and science throughout the introduction to his *Commentaries*, and although he engaged in a broadly Protestant polemic against the Roman Catholic Church, his ideas were not broadly Protestant, or even broadly Anglican, but instead specifically reflective of the ideas of those Anglicans known as latitudinarians and the preaching of this group's most prominent eighteenth-century bishop, Joseph Butler.[4]

In 1726 Butler published a compilation of fifteen sermons he had preached while serving as bishop of Rolls Chapel in London, one of England's most prominent and widely attended Anglican churches.[5] At the time of Butler's preaching, Rolls Chapel's congregation was "smart and sophisticated."[6] It was not uncommon for ministers, like Butler, to be invited to preach public sermons; the published versions of these sermons contributed significantly to eighteenth-century literary culture.[7] Following *Fifteen Sermons Preached at Rolls Chapel* (1726), Butler published *The Analogy of Religion* (1736) and *Six Sermons on Public Occasions* (1749), a compilation of sermons that were first preached in London.[8]

Latitudinarians like Butler enjoyed vast popularity, both in England and in the British colonies in North America in the 1700s. Their preaching reflected key ideas of the English Enlightenment and focused on the essential doctrines of Christianity. To discover those doctrines, the latitudinarians argued for a Newtonian epistemology. This epistemology was well summarized by John Tillotson, archbishop of Canterbury, who argued that God has "commanded us nothing in the gospel that is either unsuitable to our reason or prejudicial to our interest . . . nothing but what is easy to be understood, and as easy to be practiced by an honest and willing mind."[9] They believed that the essential doctrines of Christianity could be discovered through inductive reasoning applied to a "two books" theology—the book of revelation (the holy scriptures) and the book of nature[10]—and that man's own self-love, or the pursuit of his own real and substantial happiness, was the truest guide to that study.

The place where Butler's preaching is most reflected in Blackstone's *Commentaries* is in Blackstone's discussion of the pursuit of happiness.[11] Like Butler, Blackstone argued that man can learn about God's design for human nature by studying "the constitution and frame of humanity."[12] Blackstone argued that from the study of his nature, man could induce the purpose God has for men, which is for men to live in harmony with "the laws of eternal justice," as accomplished through the pursuit of man's "real" and "substantial" happiness. Blackstone stated that humans could choose not to live in harmony with that design, but, due to man's unique combination of "reason and freewill," that choice would be based on knowledge and free will, not ignorance or determinism.[13] In this way, both Butler and Blackstone carried out Newton's charge that the natural world was a proper starting point for epistemology, "that the most simple laws of nature are observed in the structure of a great part of the Universe, that the philosophy ought there to begin."[14]

Drawing on the epistemological notions of Butler and the latitudinarian Anglicans, Blackstone argued for the pursuit of happiness as a science of jurisprudence that would forge a middle way between what he deemed to be the two theological and philosophical extremes of his day: the Catholics' excessive focus on reason and the Enthusiasts' excessive focus on conscience. In this he is following in the steps of Bishop Richard Boyle, who claimed, "I do not think, that a Christian, to be truly so, is obliged to forego his reason; either by denying the dictates of reason [as the latitudinarians argued that Catholics would do], or by laying aside the use of it [as the latitudinarians argued that the Enthusiasts would do]."[15] Butler believed that self-love, or the pursuit of happiness, was the remedy for these two extremes.

In defining and promoting the pursuit of happiness, or one's own "self-love" as a jurisprudential science, Blackstone is speaking a language that is meaningful to his contemporaries. It is a language that affirms the latitudinarian focus on individual free will[16] and the ability of the layperson to induce first principles through study of the two books: nature and scripture. It is a language that turns away from the deductive, syllogistic reasoning of the Scholastics and turns toward the inductive, observation- and experience-based reasoning that was so appealing to the latitudinarian Anglicans of Blackstone's day. The latitudinarians had "an almost obsessive concern for design, order, and harmony as the primary manifestations of God's role in the universe,"[17] and it would not be a stretch to say that Blackstone did as well. He viewed the pursuit of happiness as a way to restore beauty and order to the common law. According to Blackstone, the English system of law and science of jurisprudence were capable of being perfected because they once had been, and increasingly could be, in harmony with and reflective of the beauty of the natural order. In making epistemological arguments based on an inductive study of nature and in appealing to the outcomes of harmony, beauty, and order, Butler and Blackstone reflected not only the philosophy of seventeenth- and eighteenth-century latitudinarian Anglicans but also the philosophy of the Scottish Enlightenment's Common Sense school.

Scottish Philosophy: The Common Sense School

Blackstone's emphasis on "our own self-love" as a "prompter to enquire after and pursue the rule of right" evokes epistemological notions present in the Scottish Enlightenment. The pursuit of happiness, for Blackstone, was not one's effort to experience a state of being happy, as we would consider it in twenty-first-century terms, but, instead, a method by which man could become most fully human. In this context, Blackstone's "real" and "substantial" happiness reflected the eighteenth-century definitions of these terms. It was real in that it was "not fictitious; not imaginary; true; genuine."[18] It was substantial in that it pertained to the substance or essence of what it meant to be fully human and, therefore, to be happy; it was, from the Latin *substantia*, "literally, that which stands under," or that which lies beneath.[19] Thus, to Blackstone, to pursue one's happiness was to pursue the essential character that lay underneath or, in other words, to pursue the natural law principles that pertained to humans and, therefore, to understand the principles that should form both the foundation and the boundary lines for all legitimate human law.

To discover these principles, the Scholastics had adopted a deductive legal science built on "syllogistic, 'geometric' reasoning."[20] In contrast, the Common Sense school of philosophy was marked by "empirical observation and careful inductive reasoning" by men who "believed that they could discover natural legal principles just as Newton had discovered the laws of nature."[21] When Blackstone described the English law as a system and a science, the science he was referring to was reflective of the Common Sense school of the Scottish Enlightenment, a school that would have been very familiar to latitudinarian Anglicans like Butler and Blackstone.

In fact, both Butler and Blackstone discussed epistemology in ways that reflect the writings of Thomas Reid, a key thinker of the Scottish Enlightenment Common Sense school, whose writings were in opposition to the skepticism of fellow Scottish Enlightenment thinker David Hume.[22] Where Hume argued that there are no innate ideas and that, instead, our constantly fluctuating perceptions form our understanding of the natural world, Reid argued for self-evident "First Principles" that form the basis for the advancement of knowledge. In both natural and moral philosophy, these first principles were discovered by induction through experiment and observation, a capability that was formed in the "original constitution of [man's] nature."[23] This philosophy not only served as a foundation for knowledge about the natural world but "could serve as a foundation for moral knowledge as well. . . . Just as our eyes enabled us to see objects and our ears enabled us to hear sounds, so too our moral sense enabled us to distinguish between right and wrong, virtue and vice."[24]

Legal historian Charles Barzun argues that the Common Sense philosophy of the Scottish Enlightenment was adapted specifically to jurisprudence, or to the science of the law. While Barzun tracks developments in early America, the ideas he articulates are those of the eighteenth-century Common Sense school that would have been very familiar to latitudinarian Anglicans, like Butler and Blackstone:

> [T]he rise of legal science cannot be fully understood unless it is seen at least in part as a response to a genuine epistemological crisis that had cast doubt on humans' ability to acquire knowledge about the world. In developing an "inductive" strand of legal science, many theorists were earnestly building a new way of thinking about legal rules, one that drew on a particular group of highly influential Scottish philosophers. These theorists believed that they could discover natural legal principles just as Newton had discovered the laws of nature.[25]

The work that Reid saw as being possible through moral sense is the same type of work Blackstone expected the pursuit of happiness to do. It explains why Blackstone believed that the holy scriptures could be a check on the pursuit of happiness: both the scriptures and the moral sense that works itself out through pursuit of happiness were means of identifying first principles of right and wrong. The inductive reasoning Blackstone encouraged through the pursuit of happiness was not pure reason, and it was not just a feeling. It was a "common intuition" woven into the fabric of man by the Creator God.[26]

Reid argued that it was possible, but not necessary, to cultivate this moral sense through education. He also argued that man's errors in moral philosophy did not indicate that first principles of right and wrong did not exist.[27] Blackstone echoed both of these ideas. First, as discussed above, Blackstone argued for education of university students in the English common law as a way to cultivate knowledge of the law as "a science, which distinguishes the criterions of right and wrong."[28] Blackstone echoed the second of these ideas when he argued for pursuit of happiness as a science of jurisprudence by which every man could identify the first principles of the common law and then use those principles to correct the common law's man-made errors, leading to its improvement and perfection over time.[29]

CHAPTER 3

Improvement and Perfection of the Common Law:
History and Architecture

A key outworking of latitudinarian thinking was the idea that knowledge of the world and an application of that knowledge in the various disciplines would lead to improvement and a movement toward perfection over time. Yet latitudinarians disagreed with one another as to what this progress might look like in the realm of religion. Could Christianity be perfected, through modern progress, over time, or was true progress in religion a return to the simplicity of ancient Christianity? This debate between modern progress and ancient simplicity as the route to improvement and perfection was echoed in law as well.

Men like Anglican minister Edmund Law argued that the avenues of learning advocated for by Francis Bacon, Isaac Newton, and John Locke had assisted men in knowing the world that God had created and the natural laws that he had created to govern it: "The more we know of the *World*, the more we view its Order, Beauty, Symmetry; the uniform Laws which it is govern'd by, the just arrangement and mutual subserviency of all its Parts, (and I need not observe how much this kind of Learning has of late encreas'd) the more we see the Glory, and Perfection of its Architect, and are more fully satisfied that he design'd its several Inhabitants for Happiness in general."[1]

Law voiced an Anglican idea of progress in language that is remarkably similar to that of Blackstone and Butler. But Law also expected "improvements in 'natural religion'" as a result of the progress in scientific learning that had taken place in modern times. Although Law approved of Butler's "perfect *Analogy* between Religion and the common course of Nature" and then applied it to the perfection of Christianity, neither Butler nor Blackstone would have agreed with Law's approach, arguing instead for the perfection of Christianity through a return to its ancient order and simplicity.[2]

Blackstone's views were shared by those legal philosophers with whom Law disagreed: latitudinarian legal philosopher Joseph Glanvill and legal theorist Sir Matthew Hale. Glanvill was "progressive" in science but "primitive" in religion, asserting "why we may imbrace what is new in Philosophy, while we reject them in Theologie." Sir Matthew Hale, too, followed this model: "Though something of a progressivist in his view of the arts and sciences, he yet could write . . . that 'if there were any Religion that was Primitive in the World, it was the true Religion and true Worship of the true God.'"[3]

Thus, while Blackstone was committed to improvement,[4] it was an improvement that, as Glanvill and Hale had argued before him, had its boundaries. For men like Law, traditional orthodoxy in religion was an impediment to improvement. For Blackstone and Butler, traditional or- thodoxy in religion—a deliberate study of and then building upon of first principles—was the road to improvement.[5] In this way, Blackstone viewed improvement in the same terms as William Worthington, vicar of Blodwel in Shropshire, who wrote, "He who has the Reins of the World's Govern- ment in his Hands will undoubtedly guide it at length to its right Course, and *improve it to the perfect Model after which he at first framed it.*" The end result of such improvement would be a return to ancient simplicity, instead of modern progress, and "a complete restoration of the world to the 'Beauty, Order, and Harmony' which had prevailed for a short time in the begin- ning."[6] To Blackstone's eighteenth-century readers, both would be indica- tive of the idea that, through experience and observation, lawmakers could induce first principles that then could be referred to in order to improve the common law over time. As the common law was improved, it would be- come more perfect; in other words, it would increasingly reflect the order, beauty, and harmony of the natural law. Blackstone articulated his hopes for the improvement and perfection of the common law in terms of history and architecture.

History: An Ancient English Common Law

In keeping with the idea of improvement as a return to ancient simplicity, Blackstone viewed his own work in teaching the laws of England in terms of revival, tracing the common law back to the Christian kings of England's Anglo-Saxon period.[7] A search for first founders was popular during the Enlightenment; following Henry VIII's break from the Roman Catholic Church and the establishment of the Church of England came a corre- sponding focus on England's distinct past, with an emphasis on the Anglo- Saxon period and King Alfred, who represented freedom.[8] Alfred was seen as the first of "the great unifying kings," whose laws were "the most famous and best preserved" over time. The Anglo-American legal tradition stems, in part, from ideas embodied in these laws. According to legal historian Daniel R. Coquillette, "If we owe to the Romans the ideas and words for 'justice,' 'legal,' 'codification,' 'judge,' 'equity,' and 'constitution,' we owe to the Anglo-Saxon the concepts of 'rights' and 'freedom.'" In fact, "the *folc riht* of the Anglo-Saxons was so important that the Norman conquerors, from William on, swore to uphold it."[9] Although some argue that King William of Normandy had "swept away virtually all Saxon Common Law and immemorial customs," others have "held that English constitutional liberties had a continuous history from Anglo-Saxon times" forward.[10] Blackstone took the latter view.

According to Blackstone, the English common law was that "admirable system of maxims and unwritten customs, which is now known by the name of the *common* law, as extending it's authority universally over all the realm; and which is doubtless of Saxon parentage."[11] Both Blackstone and his predecessor Sir Edward Coke saw King Alfred as "the *legum Anglicanarum conditor* of the early Common Law, while King Edward the Confessor [was] considered the *restitutor* thereof. . . . Alfred founded the Common Law and the Confessor restored it."[12] In seeking to revive an ancient past for the English common law, Blackstone did well to choose Edward and Alfred as his models. According to popular histories of the time, King Edward had combined the disparate Anglo-Saxon law codes into one coherent and cohesive law.[13] As an Anglo-Saxon king, Edward provided an identifiable person behind the theoretical argument of an ancient English common law.[14] And although Edward was important to Blackstone (who hailed him "our English Justinian"), his importance primarily came from reinstituting and preserving that common law that King Alfred had previously founded. Blackstone believed that King Alfred's law code contained "many of the *principal maxims of the Common Law.*"[15] Alfred's focus on training in literacy and learning, his study of the Latin language, and his emphasis on reform and renaissance[16] made him an ideal ancient founder for the English common law.

Alfred's rule is the stuff of history and of legend. As the legend goes, "King Alfred the Great was a valiant warrior, who delivered his nation from the threat of Viking conquest; a skillful ruler, who established a code of laws for his people and protected their liberties; a distinguished scholar, who cherished learning and promoted educational reform; and he was Alfred 'the truth-teller,' the paragon of virtues who shone forth as a mirror of the Christian prince."[17]

King Alfred made for an ideal symbolic figure in that he was viewed as "the greatest hero among English rulers," in part due to his enactment of "that familiar English experience, glorious national victory snatched from the jaws of shattering national defeat." The national enemies in Alfred's day were the Vikings, who were characterized as pagan, lawless pirates.[18] The national enemy, to Blackstone's way of thinking, was Rome.

Whether fact or fiction, it was this view of Alfred that was popularized from the 1500s through the 1800s. Much of the known history of Alfred affirms the characteristics present in his legendary composite. For example, Alfred sought a peace that would endure. He desired to consolidate rule to form a unified Anglo-Saxon realm, and both King Alfred's charters and publications such as *The Anglo-Saxon Chronicle* and Asser's *Life of Alfred* encouraged the development of a common Anglo-Saxon history with Alfred as a unifying king. Alfred's own writings "convey a vivid impression of his own conception of the duties of a Christian king, showing how seriously he took the responsibilities of his high office."[19] This vision of King Alfred was alive and well in Blackstone's day, and it is in Alfred's work in the realm of law, in particular, that we see parallels to Blackstone's view of himself as a professor of English law, his hopes for law reform, and the manner in which he sought to encourage that work through his teaching and the distillation of that teaching in the *Commentaries*.

As part of his program for literacy and learning, Alfred argued for the "pursuit of wisdom" not as "a wise man's option" but as "a ruler's duty."[20] Alfred's biographer Asser compared Alfred to King Solomon, with the understanding that each man "sought wisdom from God."[21] Wisdom is defined as "knowledge of what is true or right coupled with just judgment as to action; sagacity, discernment, or insight."[22] Its current meaning hails from the word's Saxon roots, where it was defined as "sapience; the power of judging rightly."[23] In other words, to pursue wisdom is first to be able to know what is true and right and then to be able to apply that knowledge to its best (right or most fit) use. Alfred believed that man's ability to reason, the pursuit of wisdom, and the proper development of the law were intertwined. Reason, an essential characteristic of a human being, was what allowed a man to engage in the pursuit of wisdom. If a ruler acted with wisdom, if he both rightly understood and rightly applied the law, then the law would develop justly. Conversely, if a ruler was not wise, if he was not able either to rightly know the law or to rightly apply it, then the law that developed would be unjust.

Alfred believed that faulty reasoning stemmed from lack of learning, and he therefore promoted literacy and learning in his realm, going so far as to order his judges either "to learn to read or quit office."[24] In the preface to his translation of Gregory the Great's *Book of the Pastoral Rule*, Alfred expressed his hope that "all free-born young men now in England who have the means to apply themselves to it, may be set to learning . . . until the time that they can read English writings properly."[25] As a further check on faulty reasoning, Alfred included revelation, the divine law as revealed by God in the holy scriptures, as a "way of knowing," describing revelation as "Mosaic Law" (a term synonymous with the law of the Old Testament) and "Christ as True Wisdom" (a phrase synonymous with both "the Law of Christ" and the teachings of the New Testament).

Historian James Campbell argues that, in spite of its symbolic strength, King Alfred's law book, with its contradictory provisions of Anglo-Saxon King Ine's law and Alfred's law, and its organization around the Mosaic Law "with little regard for the sense," would be "of little use to a judge in court."[26] But Alfred's inclusion of contradictory legal principles, his focus on wisdom (drawing on both the Mosaic Law and "Christ as True Wisdom"), his emphasis on reason as an essential human characteristic, his promotion of education and learning, and his sense of duty in properly knowing and applying the law are remarkably similar to the template Blackstone adopted for his own eighteenth-century English law reforms.

For example, Alfred's inclusion of the contradictory laws of the Anglo-Saxon King Ine (ca. 690)[27] is similar to Blackstone's inclusion of the contradictions within the common law of his day. Under the English common law, contradictions were one of two types. Either they were due to the permissible divergences that rightfully occurred with the application of first principles to local circumstances, or they were the result of faulty reasoning about the content or the application of those first principles. If the former, then such contradictions were still proper applications of first principles and were allowed as proper development of the common law.[28] If the latter, then the contradictions reached the level of deviations from first principles and therefore were repugnant to the common law and its development.[29] In his reform of legal education and jurisprudence, Blackstone wanted to correct the latter type of contradiction, and he believed that such faulty reasoning could be corrected only by turning to one of the other avenues for determining the first principles of the law: reason, revelation, or the pursuit of happiness.

Although it is not clear which type of contradiction Alfred envisioned as existing between his law and Ine's law, it is clear that Alfred, like Blackstone, viewed reason and revelation as proper jurisprudential frameworks that could remedy the defects in the law. In addition, Alfred's pursuit of wisdom strikingly parallels Blackstone's discussion of the pursuit of happiness.

As discussed previously, to pursue wisdom is first to be able to know what is true and right and then to be able to apply that knowledge to its best (right or most fit) use. Whereas Alfred advocated for the pursuit of wisdom, believing that it would, as the Saxon root of the word suggests, provide judges with the "power of judging rightly," Blackstone advocated for the pursuit of happiness as a means of discovering that which is true and right in the realm of human law. In other words, Blackstone believed that the pursuit of happiness would provide his students with a simpler, more readily accessible means of *knowing* the first principles of the law of nature as it pertains to man. If then applied in man's regulation of his own conduct, Blackstone believed that knowledge would make men happy. If that knowledge were to be applied in the realm of statutes and judicial opinions, the end result would be legal developments that were both *wise*—and made so by judges and lawmakers putting the law of nature to its best (right or most fit use) in the realm of human law—and *happy* (rightly ordered to that law).

Alfred, like Blackstone, viewed both revelation and the pursuit of wisdom (what Blackstone described as the pursuit of happiness) as jurisprudential frameworks that could remedy the defects that resulted from faulty reasoning on topics of law. Blackstone believed that remedying these defects was necessary in order to improve and perfect the ancient English common law, a process he analogized to restoring a poorly remodeled house to its original foundation and plan.

Architecture: "Solid Foundations" and an "Extensive Plan"

Blackstone's views on the improvement and perfection of the common law reflect not only his understanding of King Alfred as the ancient founder of the common law, but also Blackstone's own description of the common law itself as a house whose structure had been altered and whose ancient and true foundations had been obscured by faulty additions over time. Blackstone stated that England's "admirable system of laws" had been "built upon the soundest foundations, and approved by the experience of ages" but that the English law had been corrupted over time and was no longer in harmony with its original symmetry and simplicity.[30] According to Blackstone, these faulty additions needed to be removed so that the order, harmony, and beauty of the original blueprint could be revealed and so that the new builders could rely upon the true foundation in making additions for the future.[31]

Blackstone ascribed to future lawyers, judges, jurors, and MPs a high sense of duty in improving and perfecting the laws of England and urged them to do so by recovering the ancient foundations of the common law and the foundational principles that should guide its development.[32] The idea of perfection or improvement had its roots in the science and religion of the English Enlightenment. The philosophes of the Enlightenment looked to England and saw that "progress in one sphere generated progress in others"; they believed that "England was rich, happy, and free" and that "these characteristics depended upon and reinforced one another."[33] As John Gordon, archdeacon of Lincoln, argued, "[T]he world is . . . in a state of general improvement," with the result that "mankind at present is *wiser, happier,* and *better* than it ever was before."[34]

Blackstone believed improvement of the common law had begun with King Alfred, stating that Alfred's "mighty genius prompted him to undertake a most great and necessary work. . . . No less than to new-model the constitution; to rebuild it on a plan that should endure for ages; and, out of it's old discordant materials, which were heaped upon each other in a vast and rude irregularity, to form one uniform and well connected whole."[35] King Henry I, who restored the common law after the Norman Conquest, saw himself as paving the way for future improvements when he described himself "as providing the wood from which others may build."[36] Indeed, Blackstone described the "two books" from which first principles could be induced in architectural terms: "*Upon these two foundations,* the law of nature and the law of revelation, depend all human laws; that is to say, no human laws should be suffered to contradict these."[37]

Blackstone's choice of the architectural term "foundation" here is telling. A foundation is both the underlying building surface and the guide for the structure of the building—it both provides stability for the structure and directs its form. It is in light of this metaphor that Blackstone alternately talks about the principles upon which the common law should be built and the principles that should direct the development (and improvement and perfection) of the common law for years to come.

Historian Carol Matthews has compiled Blackstone's architectural views of the common law as they developed over time, and they are worth reproducing in full here, as they highlight a theory of jurisprudence, expressed in architectural terms, that Blackstone began articulating several years before he delivered his first law lectures and nearly twenty years before the publication of his *Commentaries*.[38]

For example, in 1746, Blackstone described the common law as a building in need of improvement. Note how he describes the common law as a physical structure, marred by faulty alterations over time, and proposes both restoration and the means of gaining the knowledge necessary for that restoration to begin:

> I have sometimes thought that the Common Law, as it stood in Littleton's Days, resembled a regular Edifice: where the Apartments were properly disposed, leading one into another without Confusion; where every part was subservient to the whole, all uniting in one beautiful Symmetry: & every Room had its distinct Office allotted to it. But as it is now, swol'n, shrunk, curtailed, enlarged, altered & mangled by various & contradictory Statutes &c; it resembles the same Edifice, with many of its most useful Parts pulled down, with preposterous Additions in other Places, of different Materials & coarse Workmanship according to the Whim, or Prejudice, or private Convenience of the Builders. By which means the Communication of the Parts is destroyed, & their Harmony quite annihilated; & now it remains a huge, irregular Pile, with many noble Apartments, though awkwardly put together, & some of them of no visible Use at present. But if one desires to know why they were built, to what End or Use, how they communicated with the rest & the like; he must necessarily carry in his Head the Model of the old House, which will be the only Clue to guide him through this new Labyrinth.[39]

Blackstone used the same analogy, in a modified version, in 1758 in his first Vinerian lecture, where he stated that the common law "has fared like other venerable edifices of antiquity, which rash and unexperienced workmen have ventured to new-dress and refine, with all the rage of modern improvement. Hence frequently its symmetry has been destroyed, its proportions distorted, and its majestic simplicity exchanged for specious embellishments and fantastic novelties."[40] Note Blackstone's use of the phrase "the rage of modern improvement" to describe the improvements of "rash and unexperienced workmen," whose efforts "to new-dress and refine" actually destroyed the symmetry, proportions, and simplicity of the ancient edifice. During the eighteenth century, "modern" had two meanings. The first definition was "Late; recent; not ancient; not antique" and certainly could be the usage Blackstone is employing. But the surrounding context suggests he may also, or alternately, be implying the second meaning of modern: "vulgar; mean; common."[41] Blackstone attaches the adjective "modern" in a pejorative way, as one might expect under either definition of the term, given his reverence for history and his admiration for simplicity. Blackstone thus distinguishes these improvements by "unexperienced workmen," which he later described as "unskilful" and which he viewed as degradations, from the seventeenth- and eighteenth-century notion of improvement that would lead to perfection—to the more whole or complete state of a thing. This latter notion of improvement stemmed from the root "-prove" and meant to "make better, raise to a better quality or condition."[42]

It is this latter definition of improvement that was included in Samuel Johnson's dictionary (1755).[43] Improvement in property law from the sixteenth century forward was somewhat more complicated, defined as "[a]n addition to property, usu. real estate, whether permanent or not; esp., one that increases its value or utility or that enhances its appearance." Thus, improvement in the context of property law encompassed a variety of meanings, including a "necessary improvement" or repair, made to ward off deterioration, versus a "voluntary improvement," "whose only purpose is ornamental."[44] Blackstone distinguishes the types of improvements made to the common law in the fourth volume of his *Commentaries*.

Here, Blackstone once more invokes the familiar architectural metaphor, specifically stating that the purpose of the *Commentaries* is to encourage his students to identify the original foundations of the common law and create a blueprint of "its extensive plan" so as to "sustain, to repair, to beautify" the structure of the common law and protect "the liberty of Britain" for years to come:

> It hath been the endeavour of these commentaries, however the execution may have succeeded, to examine [the common law's] solid foundations, to mark out its extensive plan, to explain the use and distribution of its parts, and from the harmonious concurrence of those several parts to demonstrate the elegant proportion of the whole. We have taken occasion to admire at every turn the noble monuments of ancient simplicity, and the more curious refinements of modern art. Nor have its faults been concealed from view; for faults it has, lest we should be tempted to think it of more than human structure: defects, chiefly arising from the decays of time, or the rage of unskilful

improvements in later ages. To sustain, to repair, to beautify this noble pile, is a charge entrusted principally to the nobility, and such gentlemen of the kingdom, as are delegated by their country to parliament. The protection of THE LIBERTY OF BRITAIN is a duty which they owe to themselves, who enjoy it; to their ancestors, who transmitted it down; and to their posterity, who will claim at their hands, this the best birthright, and noblest inheritance of mankind.[45]

Note how Blackstone describes the ancient elements of the law as "noble" and portraying "simplicity," with simplicity conveying, in the eighteenth century, that which is pure and uncorrupted by changes or additions over time, often in either law or religion.[46] Blackstone is careful to distinguish "the rage of unskilful improvements," which led to defects in the structure, from "the more curious refinements of modern art," which he admires. His admiration for these refinements suggests that Blackstone is using "curious" in the sense of "exact, nice, subtle" and that his use of "refinement" is meant to convey "[t]he act of purifying, by clearing any thing from dross and recrementitious matter" or "improvement in elegance or purity."[47] In this context, Blackstone's use of "art" suggests not the type of "voluntary improvement" "whose only purpose is ornamental" but, instead, a "habitual knowledge . . . of certain rules and maxims, by which a man is governed and directed in his actions."[48]

In this final architectural metaphor, we see Blackstone's belief in the common law's "ancient simplicity," which he understood to be manifest in the founding of King Alfred and the restoration of King Edward. We see his acknowledgment of the "defects" that occurred in the law over time, some of which he attributes to "unskilful improvements." We see Blackstone's desire to educate his students, so that they can make the skillful improvements necessary "[t]o sustain, to repair, to beautify this noble pile," especially for those of his students who should one day serve in Parliament. We see Blackstone's charge to these students to thus protect and then, through transmission to their posterity, preserve the "LIBERTY of BRITAIN," for years to come.

In his first architectural analogy, Blackstone argued that in order to understand the various rooms of the common law as it then stood, "to know why they were built, to what End or Use, how they communicated with the rest & the like; *he must necessarily carry in his Head the Model of the old House*, which will be the only Clue to guide him through this new Labyrinth."[49] In his final metaphor, he explained that his goal for his *Commentaries* was to "examine [the common law's] solid foundations" and then "mark out its extensive plan." With that blueprint in mind, Blackstone could then "explain the use and distribution of [the common law's] parts, and from the harmonious concurrence of those several parts to demonstrate the elegant proportion of the whole."[50]

In these two phrases, we see a distillation of Blackstone's two-part goal for legal reform in England. As evidenced by the latter phrase, he sought to provide an education in the content of the English common law at the university level, including a discussion of its different parts, and how they related to one another to create a whole. As evidenced by the former phrase, Blackstone also sought to replace the Scholastic method of deduction with a new science of jurisprudence that would enable his students to first "examine [the common law's] solid foundations," which he identified as the law of nature and the law of revelation, and, with the knowledge gained, "mark out its extensive plan." The science of jurisprudence that Blackstone believed was best suited to that task was the pursuit of happiness.

Pursuit of Happiness: A New Science of Jurisprudence

As demonstrated above, Blackstone envisioned a two-part goal for English law reform. The first part was to reform English legal education so as to include education in the common law at the university level. The second part was to reform English legal jurisprudence by replacing the Scholastic method of deduction with the inductive method of the pursuit of happiness. Blackstone's goals were articulated in his *Commentaries* in the 1760s, and in his architectural metaphors in the years prior, but they were first expressed in this portion of his poem "The Lawyer's Farewell to His Muse," which Blackstone wrote as he began his own legal studies:

> In furs and coifs around me stand;
> With sounds uncouth and accents dry
> That grate the soul of harmony,
> Each pedant sage unlocks his store
> Of mystic, dark, discordant lore;
> And points with tott'ring hand the ways
> That lead me to the thorny maze.[51]

The poem contains themes of law and jurisprudence that would define Blackstone's legal work and legal philosophy in later years. First, he describes the study of law as something that "grate[s] the soul of harmony" and is handed down by "pedant sage[s]." While "sage" is a complimentary term, referring to "a philosopher; a man of gravity and wisdom," the addition of "pedant" alters the definition completely and shows Blackstone's impatience with his law teachers, pedants who were "[men] vain of low knowledge"; "awkwardly ostentatious of [their] literature."[52] Blackstone's characterization of legal education here "brilliantly encapsulates long-standing complaints about the difficulties posed for beginning common-law students by the notorious lack of accessible and coherent introductory textbooks," yet Blackstone urges those studying the law to continue on in the pursuit of justice:

> In that pure spring the bottom view
> Clear, deep, and regularly true,
> And other doctrines thence imbibe
> Than lurk within the sordid scribe;
> Observe how parts with parts unite
> In one harmonious rule of right;
> See countless wheels distinctly tend
> By various laws to one great end;
> While mighty Alfred's piercing soul
> Pervades, and regulates the whole.[53]

As historian Wilfrid Prest argues, "These lines foreshadow a personal quest to uncover and reveal the innate reason of the common law, those coherent principles which must—or should—lie beneath the confusing jumble of legal particulars."[54] These lines also foreshadow the Common Sense methodology that Blackstone would adopt in undertaking that quest. A view that is "clear, deep, and regularly true" indicates that which can be readily observed and doctrines that can be known through observation. Blackstone urges his reader to imbibe from that clear, pure spring other doctrines than those marked out by the sordid scribe. The idea of parts uniting "in one harmonious rule of right" is a foreshadowing of Blackstone's Newtonian understanding that all human law ought to be in harmony with that one rule of right ordained by the Creator in man, which is the pursuit of happiness. Blackstone evokes Newton again with the scientific imagery of "countless wheels," an image that calls to mind the Creator God who designs the world as a clockmaker designs a clock, an analogy Blackstone later includes in his *Commentaries*. Finally, Blackstone is already looking to

King Alfred as his ancient Anglo-Saxon predecessor, the one whose "soul," which sought wisdom above all, "pervades, and regulates the whole," with "the whole" presumably being the whole of the English common law.[55]

Blackstone believed that, with a proper education in English common law and a proper science of jurisprudence, English lawyers, judges, and MPs could go about correcting the confusions and inconveniences of the English common law and English common-law teaching. For Blackstone, a new science of jurisprudence was indispensable to his overarching goals. If lawyers, judges, and MPs were to improve the law, they first had to be able to determine the first principles that lay at the foundations of law. Given what he viewed as the failings of English legal education, which began with practice instead of theory, and the Scholastic method of deduction, Blackstone urged his students to consider another means by which to identify and apply the law of nature as it pertains to man, namely, the pursuit of happiness.

To Blackstone, the pursuit of happiness reflected the ancient wisdom of Anglo-Saxon King Alfred and the moral and natural philosophy of the latitudinarian Anglicans. It embraced the Common Sense philosophy of the Scottish Enlightenment and, in so doing, avoided the undue complexities of the Scholastics and the undue emotionalism of the Enthusiasts. It provided a means by which the layperson, no less than the skilled lawyer, could induce the natural law principles that formed the foundation and framework of the common law. If the common law was a house, and Blackstone regularly described it as such, the pursuit of happiness was its cornerstone. The question that then remains is to what degree, if any, Blackstone's definition of the pursuit of happiness is reflected in the founders' use of the phrase.

Part 2 discusses the authorship of the Declaration in terms of "the founders" for two reasons. First, it places the authorship of the Declaration of Independence in its larger context. Although Thomas Jefferson drafted the Declaration, the language was debated, altered, and finally approved by John Adams, Benjamin Franklin, and additional founders who either served on the Committee of Five that drafted the Declaration or were present when it was edited and then approved by the Continental Congress (or both). The meaning of any part of the Declaration may have begun with what Jefferson intended, but ultimately depended upon what the other founders understood that language to mean as they debated, altered, and finally approved it at the Continental Congress. Second, I have referred to these men as founders as opposed to framers because they, through the Declaration,

founded the new United States of America, while the men who gathered
to create the Articles of Confederation and, later, the Constitution of the
United States framed its government.

PART II.

The Pursuit of Happiness in the Declaration of Independence

CHAPTER 4

Textual Context: Placement, Drafting, and Structure

Placement of the Pursuit of Happiness in
the Declaration of Independence

"[T]he pursuit of Happiness" is located at the beginning of the Declaration of Independence, in a two-paragraph summary on the ends of government:

> When in the Course of human events it becomes necessary for one people to dissolve the political bands which have connected them with another, and to assume among the powers of the earth, the separate and equal station to which the Laws of Nature and of Nature's God entitle them, a decent respect to the opinions of mankind requires that they should declare the causes which impel them to the separation.
>
> We hold these truths to be self-evident, that all men are created equal, that they are endowed by their Creator with certain unalienable Rights, that among these are Life, Liberty, and the pursuit of Happiness.—that to secure these rights, Governments are instituted among Men, deriving their just powers from the consent of the governed,—That whenever any Form of Government becomes destructive of these ends, it is the Right of the People to alter or to abolish it, and to institute new Government, laying its foundation on such principles and organizing its powers in such form, as to them shall seem most likely to effect their Safety and Happiness.

As shown above, the Declaration begins by assuming that "the Laws of Nature and of Nature's God" entitle men to a certain type of earthly government, one that will "secure" the unalienable rights with which men are "endowed by their Creator," including "Life, Liberty and the pursuit of Happiness." When a specific government fails to operate according to these principles, when it "becomes destructive of these ends," then it is "necessary" for the governed to separate from that government and to "assume" the "separate & equal station to which the Laws of Nature and of Nature's God entitle them," establishing a new government founded on

51

these principles, with an end goal of effecting the "Safety and Happiness" of the people. Thus, according to the Declaration, man's unalienable right to the pursuit of happiness is to be protected immediately by man's earthly government and further protected unendingly by the laws of nature and of nature's God. Should man's earthly government fail in protecting man's unalienable rights, the laws of nature and of nature's God provide that he separate from that government and form a new government that will.

As discussed previously, in his work *Commentaries on the Laws of England*, English jurist William Blackstone defines the pursuit of happiness as a means by which man could know the law of nature as it pertains to humans. If man pursued his own real and substantial happiness, he could not help but live in harmony with that law. Similarly, if man sought to live in harmony with the law of nature, he could not help but be happy.

Both Blackstone's *Commentaries* and the Declaration of Independence place the pursuit of happiness within a larger context of the laws of nature. Blackstone framed that discussion within the laws of nature, generally, and the specific laws of nature that pertain to man. The founders described these laws as "the Laws of Nature and of Nature's God." Both Blackstone and the founders then followed that discussion with the pursuit of happiness. However, where Blackstone specifically defines the pursuit of happiness, the Declaration does not.

What are we to make of the differences in Blackstone's and the founders' terminology for the laws of nature and their different contextual uses of the pursuit of happiness? Is Blackstone's understanding of the pursuit of happiness reflected in the founders' understanding and use of the phrase? Does the founders' use of "the Laws of Nature and of Nature's God" and "self-evident" "truths" provide any insight into those questions? These questions will be the focus of part 2 of this work.

Drafting of the Declaration

The drafting of the Declaration of Independence is an important and interesting aspect of its historical context. It is common to discuss the Declaration as Thomas Jefferson's original document, and, indeed, he did create the first draft. But we go astray if we consider what the document and its language meant to Jefferson alone, instead of considering how the Declaration was understood within the context of the men who drafted, edited, and approved it, including the other members of the Committee of Five, who edited the Declaration of Independence, and the Continental Congress, which debated, edited, and finally approved and signed it. The founders' views of the ideas expressed in the Declaration are evidenced by the changes they made to the document from its original draft to its final copy. As Jefferson proclaimed in his later reflections on this process, "[T]he sentiments of men are known not only by what they receive, but what they reject also."[1]

In early June 1776, the Continental Congress determined it was time to draft a document to declare independence from Great Britain.[2] It appointed a Committee of Five to complete the task by July 1 of that same year. The committee included Thomas Jefferson, John Adams, Benjamin Franklin, Roger Sherman, and Robert Livingston.[3] After some discussion (and with some later disagreement between Jefferson and Adams on the content of that discussion), it was agreed that Jefferson would draft the document.[4] Once Jefferson completed his initial draft, he sent it to Adams and Franklin for review, stating in a later letter to James Madison that Adams and Franklin "were the two members [of the Committee of Five] of whose judgments and amendments I wished most to have the benefit before presenting it to the [full] Committee."[5]

What happened from here is somewhat uncertain. The document that Jefferson later identified as his "original Rough draught" of the Declaration contains more than a few edits, many of them in his own hand, but we do not know if Jefferson was only editing his own rough draft or if he was also incorporating edits suggested by Adams and Franklin. For the most part, we also do not know the exact order in which the edits occurred. What we do know is that Adams and Franklin made at least a few changes to Jefferson's draft in their own handwriting, and those changes are merely in wording.[6] Neither Adams nor Franklin edited the phrase "pursuit of happiness" or its inclusion as an unalienable right.

Following Jefferson's, Adams's, and Franklin's initial edits, a draft was submitted to the Committee of Five and then to the Continental Congress. Adams's own remembrances here are inconclusive; as he stated in his autobiography, "[T]he Report was made to the Committee of five, by them examined, but whether altered or corrected in any thing I cannot recollect. But in substance at least it was reported to Congress."[7] We have some additional evidence in Jefferson's letter of August 30, 1823, to James Madison, where Jefferson states that, after Adams and Franklin made two to three edits, Jefferson "then wrote a fair copy, reported it to the Committee, and from them, unaltered to Congress."[8]

Historian Carl Becker makes a compelling argument for Jefferson's recollection,[9] and the surviving evidence supports his analysis. This evidence includes what Jefferson confirmed to be his own "original Rough draught" of the Declaration, edited by himself, Adams, and Franklin; a copy of the Declaration as "originally framed," presented to the Continental Congress on June 28, 1776, which Jefferson sent in a July 8, 1776, letter to Richard H. Lee; a copy of the Declaration as "originally reported" to the Continental Congress on June 28, 1776, with the edits of the Continental Congress carefully marked, which Jefferson included in his autobiography; and the final version of the Declaration, which was adopted by the Continental Congress on July 4, 1776.[10]

A study of these documents and Jefferson's and Adams's own writings about them suggests that the "original Rough draught" of the Declaration may have made several editorial passes among Jefferson, Adams, and Franklin, with the results of those editorial decisions being recorded by Jefferson, Adams, and Franklin on the document itself.[11] Becker convincingly argues that Jefferson incorporated all of these edits into a "fair copy" of the Declaration, which he then presented to the full Committee of Five. It was that fair copy, approved by the full committee in its unaltered state, that was then presented to the Continental Congress.[12]

Although we may never know the exact chronology of the editing that took place among Jefferson, Adams, and Franklin and within the Committee of Five, what we know for certain is that, by the time Jefferson's "original Rough draught" of the Declaration made it through Jefferson's own initial drafting process, Adams's review, Franklin's review, and the Committee of Five, twenty-six alterations had been made to the text. Of these changes, only three were substantive; the remaining twenty-three "were changes in phraseology" and were made by Adams, Franklin, and Jefferson himself. The substantive changes included a three-paragraph addition to the Declaration's list of grievances against the king, which Becker argues Jefferson himself added before the fair copy was given to the Committee of Five.[13] Despite their apparent willingness to edit the draft Declaration with changes large and small, not one of the committee members edited the phrase "pursuit of happiness" or its inclusion as an unalienable right.

From here, the Committee of Five submitted a clean copy of the edited draft to the Continental Congress, where it was "read and ordered to lie on the table."[14] This copy was preserved, with some differences, both in a version of the Declaration as "originally reported," which Jefferson included in his autobiography, and in a copy of the Declaration "as originally framed" that Jefferson included in his July 8, 1776, letter to Richard H. Lee. From July 1 through July 4, the Continental Congress debated the text of the proposed Declaration, incorporating its own revisions.[15] The revisions of the Continental Congress were many, and Jefferson viewed them as "depredations."[16] In fact, Jefferson became so low during the editing process that Franklin was moved to tell him a funny story in order to cheer him up.[17]

The changes made to the Declaration by the Continental Congress ranged from careful distinctions in word choice (such as replacing "unremitting" with "repeated" in a description of the injuries and usurpations suffered by the colonists) to the substantive alteration of whole paragraphs (such as the Continental Congress's deletion of the entire passage whereby the Declaration charges King George III with responsibility for the continuation of human slavery, "a market where MEN should be bought & sold," in the American colonies).[18] The record of changes suggests that every word and phrase of the Declaration was carefully considered. However, here again, we see no editing of the phrase "pursuit of happiness" and no changes to its inclusion or its placement within the Declaration.

What are we to make of the fact that the phrase "pursuit of happiness" was not edited at all, either by Jefferson, Adams, or Franklin, within the Committee of Five, or within the Continental Congress as a whole? The lack of editing here would seem to suggest one of two things: either the phrase "pursuit of happiness" really was a glittering generality with a nonsubstantive meaning to which no one would object, or it had a substantive meaning that was both understood by and agreeable to the wide variety of individuals involved in drafting and editing the Declaration. We can gain additional insights into the context of "the pursuit of happiness" and how it was understood by the founders by looking more closely at two other aspects of the Declaration's drafting: the structure of the Declaration and the purpose behind the document.

Structure and Purpose of the Declaration

Studies of the Declaration have focused heavily on the specific language of the document, often at the expense of its overall structure and purpose.[19] But the founders' stated purpose in writing the Declaration and the structure they adopted as a result matter. They matter because the purpose and structure provide context for the specific language used by the founders, and therefore offer insights into the founders' word choices and their inclusion of phrases like "the pursuit of happiness."

A close look at the various drafts of the Declaration suggest that as the founders drafted and edited the Declaration, they considered not only individual word choice and placement, but also the overall structure and purpose of the document. Indeed, Adams states in his autobiography that the

Committee of Five had drafted "Articles" to be included in the Declaration, an account that Jefferson later disputes.[20] Despite their disagreement on how the substance of the text was determined, their agreement on the substance itself is evident in the drafts of the Declaration, as well as in the overall organization and stated purposes of the text that were preserved throughout the editing process.

As stated in the Declaration's opening paragraph, the authors believed that "a decent respect to the opinions of mankind requires that they should declare the causes which impel them to the separation." The purpose of the Declaration, Jefferson would later proclaim, was to provide philosophical arguments and factual evidence to support the founders' decision to separate from English rule.[21] They chose to build that support around the analogy of slavery as the antithesis to living, at liberty, in accordance with the laws of nature. It is an analogy that reflects John Locke's argument that, under the law of nature, every man has a property right to, and therefore a right to dominion over, his own person. According to Locke, each man holds these rights within the state of nature, but man may consent to be governed in order to more fully protect and realize those rights. If a government were to exercise dominion over man arbitrarily, without proper consent or authority, the end result would be tyranny, a form of absolute power often described by the founders as despotism. One who lost dominion over his person through the actions of a tyrannical ruler would be, in the words of the founders, enslaved. This juxtaposition of tyranny and slavery was not new to Locke or the founders; as will be discussed shortly, it was a common theme in ancient philosophy.

John Adams had included a distillation of this argument in his handwritten summary of James Otis's 1761 speech against the writs of assistance, which Adams described as "[a] dissertation on the rights of man in a state of nature. He asserted that every man, merely natural, was an independent sovereign, subject to no law but the law written on his heart and revealed to him by his Maker, in the constitution of his nature and the inspiration of his understanding and his conscience. His right to his life, his liberty, no created being could rightfully contest. Nor was his right to his property less incontestable." Adams then summarized Otis as comparing a loss of liberty to slavery and proclaiming that

> the security of these rights to life, liberty, and property had been the object
> of all those struggles against arbitrary power . . . in every age. He asserted
> that our ancestors, as British subjects, and we their descendants, as British

subjects, were entitled to all those rights by the British constitution as well as by the law of nature and our provincial character as much as any inhabitant of London or Bristol or any part of England, and were not to be cheated out of them by any phantom of "virtual representation" or any other fiction of law or politics or any monkish trick of deceit and hypocrisy.[22]

Jefferson also used this analogy several years before the drafting of the Declaration. In his 1774 work *A Summary View of the Rights of British Americans*,[23] Jefferson petitioned the king for redress of "encroachments and usurpations" made against "those rights which God and the laws have given equally and independently to all." Jefferson argued here, as in the Declaration, that the rights of a "free people" are "derived from the laws of nature, and not as the gift of their chief magistrate." Jefferson claimed, "It is neither our wish, nor our interest, to separate from [Great Britain]," but simultaneously held that the grievances of the king against the rights held by free men through the laws of nature must be addressed. "Single acts of tyranny," Jefferson argued, "may be ascribed to the accidental opinion of a day; but a series of oppressions, begun at a distinguished period, and pursued unalterably through every change of ministers, too plainly prove a deliberate and systematical plan of reducing us to slavery."[24]

In the Declaration of Independence, the founders laid forth a similar charge, arguing that "the history of the present king of Great Britain is a history of repeated injuries and usurpations, all having in direct object the establishment of an absolute Tyranny over these States." They then included the list of grievances against King George III that mirrored the list Jefferson had begun in *A Summary View*. A key difference between the final copy of the Declaration and Jefferson's draft language, however, is that Jefferson's draft list of grievances culminated with this virulent passage against slavery:

[H]e has waged cruel war against human nature itself, violating it's most sacred rights of life & liberty in the persons of a distant people who never offended him, captivating and carrying them into slavery in another hemisphere, or to incur miserable death in their transportation thither. this piratical warfare, the opprobrium of *infidel* powers, is the warfare of the *Christian* king of Great Britain. determined to keep open a market where MEN should be bought & sold, he has prostituted his negative for suppressing every legislative attempt to prohibit or to restrain this execrable commerce: and that this assemblage of horrors might want no fact of distinguished die, he is now exciting those very people to rise in arms among us, and to purchase that

liberty of which *he* has deprived them, & murdering the people upon whom
he also obtruded them; thus paying off former crimes committed against the
liberties of one people, with crimes which he urges them to commit against
the *lives* of another.[25]

As historian Pauline Maier has stated, Jefferson intended for this passage "to
be the emotional climax of his case against the King." Although the Continental Congress later removed this passage on physical slavery, due to the
"Southern brethren [who] would never suffer to pass [it] in Congress," the
language of political slavery and tyranny woven throughout the remainder
of the Declaration remained.[26]

The founders bookended their discussion of the king's tyranny in the
Declaration with natural law theory. The Declaration begins with the "separate and equal station to which the Laws of Nature and of Nature's God
entitle them" and ends with a statement that, as a result of the king's tyranny, "these United Colonies are & of Right ought to be Free and Independent States." In his insightful work on how science influenced the founders,
historian of science I. Bernard Cohen argues that the term "laws of nature"
refers to scientific laws that govern the natural world.[27] Cohen argues that
these laws are distinct from the law (singular) of nature, which is the natural
law. Blackstone and the founders seem to agree and to disagree with Cohen's analysis. To consider the connections, it is worth replicating portions
of these texts in whole.

Blackstone claims that "when the supreme being formed the universe,
and created matter out of nothing, he impressed certain principles upon that
matter, from which it can never depart, and without which it would cease
to be. When he put that matter into motion, he established certain laws
of motion, to which all moveable bodies must conform." This description
lines up beautifully with the physical laws of nature that Cohen describes
in his work. But Blackstone then goes on to compare these laws to the law
of nature that governs man: "This will of his maker is called the law of
nature. For as God, when he created matter, and endued it with a principle
of mobility, established certain rules for the perpetual direction of that motion; so, when he created man, and endued him with freewill to conduct
himself in all parts of life, he laid down certain immutable laws of human
nature, whereby that freewill is in some degree regulated and restrained,
and gave him also the faculty of reason to discover the purport of those
laws."[28] As discussed previously, Blackstone's distinction here is not one of

source or purpose; both the laws of nature and the law of nature were put in place by the Creator God to govern that which has been created. Blackstone's distinction seems to one of categorization, which he utilizes in order to highlight reason as an essential characteristic of man and a key method by which man can know the law of nature as it applies to humans. In this line of thought, Blackstone is following in the footsteps of his English predecessor Richard Hooker, who described the law of nature as it pertains to man as the law of reason. In both instances, Blackstone is clear that the immutable laws of nature that pertain to the physical world (inanimate or animate, irrational creation) and the immutable law of nature that pertains to man (animate, rational creation) are put in place by a Creator God to govern all of creation.

Compared to Blackstone, Jefferson seems much more comfortable in collapsing these two categories of natural law and then engaging in political philosophy that nevertheless preserves their distinctions. So, for example, in *A Summary View of the Rights of British Americans*, Jefferson uses the plural "laws of nature" to describe a binding, natural law and then describes the ramifications of those laws for human law and governance.[29] These laws were not, for Jefferson or the founders, the laws that governed only the physical world; they were the basis by which the colonists were entitled to assume independence. We know this because, in the words of the Declaration, the colonists were assuming "the separate and equal station to which the Laws of Nature and of Nature's God entitle them." The "and of Nature's God" language is incredibly important for understanding the founders' argument here. As political theorists Kody Cooper and Justin Dyer have persuasively argued, "[T]here is strong evidence that Jefferson shared in the general consensus of the colonists, that 'Nature's God' symbolically expressed providential, moralistic theism as the essential foundation of natural rights, *precisely in virtue of* God's creation of nature."[30] In other words, and as will be discussed more fully in chapter 5, like Blackstone, the founders believed in a Creator God as the ultimate source of their natural rights.

The founders' emphasis on rights endowed by a Creator God is demonstrated in the opening of the Declaration, with a listing of truths that Jefferson initially described as "sacred and undeniable." Through his own edits or those of Franklin, this phrase was changed to "self-evident." One self-evident truth is that, as a result of their creation, "all men are created equal." Another is that "from that equal creation," men derive the inalienable rights "to the preservation of life, & liberty, & the pursuit of happiness."[31] This language is later changed to "that all men are created equal, that they are endowed by their Creator with certain unalienable Rights, that among these are Life, Liberty, and the pursuit of Happiness." Both the idea that men derive rights from their equal creation and the altered language that men are "endowed by their Creator with certain Unalienable rights" assume a Creator who imbues rights in man through creation.

Finally, the wording of the Declaration reflects Blackstone's emphasis on man's ability to use reason to determine the first principles of the law of nature as it pertains to man. The draft term "undeniable" and the final language "self-evident" both assume the role of reason in determining man's natural rights. In fact, the role of reason is included even earlier, as the Declaration states that its purpose is to share with mankind the reasons that "impel[led]" them to declare independence, and later, as the founders include an appeal "to the Supreme Judge of the world for the rectitude of our intentions." Thus, the founders submitted their reasoning on the natural law not only to the judgment of their fellow men but also to the Supreme Judge of the world, imploring the Supreme Judge to consider the rectitude or rightness of their intentions. They refer once more to the Creator God who not only creates but also sustains his creation as they close out the Declaration with a "firm reliance on the protection of divine Providence."

These natural law portions of the Declaration are not separate from the list of grievances against the king; instead, they inform it. When the founders declare that King George III has become a tyrant, they do so by declaring that he is "unfit" to rule. In other words, he is no longer operating in accordance with what it means to be a ruler, and, therefore, his governance over the colonists is void. This idea had salience in Enlightenment debates over law and governance and in the founders' own understanding of English history. Thus, after delineating the king's acts of tyranny, the founders could claim that they were not rebelling against English authority; instead, that authority had already been abdicated by the king. They declare that they are now free (no longer enslaved under tyranny) and independent (returning to "the separate and equal station to which the Law of Nature and of Nature's God entitles them"). They are reassuming their proper position under the natural law and instituting a new government—one that would protect man's unalienable rights to life, liberty, and the pursuit of happiness.

It was for the purpose of articulating to a broader world the "causes which impel them to the separation" that the Declaration was written. This purpose was further articulated by Jefferson in an 1825 letter he wrote to Henry

Lee: "When forced, therefore, to resort to arms for redress, an appeal to the tribunal of the world was deemed proper for our justification. This was the object of the Declaration of Independence. Not to find out new principles, or new arguments, never before thought of, not merely to say things which had never been said before; but to place before mankind the common sense of the subject, in terms so plain and firm as to command their assent, and to justify ourselves in the independent stand we are compelled to take."[32]

The drafting of the Declaration of Independence, its structure, its purpose, and the placement of "the pursuit of Happiness" within its text provide us with a broader context for understanding what the founders meant by including "the pursuit of Happiness" within the document. But to understand the meaning of that phrase, to understand what the founders meant by claiming—within this context and for this purpose—that man is endowed by his Creator with the unalienable right to the pursuit of happiness, we must look to the broader intellectual backdrop within which the Declaration was written.

CHAPTER 5

"No New Ideas"
Four Strands of Founding Era Thought

WHAT DID THE Declaration mean at the time of the founding? When asked about the drafting of the Declaration, both John Adams and Thomas Jefferson stated that it contained no new ideas. In an August 6, 1822, letter to Timothy Pickering, Adams stated: "As you justly observe, there is not an idea in it, but what had been hackney'd in Congress for two years before. The substance of it is contained in the declaration of rights and the violation of those rights, in the Journals of Congress in 1774. Indeed, the essence of it is contained in a pamphlet, voted and printed by the Town of Boston before the first Congress met; composed by James Otis, as I suppose—in one of his lucid intervals, and pruned and polished by Saml: Adams."[1]

When asked about Adams's recollections, Jefferson stated, in an August 30, 1823, letter to James Madison:

"[T]hat it contained no new ideas, that it is a commonplace compilation, it's sentiments hacknied in Congress for two years before, and it's essence contained in Otis's pamphlet," may all be true. of that I am not to be the judge. [Richard] H. Lee charged it as copied from Locke's Treatise on government. Otis's pamphlet I never saw, & whether I had gathered my ideas from reading or reflection I do not know. I know only that I turned to neither book or pamphlet while writing it. I did not consider it as any part of my charge to invent new ideas altogether & to offer no sentiment which had ever been expressed before.[2]

As discussed previously, Jefferson spoke further of the purpose of the Declaration of Independence and the ideas it contained, in a May 8, 1825, letter to Henry Lee, which is worth including in its fuller context here:

When forced, therefore, to resort to arms for redress, an appeal to the tribunal of the world was deemed proper for our justification. This was the object of the Declaration of Independence. Not to find out new principles, or new

arguments, never before thought of, not merely to say things which had never been said before; but to place before mankind the common sense of the
subject, in terms so plain and firm as to command their assent, and to justify
ourselves in the independent stand we are compelled to take. Neither aiming
at originality of principle or sentiment, nor yet copied from any particular
and previous writing, it was intended to be an expression of the American
mind, and to give to that expression the proper tone and spirit called for by
the occasion. All its authority rests then on the harmonizing sentiments of
the day, whether expressed in conversation, in letters, printed essays, or in
the elementary books of public right, as Aristotle, Cicero, Locke, Sidney, &c.
The historical documents you mention as in your possession, ought all to be
found, and I am persuaded you will find, to be corroborative of the facts and
principles advanced in that Declaration.[3]

If the Declaration was not intended to assert original principles or sentiments, if it was not intended to include new ideas, but, instead, was an
expression of common sense and the "sentiments of the day," what, then,
counted as old ideas and common sentiments at the time it was written?

Four key strands of thought influenced both the writing of the Declaration and the sentiments of the founding era: English law and legal theory, the history and philosophy of classical antiquity, Christianity, and the
Scottish Enlightenment's emphasis on Newtonian science. A further look
at each of these key strands leads to two conclusions. First, as historian Carl
Richard has eloquently argued, the founders did not separate these strands
of thought into distinct categories, but intermingled them in what they
understood to be an intellectually coherent fashion.[4] Second, a close look
reveals that each of these four strands includes a core thesis that is in harmony with Blackstone's understanding of the pursuit of happiness and the
use of the phrase within the Declaration of Independence. Each of the four
strands will be explored in depth below.

English Law and Legal Theory

Blackstone's *Commentaries* constituted the most comprehensive compilation
of English law in its day. It was also the most widely circulated text on
English law in the North American colonies. When Blackstone began his
Commentaries with a discussion of the law of nature and the law of God as
the sources of the immutable legal principles upon which the entire English
common law was premised, he did so within a larger eighteenth-century

understanding of natural laws that were to guide the actions of governments and men. As historian Carl Becker stated in the context of his own study of the Declaration of Independence, the concept that "there is a 'natural order' of things in the world, cleverly and expertly designed by God for the guidance of mankind; that the 'laws' of this natural order may be discovered by human reason; that these laws so discovered furnish a reliable and immutable standard for testing the ideas, the conduct, and the institutions of men—these were the accepted premises, the preconceptions, of most eighteenth century thinking, not only in America, but in England and France."[5]

In England, that understanding built on seventeenth-century constitutional struggles between Sir Edward Coke and Parliament, on the one hand, and the Stuart monarchs, on the other. These battles resulted in the English Civil War of 1642–49 and culminated with the execution of King Charles I for treason in 1649. The constitutional battles revived with the return of the Stuart monarchy in 1660 and were resolved only through the Glorious Revolution of 1688, which established parliamentary supremacy and produced the English Bill of Rights in 1689.[6] Although this view of English legal history has been both challenged and complicated by the work of more recent historians, it is the view that was promulgated by both Blackstone and the founders; it was how they viewed their own history and how they used it as evidence to support the change in law that they advocated for in their day.

The colonists looked back to the struggles between Parliament and the king in seventeenth-century England as a time in comparison with their own struggles with England.[7] Thus, English philosopher John Locke, who wrote during the time of the Glorious Revolution, not only summarized the constitutional principles vindicated in the Glorious Revolution, but also served as a model for the eighteenth-century struggles of the British colonists in North America.[8] The same could be said of Montesquieu,[9] whom many of the founders read and whom Jefferson revered in his early life. From the 1760s forward, the colonists had been petitioning Britain in terms of their fundamental rights, as understood in English law and legal theory.[10] John Adams committed this history to text in his written summary of James Otis's 1761 speech against the Writs of Assistance: "In short, [Otis] asserted these rights [of life, liberty, and property] to be derived only from nature and the Author of nature; that they were inherent, inalienable, and indefeasible. . . . These principles and these rights were wrought into the English constitution as fundamental laws. And under this head he went back to the old Saxon laws and to Magna Carta . . . to the position of rights and the Bill of Rights and the [Glorious] revolution."[11]

These comparisons involved not only theory but also practice, as constitutional struggles in England tended to have their colonial counterparts. Thus, *The Trial of the Seven Bishops in England* (1688) was followed by *The Trial of John Peter Zenger* in the colonies (1735).[12] Both cases challenged the law of seditious libel as understood in English legal precedent, and both outcomes contradicted that precedent by setting new parameters for the relationship between the people and the governmental authorities. The colonial *Writs of Assistance* case (1761), at which John "Adams saw the 'birth of the child Independence,'" raised questions about the constitutionality of colonial statutes and their relationship to English law. James Otis relied on Coke's views and English legal precedent in Bonham's Case (1610) to argue against the writs, claiming that "when an act of Parliament is against common right or reason . . . the Common Law will . . . adjudge such act to be void."[13] He referred to former constitutional struggles in England by claiming that the exercise of arbitrary power "in former periods of history cost one king of England his head and another his throne." Otis stated that the writs were "the worst instrument of arbitrary power, the most destructive of English liberty and the fundamental principles of law, that ever was found in an English law-book."[14]

As these cases demonstrate, the colonists viewed the English law as their law, and they felt free to oppose English law on its own terms, claiming that the English law was a law of liberty, as opposed to a law of tyranny or slavery. They claimed that the English law was not arbitrary but, instead, bound by a higher law, often articulated by the founders, like Otis, in language similar to that of Blackstone, as the fundamental principles of law. In his *Commentaries*, Blackstone confirmed this hierarchy of law, but qualified it, saying, "but if the Parliament will positively enact a thing to be done which is unreasonable, I know of no power that can control it."[15] While Blackstone's views on this matter were dominant in England,[16] many of the American colonists disagreed. As Jefferson later stated to James Madison, the founders held to Coke's, not Blackstone's, construction of the relationship between the English law and the higher law.[17] This disagreement regarding the corrective role of the higher law in relationship to Parliament was one "which colonial resistance would only confirm."[18]

The English common law was received in the American colonies throughout the eighteenth century,[19] and even as the colonists moved toward independence, they continued to describe their rights in terms of English law. John Adams summarized some of the key claims of James Otis's February 1761 speech against the writs of assistance as follows: "He asserted that our ancestors, as British subjects, and we their descendants, as British subjects, were entitled to all those rights by the British constitution as well as by the law of nature."[20] In his later essay titled *The Rights of the British Colonies*, Otis reiterated his argument against the general writs of assistance by claiming that the law of God was a higher authority than Parliament; if a law of Parliament contradicted the higher authority, then that law of Parliament was void.[21] Jefferson asserted similar views in *A Summary View of the Rights of British America*. Both authors framed their arguments in terms of English law. Like Otis, Jefferson made the higher-law argument, stating that the "God who gave us life gave us liberty at the same time."[22]

The English, too, viewed their relationship with the colonies in terms of English law, claiming in the 1766 Declaratory Act that both Parliament and the Crown ruled colonies. The colonists responded with the 1774 Declaration & Resolves of the Continental Congress, claiming their entitlement to all English rights, including "life, liberty, and property," as well as the common law of England and the law of the English statutes. These rights were summarized in George Mason's 1776 Virginia Declaration of Rights, already written when the Continental Congress met to debate and then declare their independence from England. Mason summarized the colonists' inherent rights as follows: "That all men are by nature equally free and independent, and have certain inherent rights, of which, when they enter into a state of society, they cannot, by any compact, deprive or divest their posterity; namely, the enjoyment of life and liberty, with the means of acquiring and possessing property, and pursuing and obtaining happiness and safety."[23] Given this extensive reliance on English law and legal theory in the founding era, the question then becomes, what impact did English legal theory have on the Declaration?

Jefferson, the original drafter of the Declaration, was a self-directed student of English history[24] and had studied English law extensively in his training as a lawyer, focusing on Coke's *Institutes* and later encountering Blackstone's *Commentaries*.[25] When Jefferson actually sat down to write the Declaration, he had two documents with him: his draft constitution of Virginia and a draft of George Mason's Virginia Declaration of Rights.[26] Jefferson's possession of Mason's work is particularly significant in that, as shown above, Mason's listing of unalienable rights included not only life, liberty, and the pursuit of happiness but also property. Mason's listing suggests that far from omitting "property" and inserting "pursuit of happiness" in its place, Jefferson was following in a tradition that viewed property and pursuit of happiness as two distinct rights.

Pauline Maier claims that with these two documents in mind, Jefferson's draft of the Declaration, and, indeed, the Declaration as a final product, should be seen not primarily as a philosophical document but as "one that concerned the fundamental authority of government."[27] In part, she is right. As both Jefferson and Adams both later claimed, the Declaration was not intended to lay out new ideas. The Declaration's structure shows it was intended to make a case for the colonies to separate from rule by England and to assume their "separate and equal station" as "Free and Independent States." As Maier argues, these are issues of the fundamental authority of government.

Yet the language the founders used to make their case is extremely philosophical, and the philosophy that language embodies is, at least in part, that of the English common law. It included a philosophy of natural rights and the ends of government articulated by English philosopher John Locke and the latitudinarian legal philosophy of Blackstone's *Commentaries.* Thus, the interesting irony of the Declaration is that the colonists declared their independence from England but did so in firm reliance on and understanding of both the English law and the higher-law principles that provided the foundation of the English common-law system. The *Commentaries* were published in London from 1765 to 1769, and an American edition was published as early as 1771–72. By the time of the Declaration, "nearly twenty-five hundred copies" of Blackstone's *Commentaries* were circulating in the American colonies, a circulation that is believed to have "rivaled that in England."[28] Only by understanding this larger English legal context, a context distilled and then distributed throughout the colonies in Blackstone's *Commentaries,* can we understand both the context and the content of the Declaration.

History and Philosophy of Classical Antiquity

A second strand of thought that influenced the founders was their knowledge of classical antiquity. The founders were deeply steeped in the history and philosophy of classical antiquity; such training in the classics was common among educated men of the time.[29] They saw the ancient Roman Republic as the ideal form of government, and they were especially familiar with the speeches and writings of the Roman philosopher and statesman-orator Cicero. Other favorites included, but were not limited to, Plutarch's biographies of great Greek and Roman leaders; Greek historian Polybius on Roman history; Roman emperor and philosopher Marcus Aurelius and philosopher Epictetus, with their shared emphasis on Stoicism (especially for Jefferson); and Joseph Addison's *Spectator* essays and eighteenth-century play based on the life of the staunch defender of the Roman Republic, Cato the Younger.[30]

The ancient historian Polybius's analysis of Rome served as a starting point for the founders as they searched for a model for their new government. Polybius saw the Roman Republic, with its "interdependence between the one, the few, and the many," as "the most outstanding example of mixed government," and the founders agreed.[31] During the American Revolution and at the time of the Constitutional Convention of 1787, the men of the founding generation promoted mixed government as the structure of government most likely to thwart tyranny. According to Carl Richard, John Adams "was the most visible and most persistent proponent of mixed government in America . . . devoted to mixed government theory throughout his life." In this as in other areas, Adams followed his model of Cicero, who, unlike the Roman historians Plutarch, Tacitus, Livy, and Sallust, "formally endorsed" Polybius's view of mixed government.[32] When asked which he would prefer among aristocracy, democracy, and monarchy, Cicero replied, "[T]here is not one of them which I approve at all by itself, since . . . I prefer that government which is mixed and composed of all these forms, to any one of them taken separately."[33]

Adams had clear ideas about mixed government as early as the 1760s, when he wrote "An Essay on Man's Lust for Power," claiming, "No simple Form of Government can possibly secure Men against the Violences of Power. Simple Monarchy will soon mould itself into Despotism, Aristocracy will soon commence on Oligarchy, and Democracy will soon degenerate into Anarchy, such an Anarchy that every Man will do what is right in his own Eyes, and no Man's life or Property or Reputation or Liberty will be safe."[34]

Although written after the Declaration of Independence, John Adams's 1787 publication *A Defence* highlights ideas he had encountered from the ancients for decades. By 1787 Adams had long solidified his adherence to mixed-government theory. In fact, *A Defence* has been called "the fullest exposition of mixed government theory by an American."[35] In writing

A Defence, Adams had two goals: First, "to defend or *conserve* certain elements of balanced government then present in most of the American state
constitutions" and, second, to "persuad[e] Americans to change or *reform*
their governments in ways that would repair inadequate constitutional
beginnings."[36]

A Defence is a tour de force of mixed-government theory, but Adams
makes clear that the source of the theory was found in antiquity.[37] The
entire framework of *A Defence* mirrors Polybius's discussion of aristocracy,
democracy, and monarchy; his search for natural laws of governance; and
the analysis of the mixed governments of Greece and Rome, ideas that
are also reflected in books 1 and 3 of Cicero's *On Laws*.[38] Following these
ideals, Adams wanted to establish "a perfect threefold balance within the
legislative power of each government, one part of the balance corresponding to the natural order of the many (a representative assembly), another
corresponding to the natural order of the few (a senate), and a third branch
headed by a single executive who would balance the first two against each
other, primarily by means of an absolute legislative veto."[39]

To this end, Adams upheld "[t]he Republics of Greece, Rome, and Car-
thage" not only as "mixed Governments" but as "[t]he best Governments
of the World."[40] Among these best governments, Adams's favorite, like that
of many of the other founders, was the Roman Republic. That the founders looked to ancient governments to determine the principles by which a
government would tend toward liberty versus slavery is reflective of their
commitment to inductive reasoning and their use of history both as an
experimental laboratory and as a field of observation useful for determining the first principles of governance. The founders used historical models
not only as they considered the best framework of government, but also as
they considered how they ought to live their own lives. Just as they could
observe, and seek to emulate, the best principles of virtuous governments
in the new United States, so could they observe, and seek to emulate, the
habits of virtuous men in their own lives.

For example, Cicero served as a model for the founders not only in his
promotion of mixed government, but also because he consistently (some
would say incessantly) spoke out against what he perceived to be tyranny
and the coming downfall of the Roman Republic. He characterized his own
fight for the preservation of Rome in terms of glory, as seen in his speech in
defense of the Roman citizenship claim of poet Archias in 62 BC. Cicero
argued that men could be motivated to live lives of merit in the face of "toil

and danger" because of the "praise and glory" that would be their reward: "If you take that away, gentlemen, what incentive do we have, in life's brief and transitory career, to involve ourselves in great undertakings?"[41]

The founders frequently characterized their own work in Cicero's terms of great undertakings that would be difficult and involve sacrifice, but would lead to glory that would live on after their deaths.[42] In a reflection of Cicero's emphasis on glory, Jefferson believed one's public life would be judged by future historians and that one ought to conduct oneself so as to gain esteem in that valuation. Further, the founders consistently looked to ancient history for men like Cicero who could be "models of personal behavior, social practice, and government form." For example, Thomas Jefferson saw much to admire in Tacitus's combination of moral and historical judgment. George Washington sought to emulate Cato as he addressed his troops. John Adams attempted to fashion himself after Cicero as an orator-statesman who used an inductive method to determine those principles of government that would most lead toward liberty and away from tyranny.[43] In an 1809 letter to Benjamin Rush, John Adams claimed that, of the men from antiquity who could have served as his model, "I chose to confine myself to Cicero." And, indeed, he had. Adams chose Cicero for his model early on and held fast to him throughout his lifetime. He "made a conscious effort to model his own public life after Cicero's glorious career," consciously copying Cicero's rhetoric and oratorical skill and seeing in the ancient man's career of law and public service a mirror of his own life.[44]

The founders looked to ancient history for models of excellence in political and public life; they modeled their own lives on ancient standards, and they evaluated the public virtues and political lives of others according to those same standards.[45] In reading the works of men like Cicero, Marcus Aurelius, and Epictetus, the founders also encountered the key principles of Stoic philosophy, many of which resonated with scientific and philosophical ideas of the Enlightenment.

The Stoic vision of the world encompasses much of the same natural law theory as that laid out by Blackstone in the introductory portion of his *Commentaries*. The Stoics argued that a "common law" and a "natural law" governed the created world, described by the Stoic Chrysippus as follows: "Our natures are part of the nature of the universe. Therefore, the goal becomes 'to live following nature,' that is, according to one's own nature and that of the universe, doing nothing which is forbidden by the common law (*nomos ho koinos*), which is right reason [*orthos logos*], penetrating all things."[46]

Stoic philosophy emphasized "exceptionless laws" that governed the universe. For a Stoic, to live the good life or the life of virtue was to live in harmony with logos, a form of "universal reason . . . that organizes and directs" the natural world and that was discernible by man through "right reason."[47] Additionally, Stoic philosophy emphasized the notion that "[h]umans should live in accordance with human nature, which is, for them, to live in accordance with human reason."[48] The human capacity for reason was described by the Stoics as being in "possession of the spark that is part of divine reason."[49] They believed that "God's reason flowed through the universe, giving order to everything."[50] That direction of logos extended to humans, as the Stoics "insist[ed] that standards of living well are based in nature, and are binding on all human beings."[51] Thus, the path to living well, or "virtue lay in 'living agreeably to nature in the exercise of right reason.'"[52] To the Stoics, "virtue and the good life were indistinguishable, in speaking of one, one spoke of the other also."[53] Stoic philosophers defined virtue as "the skill of putting other things to their correct use" and believed that "virtue is sufficient for happiness."[54] Humans could choose the path of virtue by exercising their reason, which was "connected to the divine reason."[55] In this sense, the Stoic understanding of virtue comports with Blackstone's understanding of pursuit of happiness as the pursuit of a virtuous or rightly ordered life.

The founders encountered Stoic philosophy not only through Cicero but also through later Stoics such as Marcus Aurelius and the former slave turned philosopher Epictetus, who was a particular favorite of Jefferson, perhaps due to his emphasis on putting theory into practice.[56] Stoicism and a theory of mixed government to protect liberty and oppose tyranny were two key lines of thought from classical antiquity that were reflected in the Declaration. A third key line of thought from classical antiquity that was reflected in the Declaration was the ancient view of slavery.

Slavery was a broader and more fluid concept in the ancient world than in the British colonies in North America. In antiquity slavery was the antithesis of freedom and could occur through a variety of means, indebtedness and warfare being the greatest two. The ancient Greeks and Romans believed an enslaved man was, by the very fact of his enslavement, unable to live a virtuous, or rightly ordered, life. Slavery was contrary to nature; while a free man could choose to live in harmony with his human nature, a slave did not have that choice.[57] For Epictetus, who had been born a slave, to live in harmony with nature was both the goal of one's life and "the virtue of the happy man."[58]

The Stoics distinguished the effects of physical slavery and the effect of a slavery that took away one's freedom to live wisely, which was to live in accord with human nature, stating, "The wise may have their body put in chains, but you will never chain their soul."[59] The founders consistently employed the classical understanding of slavery as the antithesis to liberty in their struggles with Britain. The Declaration asserted that the tyranny of the British government threatened man's unalienable rights. These included the colonists' unalienable right to life, which was self-preservation—the first law of nature.[60] Tyranny threatened liberty, which, in the ancient world, was defined in terms of status, as "the freedoms of the ordinary citizen," including "freedom opposed both to the state of slavery and to domination by the powerful."[61] Tyranny also threatened the pursuit of happiness, an idea that is even more compelling when both tyranny and the pursuit of happiness are understood in a classical sense. In the classical sense, to pursue happiness is to pursue virtue—to pursue a life that is rightly ordered in relation to the first principles, summarized by the founders as "the Laws of Nature and of Nature's God." And in the classical sense, this pursuit was not possible among those who were enslaved.

As discussed earlier, in his "original Rough draught" of the Declaration, Jefferson's list of grievances against the king culminated with a virulent passage against slavery. The charge of slavery was the high point of Jefferson's argument.[62] This charge makes sense when viewed within the overall structure of the Declaration and within the classical philosophy that informed its content. Jefferson's basic argument is that King George III has become a tyrant and therefore "is unfit to be the ruler of a free people." The colonists believed they were enslaved by this tyranny and therefore no longer able to exercise their unalienable rights of life, liberty, and the pursuit of happiness. As a result, the colonists had the right to dissolve their government and return to their "separate and equal station" in the universe. The colonists once more would be at liberty, governed by "the Laws of Nature and Nature's God," free from the rule of tyranny, and fully able to exercise their unalienable rights. Carl Richard confirms the founders' classical connection between tyranny and the inability to live a virtuous, or rightly ordered, life, stating:

> Classical republicans feared conspiracies not so much because tyranny deprived citizens of their liberty as because it robbed them of their virtue. As we have seen, the founders repeatedly contended that tyranny corrupted citizens by dehumanizing and degrading them. Perhaps more than any argument this

assumption produced the desire for independence from Great Britain. If the cunning prime ministers of Britain could ever convince the American public to accept the smallest unconstitutional tax, Americans would eventually lose not only the power, but the very will, to resist. Americans would then be no more than slaves, subject to the whims of distant masters.[63]

Christianity

The third strand of thought that influenced the founders in the Revolutionary era is Christianity. Perhaps no question has been so fraught in founding-era scholarship than "Were (or were not) the founders Christian?" Two recent works that have accomplished a great deal in expanding our understanding of the role of Christianity in the founding era did so by changing the question altogether. Thus, both Carl Richard, in *The Founders and the Bible*, and Daniel Dreisbach, in *Reading the Bible with the Founding Fathers*, broadened the inquiry by exploring how the Bible might have influenced the founders in their personal lives and political thought. The result, in both instances, is an informative, refreshingly nuanced, and incredibly well-researched discussion of the intricacy, complexity, and diversity of the Bible's influence in early America.

A cursory read of legal and political literature of the founding era demonstrates that the founders continually invoked the Christian God, specifically, or a theistic God, more generally, in their founding-era judicial arguments and opinions, petitions, and declarations of rights.[64] In so doing, they were reflecting the discourse of their time. We see these same types of references in the Declaration of Independence.

The Declaration begins with a discussion of a Creator who endows individuals with "certain unalienable rights." The Declaration's Creator is in the image of a divine clockmaker, who establishes laws to govern his creation. The English deists used this imagery to describe a "God who had endowed the world at the beginning of time with ethical laws that every individual can discover for himself through the use of his unaided reason."[65] But Blackstone used the same image to describe the manner in which the Christian God had created the laws of nature to govern his creation:

> Law, in its most general and comprehensive sense, signifies a rule of action; and is applied indiscriminately to all kinds of action, whether animate or inanimate, rational or irrational. Thus we say, the laws of motion, of gravitation, of optics, or mechanics, as well as the laws of nature and of nations. And

it is that rule of action which is prescribed by some superior, and which the inferior is bound to obey.

Thus, when the supreme being formed the universe, and created matter out of nothing, he impressed certain principles upon that matter, from which it can never depart, and without which it would cease to be. When he put that matter into motion, he established certain laws of motion, to which all movable bodies must conform. And, to descend from the greatest operations to the smallest, when a workman forms a clock, or other piece of mechanism, he establishes, at his own pleasure, certain arbitrary laws for it's direction; as that the hand shall describe a given space in a given time; to which law as long as the work conforms, so long it continues in perfection, and answers the end of it's formation.[66]

Blackstone specifically identified the supreme being as the Christian God who, through "divine Providence," revealed the "holy scriptures" as the unfailing means by which one could know the law of nature as it pertains to man.[67] Both Coke and Blackstone believed Christianity to be the foundation of the English common law; they discussed it as a fact. Although later repudiated by Jefferson, this belief in the Christian underpinnings of the common law was widely held by many of the colonists in British North America at the time of the founding.[68]

Although the Declaration's later references to God may appear to reflect a more general theism, seemingly general terms such as "Almighty God" and "Providence" were specific names for the Christian God, as included in the doctrinal teachings of the eighteenth-century Anglican and Presbyterian Churches in America, including the Anglican Church's *Articles of the Christian Religion* and *The Book of Common Prayer* and the Presbyterian Church's *The Westminster Confession of Faith*.[69] The Westminster Assembly was called by Parliament and met at Westminster Abbey in London from 1643 to 1648, a time period in English history that the founders continually compared with their own. The assembly's work culminated in *The Westminster Confession of Faith*, which was largely adopted by the Presbyterian Church. A great many of the founders were schooled by Scottish Presbyterian tutors or at the Presbyterian College of New Jersey, which graduated "ten cabinet officers, thirty-nine congressmen, twenty-one senators, twelve governors, thirty judges (including three Supreme Court justices), and fifty state legislators" under the leadership of President John Witherspoon.[70]

The Continental Congress added to the Declaration an appeal to "the protection of divine Providence." As will be discussed further, "divine

Providence" could possibly reflect the ancient conception of Providence as "first cause" or "first mover," but likely reflects a more robust, interventionist, Christian conception of Providence as the means by which God upholds all things and where God himself is defined as "the first cause."[71] In additional language edited in by the Continental Congress, the founders appeal to "the Supreme Judge of the world for the rectitude of our intentions." "Supreme Judge" is a name attributed to the Christian God in the Presbyterian *Westminster Confession of Faith*. "Rectitude" means rightness and again evokes the idea of a correct order of things, the idea of a fit relationship to one's world. Finally, the language of slavery throughout the Declaration not only had its roots in classical conceptions of slavery versus liberty, but also was reflective of the persistent narrative of slavery in the Old Testament history of the Israelites, a narrative that was particularly compelling to the founders.[72]

To what extent were the founders familiar with the Christian teachings embodied in these phrases? Although personal religious belief is difficult to determine, evidence demonstrates that the founders were, at the very least, steeped in Christianity in an intellectual, academic sense.[73] As part of their college entrance requirements, the founders were required to know Greek, so that they could study the New Testament in its original language, and, indeed, many continued to study the Bible in its original languages for their own education and pleasure later in life.[74] The New Testament is replete with language demonstrating significant harmony not only between the Christian God and the first cause of Stoic philosophy, but also between the Christian God and the Creator as described in the Declaration. For example, in the book of Colossians, Paul describes a Creator who, like the Creator in the Declaration, governs the universe through the law of nature: "[Christ] is the image of the invisible God, the firstborn over all creation. For in him all things were created: things in heaven and on earth, visible and invisible, whether thrones or powers or rulers or authorities; all things have been created through him and for him. He is before all things, and in him all things hold together."[75]

This natural law understanding of how the Christian God created and ordered the world is evident throughout the New Testament. For example, in the book of Romans, Paul claims that "since the creation of the world God's invisible qualities—his eternal power and divine nature—have been clearly seen, being understood from what has been made."[76] Thus, the observation of creation provides insight into the attributes of the Creator God, an idea that formed the basis for inductive reasoning through the "nature" book of "two-book" theology that had been articulated by Christian theologians and legal scholars for centuries.

Perhaps the most prominent passage connecting Christianity and classical notions of a Creator occurs in the Gospel of John, which was included in translation requirements for entrance into King's College (now Columbia University), the College of New Jersey (now Princeton), and Brown University. Alexander Hamilton and John Jay went to King's College, which was Anglican. When Jay entered in 1760, he was required to "translate the first ten chapters of John into Latin." At the time of John Adams's entrance, Harvard required the ability to "parse ordinary Greek, as in the New Testament." The Presbyterian College of New Jersey schooled a disproportionate number of the founders and required translation of "the Greek gospels" for entrance.[77] This passage from the Gospel of John was a common translation requirement: "In the beginning was the Word, and the Word was with God, and the Word was God. He was with God in the beginning. Through him all things were made; without him nothing was made that has been made. In him was life, and that life was the light of all mankind."[78] In this passage, "the Word" is an English translation of the Greek term "logos," "the governing power behind all things."[79] John uses "the Word" as a synonym for Christ, thereby instructing his readers that what they understood as the Greek concept of logos, the first mover behind all of creation, was embodied and fully realized in the person of Jesus Christ.

The early Christians believed that Christ was "the governing power behind all things" not only in the created world but also among mankind. Following his discussion of the principles of God made known in the created order in Romans 1, Paul proclaims that the law of God is written on the heart of man and that man's conscience bears witness to this fact.[80] These passages demonstrate what Paul so eloquently proclaimed to a group of Stoic and Epicurean philosophers when he met with them in Athens. The Greek philosophers saw his words as a "new teaching," but Paul proclaimed that his teachings were very old: "[T]he very thing you worship," Paul proclaimed, "this is what I am going to proclaim to you."[81] Paul then defined the Christian God in Greek philosophical and intellectual terms, making a case that what his listeners had identified as the Stoic first mover, or logos, was actually the providential Christian God:

> The God who made the world and everything in it is the Lord of heaven and earth and does not live in temples built by human hands. And he is not served by human hands, as if he needed anything. Rather, he himself gives men life

and breath and everything else. . . . [H]e marked out their appointed times in history and the boundaries of their lands. God did this so that they would seek him and perhaps reach out for him and find him, though he is not far from any one of us. "For in him we live and move and have our being." As some of your own poets have said, "We are his offspring."[82]

English legal theorists followed this trend as they interpreted the English law through a combination of classical Stoicism and Christianity. And they were not alone. Montesquieu argued, in language that reflects elements of both Stoicism and Christianity, that "God is related to the universe as Creator and Preserver; the laws by which He created all things are those by which he preserves them. He acts according to these rules, because He knows them; He knows them, because He made them; and He made them, because they are in relation of His Wisdom and power. . . . The law which, impressing on our minds the idea of a Creator, inclines us toward Him, is the first in importance, though not in order, of natural laws."[83]

Yet this overlap of ideas between Stoicism and Christianity went only so far. Not one of the gospel writers would have claimed that the God who created, sustained, and actively intervened in his creation was fully represented by the Stoic first mover. Where ancient philosophy envisioned "impersonal forces that did not concern themselves with individuals and their lives," Christianity envisioned a "wise and loving form of divine intervention."[84] It a conception of the providential God as first mover that we see in the writings of Jean-Jacques Burlamaqui, whose legal philosophy not only was heavily mirrored in Blackstone's *Commentaries*, but also was quite compelling to the founders. "It is beyond doubt," Burlamaqui wrote,

> that he who exists necessarily and of himself, and has created the universe, must be invested with an infinite power. As he has given existence to all things by his own will, he may likewise preserve, annihilate or change them as he pleases. But his wisdom is equal to his power. Having made every thing, he must know every thing, as well the causes as the effects from thence resulting. We see besides in all his works the most excellent ends, and a choice of the most proper means to attain them; in short, they all bear, as it were, the stamp of wisdom. Reason informs us, that God is essentially good; a perfection which seems to flow naturally from his wisdom and power. . . . But let us enter into ourselves, and we shall actually find, that what we ought to expect in this respect from the divine wisdom and goodness, is dictated

by right reason, and by the principles engraved in our hearts. If there be any speculative truths that are evident, or if there be any certain axioms that serve as a basis to sciences; there is no less certainty in some principles that are laid down in order to direct our conduct, and to serve as the foundation of morality. For example; *That the all-wise and all bountiful Creator merits the respects of the creature; That man ought to seek his own happiness.*[85]

In his study of thirty key leaders in the founding era, Richard concluded that the founders would have held to this more robust form of divine Providence:

[A]ll of the founders embraced the biblical concept of an omniscient, omnipotent, caring God who not only created the universe but also intervened in it. They believed that the Creator invested each individual with inalienable rights and guided the affairs of individuals, societies, and nations to enforce those rights, as well as to advance other goods necessary to human happiness. The work of this "divine Providence" was mysterious. A few of the founders believed that God carried out His will through natural causes alone, but most were willing to speak of miracles.[86]

Jefferson, Franklin, and Adams each held to a sustaining, interventionist view of divine Providence, even as they were quite unorthodox in other aspects of their faith.[87]

It was not unusual for the founders to follow these earlier trends and view classical virtue through a Christian lens as well.[88] Thus, in the 1760s, Samuel Adams described the constitution of England as "founded 'On the Law of God and the Law of Nature,' as interpreted by Cicero, the Stoics, and James Otis.'"[89] James Otis, as we saw earlier, adopted Coke's view that the common law of England was governed by the higher law of God. His intermingling of law, philosophy, and theology is evident in his speech against the writs of assistance. Otis states that man, outside of society and in a state of nature, was "subject to no law but the law written on his heart"; it is a fascinating statement that combines John Locke on the state of nature with Paul's description of the law of God written on the heart of man. In language reflective of eighteenth-century Anglicanism and the Scottish Enlightenment, Otis stated that the law written on the heart of man was "revealed to him by his Maker, in the constitution of his nature and the inspiration of his understanding and his conscience."[90] Even as Jefferson,

Adams, and Franklin were unorthodox in their religious views, they continually advocated for the importance of Christian teachings for the incul-
cation of virtue and, especially for Adams and Franklin, the preservation of
the republic.[91] With this idea that there were interrelated lines of thought in
the eighteenth century that were then combined in the Declaration, Jefferson agreed, stating of the Declaration that "[a]ll its authority rests, then, on
the harmonizing sentiments of the day."[92]

The Scottish Enlightenment's Focus on Newtonian Science

In addition to English law and legal theory, the history and philosophy of
classical antiquity, and Christianity, a fourth key strand of thought influential in the founding era was the Scottish Enlightenment's focus on Newtonian science.[93] Much has been written on the moral philosophy of the
Scottish Enlightenment and its impact on the founding.[94] The founders im-
bibed the Scottish Enlightenment philosophy of an ordered universe from
their Scottish grammar school tutors and through their college educations
under men like the College of New Jersey's president John Witherspoon.
The founders did not see in the Scottish Enlightenment ideas that they had
never before encountered; they saw in it ideas with which they were already
intimately familiar. From their grammar school days under Scottish tutors
through their college studies of the classics, the New Testament, and moral
and political philosophy, the founders had become familiar with a combination of English liberty, classical history and philosophy, and Christianity
that they did not believe to be inconsistent. The founders saw one tradition
of liberty, tracing from antiquity to England to America, and it was a tradition that combined both classical and common-law understandings of that
term.[95] Thus, the Scottish Enlightenment revitalized ideas already held by
the founders.

Perhaps the most significant contribution of the Scottish Enlightenment
to founding-era thought came through the Scottish Enlightenment's Common Sense school, which harmonized philosophy and Newtonian science.
As discussed previously, the Common Sense school held to the idea that
one could induce first principles through observation of nature, an epistemology or way of knowing that mirrored not only the "book of nature" of
two-books Christian theology, but also the work of English scientist Isaac
Newton.

Newton made use of the scientific method to explore the natural world
and, in 1687, published his work on the history of science, *Mathematical*

Principles of Natural Philosophy.[96] That Jefferson thought much of Newton's methods and conclusions is demonstrated in his inclusion of Newton in his "noble trinity" of great men: Francis Bacon, Isaac Newton, and John Locke. In his esteem of Bacon, Newton, and Locke, Jefferson was not alone.[97] These three men have been described as "patron saints" of the Enlightenment whose "splendid reputations on the Continent" helped create what intellectual historian Peter Gay has termed a mid-eighteenth-century "Anglomania," with an accompanying "[advocacy] of experimentation and [criticism] of metaphysics."[98]

Like Newton, the English philosopher Francis Bacon called for a "more perfect use of reason in the investigation of Nature," the type of induction of self-evident first principles through experimentalism that drew from Newtonian science and became a hallmark of the Scottish Common Sense school.[99] Bacon's fellow Englishman John Locke similarly argued for man's ability to "discover" the law of nature, which he described as "law enacted by a superior power and implanted in our hearts" and as "the decree of the divine will discernible by the light of nature and indicating what is and what is not in conformity with rational nature, and for this very reason commanding or prohibiting."[100] As eighteenth-century Anglican priest Edmund Law stated: "[T]he Avenues to Learning of all kinds have been plan'd out and open'd by Ld. *Bacon*, the Nature and most intimate Recess of the Human Mind unfolded and explain'd by *Locke*, the Frame and Constitution of the Universe by *Newton* . . . in a more perfect Manner than ever was done or attempted since the Foundation of the World."[101]

Newton believed the laws of nature could be determined through observation and that such observations ought to be the starting point of philosophy.[102] His method was inquiry, guided by reason, and his object was "the discovery of the natural order of things." Newton believed that there was an order to the created world and that happiness consisted in living in accordance with that order,[103] a belief that is in tandem with the classical and Christian understanding of the law of nature. Indeed, Newton, a lifelong scholar of both the classics and the Bible, was convinced of a harmony between science and religion, a harmony that he shared with many of his contemporaries.[104] Newton saw the wisdom of God as he studied the natural world, and the principles he discovered in his scientific explorations led him to look on creation with a sense of awe.[105]

Newton is perhaps best known for his contributions to science and mathematics. But the works of historian of science I. Bernard Cohen, historian

Arthur Herman, political scientist John E. Paynter, and historian Garry Wills have highlighted how Newton's scientific theories of an ordered universe contributed to eighteenth-century political philosophy and principles of governance. The founders believed that, just as there existed laws of nature to direct the natural world, so did there exist laws of nature to direct proper governance. Newton provided them with a scientific model that "exalted a divine Creator [and] gave assurance that the laws of nature were universal, harmonious, and beneficent."[106] Franklin's favorite portrait of himself was one in which he "sat deep in thought in front of a bust of Newton, who watched his protégé approvingly."[107] Jefferson had Newton's portrait on display in his study and, in keeping with Newton's philosophy, believed that "all things work by the laws of Nature and Nature's God."[108] He believed Newton's "empirical science" was adaptable not only to the physical sciences but also "in all fields, the moral and social together with the physical."[109] John Adams agreed, applying Newton's science to the study of political systems.[110] Adams looked to governments over time as experiments, and he studied them in that context. He then compiled the key principles of governance that had led toward liberty, as opposed to tyranny, in his work *A Defence of the Constitutions of the United States*, all with the end goal of applying those principles to the Constitution of the United States.[111] James Madison also believed that good government could be secured by determining the principles that would encourage government to operate as it was intended to operate. He, too, conducted an intensive historical study of governments in order to identify those principles and apply them to the new government of the United States. The results of Madison's study of the principles of government are contained in his "Notes on Ancient and Modern Confederacies" and "Vices of the Political System of the United States."[112]

In so doing, the founders were following in the Common Sense school of the Scottish Enlightenment. As historian Arthur Herman so eloquently stated, the founder of the Common Sense school, Thomas Reid, argued, "The world was not a mysterious maze. . . . It was an open and well-lit vista, rich with material for making clear judgements about up and down, black and white and right and wrong. 'Settled truth,' [Reid] wrote, 'can be attained by observation.' Reality is not one step removed from us by our own limitations, but knowable and graspable by our own experience. All it took was ears to listen and eyes to see."[113] In combining Newton's scientific findings and inductive method with their studies on government, the founders agreed, thereby embarking on a fascinating search for political first principles—a search whose results were not only "attainable by observation," but also directly applicable to the founders' current circumstances. In this way, especially, the Scottish Enlightenment's focus on Newtonian science, as exemplified by Reid's Common Sense philosophy, formed part of the founders' intellectual world.

The questions that then remain are these: Which, if any, of these four strands of thought were evidenced in the lives of the primary drafters and editors of the Declaration of Independence, Thomas Jefferson, John Adams, and Benjamin Franklin? And which, if any, of these four strands of thought influenced their understanding of the pursuit of happiness?

CHAPTER 6

Intermingling of the Four Strands

As the philosophes of the English Enlightenment surveyed the struggles between the American colonies and England in the years leading up to and following the American Revolution, they did so with hope that the "practical science" of freedom "might be realized" in America. As they observed the American Revolution and the founding of the new American republic from across the Atlantic, the European Enlightenment thinkers began to describe America as "the hope of the human race" and "its model." They applauded American practicality and, especially, what they perceived to be the full embodiment of liberty on American soil. To the Europeans who looked on, America was the new ideal in liberty and the best example yet of "the program of enlightenment in practice."[1]

That key figures of the Enlightenment would feel such hope and joy at the progress of the British colonies in North America—and then the new United States—is the flip side of the American Enlightenment's own mid-eighteenth-century reverence for its French and English counterparts. Americans adapted this Enlightenment thinking to their own situation.[2] As a result, when the Americans ultimately decided to split from England, they did so with an understanding that they were furthering, not hindering, the great English tradition of liberty.

As historians Carl Richard and Peter Gay and legal historian Charles Barzun have aptly shown, in arguing for their cause, the founders intermingled in their rhetoric key intellectual strands of the European Enlightenment, including English law and legal theory, the history and philosophy of classical antiquity, Christianity, and the Scottish Enlightenment's emphasis on Newtonian science and Common Sense philosophy.[3] It was an "enlightened, Europe-centered ideology" that they promoted.[4] This intermingled ideology was evidenced in founding-era thought. Furthermore, these ideas converged in a way that tells us something interesting not only about the structure, purpose, and meaning of the Declaration of Independence, generally, but also about the pursuit of happiness, more specifically.

The founders were influenced by a mixture of these ideas, and they did not separate them out as mutually exclusive categories, as we tend to today. Instead, they believed that ancient law and philosophy were expressed within the English common law and would be perfected by the new United States. Many understood Christianity as the foundation of the common law and the fulfillment of ancient ideals, as seen in John's claim in the New Testament Gospel of John that Christ is logos, the term applied to the first mover of Stoicism, and Paul's claim in the book of Acts that the Christian God fulfills the pagan philosophy and religion of the ancient world.[5] Men like Jefferson, Adams, Franklin, and their contemporaries

> poured out broadsides, pamphlets, and books by the hundreds; voluble preachers printed sermons touching on high principles of political obligation; ambitious lawyers and aspiring politicians denounced intolerable corruption, confiscatory taxation, oppressive vetoes, tyrannical ministers, and invoked heroes of antique and modern times—Cato, Cicero, Machiavelli, Locke, Trenchard and Gordon, and Montesquieu—with the ease of educated men knowing that they have an educated audience. When the colonists decided, regretfully but irrevocably, that it had become necessary to dissolve their political bonds to the British crown, and to assume, among the powers of the earth, the separate station to which they thought the laws of nature and of nature's God entitled them, they found that the world was listening.[6]

One of the most intriguing examples of this intermingling of ideas is to be found in the works of eighteenth-century author and playwright Joseph Addison. Addison was popular in both England and the American colonies, with Franklin, Adams, and Jefferson counted among his admirers.[7] Addison's series of essays written with Richard Steele, known as the *Spectator*, were published from 1711 to 1712.[8] In the *Spectator*, Addison intermingled Christianity, classical history, and political philosophy, with topics as wide ranging as "patriotism, virtue, fame, liberty, prudence, fortune, integrity, the nature of government, honor, faction, and education."[9] In 1776 an advertisement for a new edition of the *Spectator* claimed, "The Book thus offered to the Public is too well known to be praised: It comprizes precepts of criticism, sallies of invention, descriptions of life, and lectures of virtue. It employs wit in the cause of truth, and makes elegance subservient to piety: It has now for more than half a century supplied the English nation, in great measure, with principles of speculation, and rules of practice; and given Addison a claim to be numbered among the benefactors of mankind."[10]

Like so many of his contemporaries, Addison believed that he could know his present day more fully if he studied the ancient past, as embodied in the classics.[11] His play *Cato, a Tragedy* brought that history to life through his portrayal of Cato the Younger, a virtuous leader in the Roman Republic whose life was chronicled in Plutarch's *Parallel Lives*, a favorite read of the founders. Cato "exemplified the life led in accordance with Stoic ideals. Identifying the virtuous life with happiness."[12] The play set forth the idea of a providential God in scene 1 of act 5, where Cato addresses the Stoic Plato. As will be highlighted in part 3, this passage so influenced Benjamin Franklin that he included it in his autobiography as a motivation for the pursuit of virtue and, therefore, happiness.[13]

Cato, a Tragedy was wildly popular among the founders.[14] But they enjoyed *Cato* not only for its portrayal of classical history and a Stoic ideal, but also for what they viewed as its contemporary applications in law and political theory. In Cato's struggle against the corrupt tyranny of Julius Caesar (one of the founders' chief classical villains), the founders saw their own struggle against the corrupt tyranny of King George III. The play was immensely popular in the Revolutionary era, with George Washington even ordering a production of it at Valley Forge to motivate his troops to fight to overthrow English tyranny. In Addison's works, the founders' philosophical intermingling of classical history and philosophy and English legal theory found practical expression.[15]

Like Addison's *Spectator*, Blackstone's *Commentaries*, the key text on English law in early America,[16] combined ideas from Christianity, classical history and philosophy, and English history and legal theory. And, like *Cato, a Tragedy*, the *Commentaries* was adapted by the founders in support of their revolutionary ideals. Blackstone's *Commentaries* had its roots in England and was a response to Rome. Just as Emperor Justinian sought to create a harmonious compilation of the Roman law and a simplified textbook for students of the law, so did Blackstone seek to compile the English law in a harmonious and more accessible format. Blackstone's *Commentaries* began with a conception of natural law that, much like the work of his contemporary Burlamaqui, reflected key tenets of Stoic philosophy, Christian theology, and Newtonian science. The founders looked to the *Commentaries* to form their understanding of English law, and this understanding greatly influenced not only the law of the new United States,[17] but also the debates between England and the colonists that led to the Declaration of Independence in the first place. So, for example, while founders like James Wilson disagreed with Blackstone's belief that Parliament remained a supreme authority over the colonies, they did not throw him out as a whole. Instead, they disagreed with Blackstone on that point and then used his own words to show him why he was wrong, stating that the authority of Parliament was inferior to that of the higher law because, in the words of Blackstone, the colonists were first and foremost obliged to obey "the law of nature [which] is superior in obligation to any other."[18]

The founders also looked to English history for the story of their own origins.[19] In both England and the colonies, King Alfred was celebrated as the founder of English law. The American colonists revered King Alfred and what they believed to be a "golden age" of Saxon liberty, a liberty that they wanted to reestablish and preserve in the American colonies. During the American Revolution, the colonists upheld King Alfred as the symbol of the liberty for which they fought, going so far as to rename the leading American warship in Alfred's name.[20]

The three men who drafted and edited the rough draft of the Declaration of Independence blended these four strands of thought in their personal philosophies as well.[21] As discussed previously, Thomas Jefferson created the first draft of the Declaration and then sent it to John Adams and Benjamin Franklin for review. Jefferson had made a careful study of English law.[22] However, he was no fan of William Blackstone, labeling him a "honeyed" Tory and preferring the works of Sir Edward Coke, which he believed to be more challenging.[23] Yet Jefferson "was European to the bone," drawing ideas from both England and France, which he then applied to his own experiences in Virginia.[24] Jefferson read Anglo-Saxon history and law codes enthusiastically, looking to Anglo-Saxon precedents for his views on religious freedom and governance.[25] In contemplating the Great Seal of the United States, Jefferson went so far as to suggest that it should bear the portraits of "the first Anglo-Saxon kings, 'from whom we claim the honor of being descended, and whose political principles and form of government we have assumed.'" Like Blackstone, Jefferson looked to Anglo-Saxon legal principles as a foundation for law and advocated for a "restitution of the ancient Saxon laws."[26]

Jefferson also was a skilled classicist, self-taught and then trained both by the Reverend James Maury, where he read in the original Greek and Latin, and by George Wythe at the College of William and Mary.[27] Jefferson greatly admired Stoic philosopher Epictetus and was a proponent of the scientific ideals of the Scottish Enlightenment, perhaps due to his studies under William Small, who taught Jefferson math and science, including

Newtonian scientific theory and the mathematical order of the universe.[28] Jefferson was so taken with Thomas Reid's Common Sense philosophy that Jefferson added Reid to his recommended reading list and included Reid in Jefferson's proposed curriculum for the University of Virginia.[29] Jefferson included both Wythe and Small among the three contemporary men who had had the greatest influence on him (Peyton Randolph, chair of the First and Second Continental Congress, was the third).[30]

Jefferson rejected some key principles of traditional Christian orthodoxy, such as the divinity of Christ, but remained consistent in his admiration of Christ as a moral teacher.[31] He cut apart his Bible, paring it down to the ethical teachings of Christ, which he then compiled into a text he titled "The Life and Morals of Jesus." Yet he also contributed money to the American Bible Society. His motivations here seem to stem, in part, from a combination of his religious, scientific, and political philosophies. So, for example, he encouraged biographers to discredit those portions of the life of Jesus that ran against "the physical laws of nature" but promoted the adult reading of the Bible for purposes of morality.[32]

Jefferson's piecemeal integration of classical philosophy and Christian theology is fascinating and is perhaps best described as Jefferson having "attempted to wed moral and metaphysical Epicureanism with a rationalized, theistic metaphysics and a Christian ethics."[33] Thus, he "called himself 'an Epicurean,'" while also devoting himself to a careful study of the writings of Jesus and denying the Epicurean doctrine of divine nonintervention.[34] He believed in divine Providence, a Creator God who actively intervened in his creation, including active intervention in the affairs of men. In an October 31, 1819, letter to William Short, Jefferson wrote, "Epictetus & Epicurus give us laws for governing ourselves, Jesus a supplement of the duties & charities we owe to others."[35] In the possibility of a world to come, Jefferson departed from the ancients once again, as he wrote frequently and, oftentimes, poignantly of his expected reunification with departed friends and loved ones in the afterlife.[36]

Like Jefferson, John Adams was unorthodox in his religious views. A self-proclaimed Unitarian, he was nevertheless a lifelong advocate of the Bible, endeavoring to continue his study of both the classics and the Bible throughout his life.[37] Adams held to a Christian notion of a providential God who "continually preserved and directed the universe."[38] He was a skilled classicist and English constitutional scholar.[39] In his early years, Adams consciously adopted Cicero's own philosophy of service in the study and practice of law, which he articulated as "to procure Redress of Wrongs, the Advancement of Right, to assert and maintain Liberty and Virtue, to discourage and abolish Tyranny and Vice."[40] In later years, Adams combined political theories from English law and classical thought and inductive science from the Scottish Enlightenment in his exploration of the principles of government. He joined an ongoing chorus of "[e]ighteenth-century intellectuals [who] admired the English constitution so much because it seemed to have nicely mixed and balanced the three simple forms of government, monarchy, aristocracy, and democracy, in the Crown, House of Lords, and House of Commons."[41] He relied on Enlightenment thinkers in his arguments, with his "political outlook [owing] much to Harrington, Locke, Montesquieu; [and] his view of human nature [owing] much to Hutcheson, Ferguson, Bolingbroke."[42]

Adams, like his fellow Englishmen before him, believed in a westward movement of empire—from Greece and Rome to France and Great Britain—and he distinguished himself from his former countrymen with his belief that this westward empire, and the liberty it embodied, would be received, and perfected, in the new United States. In his writings, he makes clear that he saw his work here to be like that of Moses, leading the Israelites out of slavery, thus equating the colonists' separation from Great Britain with the work of divine Providence, an analogy that Jefferson and Franklin articulated as well.[43] Through *A Defence*, Adams argued that a modified Roman Republican mixed-government structure provided the best model on which to base that perfection of liberty.[44] "'Liberty,' he said, 'depends upon an exact Ballance, a nice Counterpoise of all the Powers of the state. . . . The best Governments of the World have been mixed.'"[45]

With this in mind, Adams considered how the corruptions of the English constitution could be improved and perfected by applying elements from "[t]he best Governments of the World" in the new United States. In an early form of political science, Adams applied Newtonian principles of empirical study to his search for the natural principles or laws of good governments.[46] He used history as a laboratory, looking to past experience for evidence that he could apply to new experiments.[47] In so doing, he made use of the ancient rhetorical device of induction, one of the key rhetorical strategies outlined by Cicero in *De Inventione*, the Scottish Enlightenment's Common Sense focus on inductive reasoning, and the Stoic and Christian ideal of finding natural principles, known as "exceptionless laws" or "the Laws of Nature and of Nature's God" that governed the natural order of things.[48] He even articulated his work leading up to the Declaration of Independence in scientific terms, confiding in his wife, Abigail, "that I may have been instrumental in touching some Springs and turning some small Wheels which have had and will have such Effects, I feel and Awe upon my Mind which is not easily described."[49]

Benjamin Franklin is perhaps the most interesting. He developed a reputation first as a scientist and then as a philosophe.[50] He studied Joseph Addison's *Spectator* papers and "perfected his knowledge of modern science by studying the English Newtonians."[51] Franklin corresponded heavily with the "luminaries" of the Scottish Enlightenment and frequently visited its epicenter, Edinburgh, where he was so well regarded by his Scottish contemporaries that he was inducted into Edinburgh's Royal Society in 1783; Franklin was the first foreigner to receive this honor.[52]

Franklin was not trained in English law, but, prior to the Declaration, he conducted a significant study of "all that had been written, pro and con, about the respective rights and prerogatives of British and colonial legislatures." While Franklin and Adams disagreed on the best form of government, Franklin shared Adam's methodology; prior to the Constitutional Convention, Franklin hosted "the Society for Political Enquires," which met weekly to study the science of political life. Franklin's influence in the natural and political sciences was evident in the years leading up to the American Revolution. He visited France repeatedly, and the French so admired Franklin as a scientist and a philosophe that they elected him, in 1772, to the French Royal Academy of Science.[53]

Although Franklin received only two years of formal education, he was a voracious reader across many genres, including Plutarch's *Parallel Lives* and Joseph Addison's *Spectator*, which Franklin saw as "a tool for self-improvement." He taught himself to read in several languages, including Latin and French.[54] Franklin opposed a broad classical languages requirement, reserving such education for students advancing on to studies in areas such as law, medicine, and divinity. Yet he enjoyed reading the classical authors in translation and included such reading in his proposal for the Philadelphia Academy.[55] Franklin even voiced his intention to include "a Latin motto, which carries a charm in it to the Vulgar, and the Learned admire the pleasure of construing" in each edition of his newspaper, the *New England Courant*.[56]

Franklin, too, was unorthodox in his Christian faith. He did not believe in the divinity of Christ, but he supported Christ's moral teachings and was a lifelong advocate for the Bible.[57] He evidenced a particular affinity for the Bible's teachings on wisdom, especially in the book of Proverbs. In his 1732 essay "On the Providence of God in the Government of the World," Franklin used reason to argue for a God of "great wisdom, goodness and power"—the same three attributes of God that Blackstone highlighted in the introduction to his *Commentaries*—who actively intervenes in the affairs of men. It is a conception of divine Providence that Franklin would hold throughout his life.[58]

In his autobiography, Franklin included a discussion of his earlier call for a "united Party for Virtue," and his proposed creed for such a party gives us some insight into his religious beliefs. That creed included "the belief that there was 'one God' who 'governs the World by his Providence'; that the way to serve God was to do good to man; that 'the Soul is immortal'; and 'that God would certainly reward Virtue and punish Vice either here or hereafter.'" When asked about his religious views in 1790, Franklin answered in language similar to the creed he had proposed earlier when he stated his belief "in One God, Creator of the Universe. That He governs it by his Providence. That he ought to be worshipped. That the most acceptable Service we can render to him, is doing Good to his other Children. That the Soul of Man is immortal, and will be treated with Justice in another Life respecting its Conduct in this." Franklin's views of Christ as a moral teacher mirrored those of Jefferson, and he stated that he "believed Jesus's 'System of Morals and his Religion as he left them to us, the best the World ever saw, or is likely to see.'"[59]

A close look at the men we identify as the founders shows a great diversity of thought, even as they inhabited the same intellectual world. Yet a close look at the writings of the three men who initially drafted the Declaration of Independence—Jefferson, Adams, and Franklin—reveals many similarities as well. These include a broad understanding of English law and legal history; a deep appreciation for classical history and philosophy; a lack of Christian orthodoxy, combined with a commitment to biblical morality and a firm belief in a Creator God and a Christian view of divine Providence; and an enthusiasm for Newtonian science and its ramifications for political thought. Despite the variances within and between the philosophies of these three men (and there are many), not one of these men altered "the pursuit of happiness" as an unalienable right as they meticulously reviewed and edited the initial draft of the Declaration of Independence. Despite the variances within and between the broader group of founders assembled on the Committee of Five and in the Continental Congress, the phrase continued, unaltered. This lack of editing suggests not only that the founders intermingled these four strands in their founding-era thought, but also that these four strands specifically converged in such a way as to give meaning to the phrase "pursuit of happiness"—a meaning that was apparent and acceptable not only to Jefferson, Adams, and Franklin but also to the larger group of men who edited and finally approved the Declaration in the Continental Congress. It is William Blackstone's discussion of the pursuit of happiness that best fits this definition.

CHAPTER 7

Convergence of the Four Strands: The Pursuit of Happiness

BLACKSTONE WAS THE most widely read English jurist in the Revolutionary era. It follows that Blackstone's writings would inform both the structure and the content of the Declaration of Independence, the foundation of which was English law. And, indeed, they do. As historian Julius S. Waterman has emphasized:

> Paradoxically, those same Commentaries furnished to the American Colonies a most effective weapon in their revolution against the mother country. . . . The philosophy of the Declaration of Independence usually is ascribed to Locke and Paine. But it appears to me that one may clearly trace the influence of Blackstone's Commentaries on the mind of Jefferson, in the affirmations of the Declaration that all men are born with certain unalienable rights. . . . The counts in the indictment of George the Third, contained in the Declaration of Independence, in the main are sustained by Blackstone's description of the rights of Englishmen and the principles of the British Constitution. . . . Little did the Great Commentator realize when he read his lectures to a polite and scholarly audience at Oxford of the weapon he unwittingly was forging for the Colonists in North America.[1]

As Waterman points out, the colonists were influenced by then current notions of natural rights and the law of nature, and while they agreed with Blackstone that "a fundamental law of nature" existed that was "superior to human law," they strongly disagreed with Blackstone's assertion that man's natural rights could be "subject to the supreme power which Blackstone said existed in every government."[2] The former ideas are Whiggish in nature; the latter are Tory. Indeed, later in life, Jefferson decried Blackstone as a Tory and took pains to emphasize that it was Coke on Littleton and not the "honied Mansfieldism of Blackstone" that "was the universal elementary book of law students, and a sounder whig never wrote, nor of profounder learning in the orthodox doctrines of the British constitution, or in what were called English liberties."[3]

The Declaration begins where Blackstone began—with natural rights theory, articulated by the founders as "the Laws of Nature and of Nature's God." The Declaration then enumerates three unalienable rights: life (understood in Newtonian science to be in keeping with the first law of nature, which was self-preservation), liberty (understood in the classical world to be a status of freedom opposed both to slavery and to domination by those more powerful), and the pursuit of happiness (understood in the natural law sense of man's right to live a rightly ordered or virtuous life in accordance with the law of nature as it pertains to man).[4] But the Declaration is best understood not as the expression of ideas contained in Blackstone's *Commentaries* but as Blackstone mediated by the founders' understandings not only of English law and legal theory but also of the history and philosophy of classical antiquity, the providential theology and morality of Christianity, and the epistemology of the Scottish Enlightenment, as contained in its Common Sense application of the inductive methods of Newtonian science.

The most fascinating thing about these four strands of thought is not where they diverge but where they converge. If we remove the first mover in each strand of thought (nature for the Newtonian scientists, God for Christianity, God and the king for the English common law, and logos for the Stoics), all four strands of thought posit a world that is governed by laws of nature, in which to live rightly or virtuously is to live in accordance with that law. And in each line of thought, to live in accordance with the law of nature is to be happy, as understood in the Greek sense of *eudaimonia*, translated to the English as "flourishing" or "well-being."

Thus, all four lines of thought are in harmony with Jefferson's use of pursuit of happiness as an unalienable right and Blackstone's definition of that phrase in his *Commentaries*. Jefferson may not have looked to Blackstone to define the phrase pursuit of happiness, but Blackstone seems to have articulated the phrase's meaning as it was widely understood within the four ideological strands present at the time of the founding. The convergence of these four strands meant that founders with very different personal and political philosophies could nevertheless affirm the language of the Declaration because the language chosen reflected the commonalities among these four strands.

Looking at the pursuit of happiness in its historical context tells us quite a bit about the meaning of the phrase. It also tells us quite a bit about founding-era thought. In contrast to studies suggesting that the Declaration reflects either a single ideological strand or several distinct ideological strands, one of which is predominant, this study suggests that the founders drew from a variety of intellectual inspirations, combining them in ways that may sometimes seem incoherent to us. This incoherence, as we see it today, may lead us to determine that the founders saw incoherence as well, but a contextual study of the pursuit of happiness reveals that the founders saw a convergence of ideas that conveyed substantive meaning. When these ideas are explored together, they reveal what Jefferson described as the "harmonization of the ideas of the day," as embodied in eighteenth-century thinking about English law and legal theory, the moral teachings and divine Providence of Christianity, the history and philosophy of classical antiquity, and the Scottish Enlightenment's focus on Common Sense epistemology and Newtonian science. Studying the pursuit of happiness in historical context suggests that Blackstone and the founders agreed on much about the nature of law and jurisprudence, even as they disagreed about the right of a people to overthrow a government that they believe has become tyrannical. The study of the pursuit of happiness highlights the influence of Isaac Newton's scientific theories on founding-era documents, adds to the ongoing debate regarding whether the founders' and framers' references to classical antiquity were substantive or merely window dressing, and affirms the work of recent scholars on both the influence of the Bible and the complexity of that influence in the personal lives and political theory of the founders.[5]

That the founders viewed happiness at the place where these four strands of thought converged is evidenced not only in the unalienable rights language at the beginning of the Declaration, but also in the use of "happiness" in latter portions of the text. The word "happiness" first appears in the Declaration at the beginning of the document, where "the pursuit of Happiness" is listed as an unalienable right. The second time "happiness" appears in the Declaration is toward the end of that same passage. The founders declare that when governments cease to protect man's unalienable rights, including "Life, Liberty and the pursuit of Happiness," men should put in place new governments "to effect their Safety and Happiness." This combination of "safety" and "happiness," and the idea that to effect the safety and happiness of the people is the proper end of government, is not unique to the Declaration. This language was mirrored prior to the Declaration (both in George Mason's 1776 Virginia Declaration of Rights and in a May 10,

1776, resolution of the Second Continental Congress recommending that the colonies adopt new governments that will "best conduce to the happiness and safety" of the people) and after the Declaration (in the preamble to John Adams's 1780 draft of the Constitution of the Commonwealth of Massachusetts).[6] In each of these passages, the end goal of effecting safety seems to be shorthand for a belief that the purpose of government is to act as a security or safeguard for the rights of the people.[7] To "conduce to" or to "effect" the happiness of the people indicates that government has a responsibility to govern in a way that will be conducive to the people's well-being. While a government purpose of acting as a security or safeguard for the people's rights and a government purpose of conducing or effecting the happiness of the people are different from man's unalienable right to the pursuit of happiness, the three concepts are both complementary and interdependent. These connections between safety, happiness, and the pursuit of happiness will be discussed more in depth in part 3.

The third time "happiness" appears in the Declaration is in earlier draft versions only. It occurs at the end of the document, where Jefferson describes separation from Britain, although initially painful, as the road "to happiness and to glory."[8] This passage, with its accompanying "happiness" reference, was removed by the Continental Congress. But its use of the term is revealing nevertheless. This phrase refers to an ancient concept of "glory" or "fame," which is understood as the renown of future generations.[9] "Glory" or "fame" was achieved by living a life of virtue and distinction. The founders, like the ancients, believed that to live a life of virtue was to be happy and that to pursue glory through a life of virtue was to be lauded. Thus, glory and happiness, where happiness is obtained through a rightly ordered life, were intimately interconnected.

In his original draft, Jefferson wrote the phrase as "to glory and to happiness." Either John Adams or Jefferson himself changed the phrase "to happiness and to glory," and rightly so.[10] First of all, the founders believed one should not seek glory, or renown, so that one could live a happy or virtuous life, but that one should seek to live a happy or a virtuous life, so that one would receive glory or renown in future generations. Second, happiness must precede glory in the sense that a rightly ordered life of virtue (which leads to happiness) is the necessary precursor to receiving the glory, or renown, of future generations. As will be discussed in chapter 9, Jefferson believed that perfect happiness was not attainable on earth. It might make sense, then, for Jefferson to place "glory" before "happiness," suggesting in his draft of the Declaration that the glory that man would receive for having sought to live a virtuous or happy life on earth (for having pursued happiness) would then be followed by the attainment of perfect happiness in the afterlife.

Understanding happiness as the result of virtuous living explains not only its connection to glory in this phrase, but also the reason Adams or Jefferson rearranged the order of "glory" and "happiness" when editing an early draft of the Declaration. Furthermore, describing separation from Britain as "the road to happiness and to glory" would have reminded the founders of their inherent inability to achieve either happiness or glory while under tyranny. Separating from Britain would allow the founders to throw off the tyrannical rule of King George III and would restore them to a status of liberty, wherein they could, in the words of the Declaration, "institute new Government, laying its foundation on such principles and organizing its powers in such form, as to them shall seem most likely to effect their Safety and Happiness." A key purpose of that new government would be to protect man's unalienable right to the pursuit of happiness.

PART III.

The Pursuit of Happiness:
A Private Right and a Public Duty

A Single Definition with Dual Applications

For [the Creator] has so intimately connected, so inseparably interwoven the laws of eternal justice with the happiness of each individual, that the latter cannot be attained but by observing the former; and, if the former be punctually obeyed, it cannot but induce the latter. In consequence of which mutual connection of justice and human felicity, he has not perplexed the law of nature with a multitude of abstracted rules and precepts, referring merely to the fitness or unfitness of things, as some have vainly surmised; but has graciously reduced the rule of obedience to this one paternal precept, "that man should "pursue his own happiness." This is the foundation of what we call ethics, or natural law.

—William Blackstone, *Commentaries on the Laws of England* (1765)

We hold these Truths to be self-evident, that all Men are created equal, that they are endowed by their Creator with certain unalienable Rights, that among these are Life, Liberty, and the pursuit of Happiness. —That to secure these rights, Governments are instituted among Men, deriving their just powers from the consent of the governed, —That whenever any Form of Government becomes destructive of these ends, it is the Right of the People to alter or to abolish it, and to institute new Government, laying its foundation on such principles and organizing its powers in such form, as to them shall seem most likely to effect their Safety and Happiness.

—Declaration of Independence (1776)

Eighteenth-century dictionaries state that to be happy is to be lucky or fortunate or to be in a state of felicity.[1] The former meaning stems from a fourteenth-century meaning of the word, with the root word "hap" meaning "by chance or accident." The latter meaning demonstrates how the meaning of "happy" changed over time so that, by the eighteenth century, its primary definition came to mean "a state of felicity" or "very glad" or "pleased and content."[2] By the early 1700s, the definition also came to include the synonym "blessed," defined as "to wish success to," "to consecrate to God," and "to make happy."[3]

At first glance, it would seem that the idea of happiness as felicity supports the notion of the pursuit of happiness as an unalienable right, if to be happy is to feel good. But happiness as it was used in the natural, moral, and legal philosophy of the eighteenth century embodied not only an understanding of "happy" as very glad, pleased, and content, but also an understanding of that which had the capability of making one very glad, pleased, and content in the truest sense of the words. Enlightenment thinkers contrasted fleeting and temporal happiness with "real" and "substantial" happiness and borrowed from ancient thinkers to argue that true happiness—real and substantial happiness—came from living a life of virtue, a life that was fit or rightly ordered in relation to the natural law. In other words, Enlightenment thinkers understood true happiness in the ancient sense of *eudaimonia*, or human flourishing, which was to be achieved through a life of virtue and which had both private (pertaining to an individual person) and public (pertaining to the community) applications.

A variety of Enlightenment thinkers discussed happiness as both a public duty and a private right. In doing so, they also explicitly connected the pursuit of happiness with the practice of virtue. English natural, moral, and legal philosopher Francis Bacon stated that goodness or "the affecting of the weal of men" is the greatest of all virtues and "imprinted deeply in the nature of man."[4] Scottish philosopher David Hume argued for a form of government "by which liberty is secured, the public good consulted, and the avarice or ambition of particular men restrained and punished."[5] Francis Hutcheson, a key leader in the Scottish Enlightenment, asked, "May not another instinct toward the Publick, or the Good of others, be as proper a Principle of Virtue, as the Instinct toward private Happiness? And is there not the same Occasion for the Exercise of our Reason in pursuing the former, as the latter?"[6] John Locke asserted that "the *golden age* [the Anglo-Saxon period] . . . had more virtue, and consequently better governors, as well as less vicious subjects" and stated, in words strikingly similar to those of Blackstone, that "God having, by an inseparable connexion, joined virtue and public happiness together, and made the practice thereof necessary to the preservation of society, and visibly beneficial to all with whom the virtuous man has to do; it is no wonder that every one should not only allow, but recommend and magnify those rules to others, from whose observance of them he is sure to reap advantage to himself."[7] Locke believed that "Nature . . . has put into man a desire of happiness, and an aversion to misery" and that "the highest perfection of intellectual nature lies in a careful and constant pursuit of true and solid happiness; so the care of ourselves, that we mistake not imaginary for real happiness, is the necessary foundation of our liberty."[8] Similarly, in his work *The Reasonableness of Christianity*, Locke argued that revelation was simply an expansion of reason and that God had harmonized the physical and the moral worlds such that the true and knowable causes of true and enduring human happiness were identical to virtue.[9]

Thus, in pursuing happiness, one could gain knowledge of the self-evident principles that formed "the most simple laws of nature."[10] Following those principles would lead to a life of virtue, rightly ordered within the natural law. Collections of legal maxims asserted this connection between law and virtue in statements such as "Law favoreth charity," "Law favoreth honor and order," "Law favoreth justice and right," and "Law favoreth things for the commonwealth."[11] We see these same connections between the pursuit of happiness as a private right and a public duty—and, as will be discussed later, a connection between happiness and virtue—in both the *Commentaries* and the Declaration of Independence.

Blackstone emphasized the public duty to pursue happiness as a science of jurisprudence, claiming "so graciously has providence interwoven our duty and our happiness together"; yet even here, Blackstone emphasized "the enobling of the human species, by giving it opportunities of improving it's *rational* faculties, as well as of exerting it's *natural*."[12] And, in fact, the pursuit of happiness is first discussed in Blackstone's *Commentaries* in this individual application—as an epistemology or a way of knowing the law of nature that the Creator had built into the constitution of each man. Blackstone then used that individual application as a jumping-off point to promote the pursuit of happiness as a public duty. Just as individuals could determine the law of nature as it pertains to man by consulting what makes them truly and substantially happy, so, too, could lawyers, judges, jurors, and MPs use that same science of jurisprudence to fulfill their public duty, which was to improve the common law, perfecting it as the foundation of a good or fit government. The private right to pursue happiness informed—and made possible—the public duty to do the same.

The Declaration discusses the pursuit of happiness in its individual application when it lists the pursuit of happiness among man's unalienable rights—those rights that are so important that we obtain them simply by

being human and that are so essential to our humanity that we cannot alienate them from our persons. In its inclusion of the pursuit of happiness as one
of the unalienable rights bestowed upon man by his Creator, the Declaration emphasizes the individual-right application of the phrase.

While the Declaration's emphasis is on the pursuit of happiness as an
individual unalienable right, this is not to say that the Declaration is void
of the public-duty implications of the phrase. In fact, in an Enlightenment
understanding of rights, which necessarily indicated correlating duties, it
would be surprising to see otherwise. That the founders agreed with both
a private-right and a public-duty application of the pursuit of happiness is
evidenced by their writings. As discussed previously, the founders argued,
in language that is remarkably reflective of Blackstone's architectural anal-
ogies, that when a government ceases to protect man's unalienable rights,
"it is the Right of the People to alter or abolish it, and to institute new
Government, laying its Foundation on such Principles, and organizing its
Powers in such Form, as to them shall seem most likely to effect their Safety
and Happiness." From this passage of the Declaration of Independence, they
transitioned into King George III's "train of abuses," describing him as "a
Tyrant . . . unfit to be the ruler of a free people." To be unfit was to be the
opposite of virtuous; it was to be no longer capable of effecting the safety
and happiness of the people.

The founders affirmed the pursuit of happiness as an individual unalienable right in the Declaration. But, as highlighted by the language above,
they also appealed to the necessity of a happy (fit, virtuous) form of government, as well as a government that would effect the happiness of the people,
a theme they had articulated in a variety of ways prior to the Declaration.
For example, in *Resolutions of the Continental Congress* (1765), the founders
stated, "That the increase, prosperity, and happiness of these colonies, depend on the full and free enjoyment of their rights and liberties, and an
intercourse with Great-Britain mutually affectionate and advantageous."[13]

The founders echoed Blackstone's discussion of the English foundations
of law, the laws of nature, and happiness as an end of good governance
when, in the *Declarations and Resolves of the First Continental Congress* (1774),
they claimed that they were writing "as Englishmen . . . asserting and vin-
dicating their rights and liberties," which they held "by the immutable laws
of nature, the principles of the English constitution and the several charters or compacts," requesting that Great Britain "restore us to that state,
in which both countries found happiness and prosperity."[14] The next year,

the colonists again raised the themes of the foundations of law and the happiness or welfare of the people, claiming in *The Causes and Necessity of Their Taking Up Arms* (1775) that "Reverence for our Creator, principles of humanity, and the dictates of common sense, must convince all those who reflect upon the subject, that government was instituted to promote the welfare of mankind, and ought to be administered for the attainment of that end."[15] Finally, and as discussed previously, George Mason's Virginia Declaration of Rights (1776) stated that all men have "inherent rights," including "pursuing and obtaining happiness and safety." Mason went on to write that "government is, or ought to be, instituted for the common benefit, protection, and security of the people, nation or community; of all the various modes and forms of government that is best, which is capable of producing the greatest degree of happiness and safety and is most effectually secured against the danger of maladministration." Mason then identified "virtue" and "frequent recurrence to fundamental principles" as the means of preserving a government with that end: "That no free government, or the blessings of liberty, can be preserved to any people but by a firm adherence to justice, moderation, temperance, frugality, and virtue and by frequent recurrence to fundamental principles."[16]

The founders included themes of happiness as a private right and a public duty in their individual writings as well. For example, Benjamin Franklin stated that "[t]he desire of happiness in general is so natural to us that all the world are in pursuit of it," and although men may attempt to achieve happiness in different ways, the reality is that "[i]t is impossible ever to enjoy ourselves rightly if our conduct be not such as to preserve the harmony and order of our faculties and the original frame and constitution of our minds; all true happiness, as all that is truly beautiful, can only result from order." Therefore, according to Franklin, if we pursue happiness through passion instead of reason, we achieve only an "inferior" and "imperfect" happiness, because "[t]here is no happiness then but in a virtuous and self-approving conduct."[17] As he said in a September 17, 1787, speech before the Constitutional Convention, "Much of the Strength and Efficiency of any Government in procuring and securing Happiness to the People depends on Opinion, on the general Opinion of the Goodness of that Government as well as of the Wisdom and Integrity of its Governors."[18]

John Adams held similar views, affirming in a 1763 letter to the *Boston Gazette* that "truth and virtue, as the means of present and future happiness, are confessed to be the only objects that deserve to be pursued."[19] Adams claimed to study "magistracy and legislation . . . as means and instruments of human happiness," concluding that "the liberty, the unalienable, indefeasible rights of men, the honor and dignity of human nature, the grandeur and glory of the public, and the universal happiness of individuals, was never so skilfully and successfully consulted, as in that most excellent monument of human art, the *common law* of *England*."[20] In his work "Thoughts on Government" (1776), Adams stated:

> We ought to consider what is the end of government before we determine which is the best form. Upon this point all speculative politicians will agree, that the happiness of society is the end of government, as all Divines and moral Philosophers will agree that the happiness of the individual is the end of man. From this principle it will follow, that the form of government, which communicates ease, comfort, security, or in one word happiness to the greatest number of people, and in the greatest degree, is the best. All sober inquirers after truth, ancient and modern, pagan and Christian, have declared that the happiness of man, as well as his dignity, consists in virtue. . . . If there is a form of government then, whose principles and foundation is virtue, will not every sober man acknowledge it better calculated to promote the general happiness than any other form?[21]

Adams again emphasized the connection between the frame of government and the happiness of the people in his fourth annual message on November 22, 1800, proclaiming, "May this territory be the residence of virtue and happiness," before going on to encourage the House of Representatives to continue in their "labors to promote the general happiness."[22]

Jefferson voiced similar connections between private and public happiness in his own writings. In his *Summary View of the Rights of British America* (1774), Jefferson stated that the colonists came to America and created "new societies, under such laws and regulations as to them shall seem most likely to promote public happiness."[23] In 1770 he stated that it was the "indispensable duty of every virtuous member of society to prevent the ruin, and promote the happiness, of his country, by every lawful means."[24] Jefferson revisited themes of public happiness throughout his presidential inaugural addresses and annual messages to Congress, discussing the "true principles" of the Constitution, urging a combination of "action" and "sentiment" that would be "auspicious to [the people's] happiness and safety" and emphasizing the legislature's role in "lay[ing] the foundations of public happiness in wholesome laws."[25] Jefferson wrote to John Adams in 1794, closing with "wishes of every degree of happiness to you both public and private" and in 1796 sent to Adams a wish "that your administration may be filled with glory and happiness to yourself and advantage to us."[26]

In their discussions of private and public happiness, Jefferson, Adams, and Franklin often tied together happiness and virtue. Franklin argued that "the Science of Virtue is of more worth, and of more consequence to [man's] Happiness than all the rest [of the sciences] put together."[27] Furthermore, Franklin stated, "I believe [God] is pleased and delights in the Happiness of those he has created; and since without Virtue Man can have no Happiness in this World, I firmly believe he delights to see me Virtuous, because he is pleas'd when he sees me Happy."[28] In his autobiography, Franklin listed the following virtues, which he had endeavored from a young age to follow as part of his "bold and arduous project of arriving at moral perfection":

1. Temperance. Eat not to dullness; drink not to elevation.
2. Silence. Speak not but what may benefit others or yourself; avoid trifling conversation.
3. Order. Let all your things have their places; let each part of your business have its time.
4. Resolution. Resolve to perform what you ought; perform without fail what you resolve.
5. Frugality. Make no expense but to do good to others or yourself; i.e. waste nothing.
6. Industry. Lose no Time. Be always employ'd in something useful; cut off all unnecessary actions.
7. Sincerity. Use no hurtful deceit; think innocently and justly; and, if you speak; speak accordingly.
8. Justice. Wrong none by doing injuries, or omitting the benefits that are your duty.
9. Moderation. Avoid extremes; forbear resenting injuries so much as you think they deserve.
10. Cleanliness. Tolerate no uncleanness in body, cloaths, or habitation.
11. Tranquility. Be not disturbed at trifles, or at accidents common or unavoidable.
12. Chastity. Rarely use Venery but for Health or Offspring; Never to Dullness, Weakness, or the Injury of your own or another's Peace or Reputation.
13. Humility. Imitate Jesus and Socrates.[29]

Franklin's discussion of the virtues in his autobiography evidences scientific thinking, as he first compiled and then recategorized lists of virtues
from a variety of sources, ultimately creating a chart whereby he could track
his progress in developing the virtues as habits over time.[30] His adoption
and intermingling of a variety of philosophies are evident in the list he
ultimately compiled and in his framing of the endeavor. Franklin's notion
that one could progress toward moral perfection through practice would
comport with Aristotle's notion that "moral excellence is the result of habit
or custom. . . . The virtues, then, come neither by nature nor against nature, but nature gives the capacity for acquiring them, and this is developed
by training."[31] Franklin seems optimistic that moral perfection could ensue
and cites Jesus as inspiration for the virtue of humility, even as Franklin's
suggestion that moral perfection could be achieved in man's lifetime is in
contrast with Christianity's doctrine of original sin and the fall of man.

Franklin's intermingling of philosophies is present also in the excerpts
he included to urge him forward in his quest. First, Franklin included with
his chart a "motto" from Addison's *Cato, a Tragedy* that ties together themes
from two-books theology and Common Sense epistemology in a way that
would comport with either Stoicism or Christianity:

> Here will I hold. If there's a power above us
> (And that there is, all nature cries aloud
> Thro' all her works), He must delight in virtue;
> And that which he delights in must be happy.[32]

Franklin also quoted from the Old Testament book of Proverbs, "speaking of wisdom or virtue: 'Length of days is in her right hand, and in her left
hand riches and honour. Her ways are ways of pleasantness, and all her paths
are peace.' Iii. 16, 17."[33]

Finally, Franklin included a prayer for assistance in his efforts to practice
the virtues. He included the substance of the prayer in his autobiography,
as follows: "And conceiving God to be the fountain of wisdom, I thought
it right and necessary to solicit his assistance for obtaining it; to this end I
formed the following little prayer, which was prefix'd to my tables of ex-
amination, for daily use. 'O powerful Goodness! bountiful Father! merci-
ful Guide! Increase in me that wisdom which discovers my truest interest.
Strengthen my resolutions to perform what that wisdom dictates. Accept
my kind offices to thy other children as the only return in my power for thy

continual favours to me.'" Franklin then included an alternate prayer that highlighted the same themes:

> I used also sometimes a little prayer which I took from Thomson's Poems, viz.:
>> Father of light and life, thou Good Supreme!
>> O teach me what is good; teach me Thyself!
>> Save me from folly, vanity, and vice,
>> From every low pursuit; and fill my soul
>> With knowledge, conscious peace, and virtue pure;
>> Sacred, substantial, never-fading bliss![34]

Franklin tied his efforts to exercise virtue and thereby increase his private happiness to public happiness when he wrote that the improvement of "private character" would assist the development of "all happiness both public and domestic" and that "most necessary to increase the Happiness of a Country . . . is the promoting of Knowledge and Virtue."[35]

John Adams also spoke of both private and public happiness in terms of virtue. In a 1775 letter to his wife, Abigail, Adams argued for education in the public virtues of "Benevolence, Charity, Capacity and Industry," stating that the same virtues that made for a happy private life would make for a happy public life as well.[36] In his March 4, 1797, inaugural address in the city of Philadelphia, Adams continued these themes, arguing that the propagation of "knowledge, virtue, and religion among all classes of the people" would further "not only . . . the happiness of life in all its stages and classes, and of society in all its forms, but [also] as the only means of preserving our Constitution."[37] In this line of thinking, Adams included a call for broad-based public education that culminated in a list of virtues that the government ought to "countenance and inculcate" in the Massachusetts Constitution of 1780, section 2, "The Encouragement of Literature, etc.":

> Wisdom and knowledge, as well as virtue, diffused generally among the body of the people, being necessary for the preservation of their rights and liberties; and as these depend on spreading the opportunities and advantages of education in the various parts of the country, and among the different orders of the people, it shall be the duty of legislators and magistrates, in all future periods of this Commonwealth, to cherish the interest of literature and the sciences, and all seminaries of them; especially the university at Cambridge, public

schools, and grammar schools in the towns; to encourage private societies and public institutions, rewards and immunities, for the promotion of agriculture, arts, sciences, commerce, trades, manufactures, and a natural history of the country; to countenance and inculcate the principles of humanity and general benevolence, public and private charity, industry and frugality, honesty and punctuality in their dealings, sincerity, good humour, and all social affections and generous sentiments among the people.[38]

The connection Adams drew between virtue and good governance was one he had mulled over more than twenty years earlier, when he included this entry in his diary on Sunday, February 22, 1756:

Suppos a nation in some distant Region, should take the Bible for their only law Book, and every member should regulate his conduct by the precepts there exhibited. Every member would be obliged in Concience to temperance and frugality and industry, to justice and kindness and Charity towards his fellow men, and to Piety and Love, and reverence towards almighty God. In this Commonwealth, no man would impair his health by Gluttony, drunkenness, or Lust—no man would sacrifice his most precious time to cards, or any other trifling and mean amusement—no man would steal or lie or any way defraud his neighbour, but would live in peace and good will with all men—no man would blaspheme his maker or prophane his Worship, but a rational and manly, a sincere and unaffected Piety and devotion, would reign in all hearts. What a Eutopa, what a Paradise would this region be. Heard Thayer all Day. He preach'd well.[39]

Jefferson evidenced similar themes in his own writings. In an October 31, 1819, letter to William Short, Jefferson summarized Epicurean doctrine on virtue as a path to happiness, stating that virtue consisted of prudence, temperance, fortitude, and justice, whose opposites were folly, desire, fear, and deceit.[40] In his *Notes on the Doctrine of Epicurus*, Jefferson wrote that happiness is the aim of life, and virtue the foundation of happiness, a theme he articulated in an 1814 letter to philosopher and scientist José Corrêa da Serra, stating that it was "the order of nature to be that individual happiness shall be inseparable from the practice of virtue."[41] He went on to state, in an 1816 letter to Amos J. Cook, "Without virtue, happiness cannot be."[42]

CHAPTER 9

Improvement and Perfection from the
Commentaries Forward

FOR BLACKSTONE, THE pursuit of happiness was the primary method by which man could determine the law of nature as it pertained to man. To live in harmony with that law was to be happy. Blackstone argued for the pursuit of happiness not only as an individual pursuit but also, and perhaps more important, as a science of jurisprudence, by which his students could know, and then rightly apply, the first principles of the common law in their later work as judges, jurors, lawyers, or members of Parliament. Blackstone believed that, through the identification and application of first principles, the English common law could be improved and perfected over time, bringing it ever more closely in alignment with the law of the Creator.

Jefferson articulated a similar relationship between happiness and the principles of good or just governance as he drafted the Declaration of Independence, stating not only that governments were created to secure man's unalienable right to the pursuit of happiness but also that it was the right of the people to lay the foundation of their government on those principles that would "seem most likely to effect their Safety and Happiness." Jefferson did not set forth an epistemology or jurisprudence of the pursuit of happiness as overtly as Blackstone did in his *Commentaries*, but a close reading of Jefferson's works on legal reform allows us to see his commitment to these methodologies just the same. As will be discussed in depth in the pages that follow, Jefferson's writings consistently reveal a commitment to an epistemology of the pursuit of happiness (the inductive use of experimentation and observation to determine what the "Laws of Nature and of Nature's God" require for both men and governments) and a jurisprudence of the pursuit of happiness (the use of that information about first principles so gleaned to improve and then perfect the law over time).

Blackstone and Jefferson are commonly viewed as intellectual enemies and political foes. Yet their writings on legal philosophy and legal reform demonstrate that, while Jefferson vehemently disagreed with Blackstone's political views, he nevertheless shared Blackstone's understanding of the pursuit of happiness and Blackstone's belief that it was through an epistemology and jurisprudence of the pursuit of happiness that the law could be improved and perfected over time. Perhaps the most telling—and most concrete—example of Blackstone's and Jefferson's shared theoretical understandings of the pursuit of happiness as a science of jurisprudence is in each man's attempt to improve and perfect the criminal law through the legal reforms they promoted in their lifetimes. It is in those endeavors, in particular, that we begin to see Jefferson and Blackstone, somewhat surprisingly, and perhaps unwittingly, not merely as political foes but also as intellectual allies.

Both Blackstone and Jefferson articulated an idea of improvement and perfection that took hold strongly in the Enlightenment era, where philosophes and religious leaders advocated for a world in a continual state of progress. To improve was "[t]o advance any thing nearer to perfection; to raise from good to better."[1] As Samuel Johnson emphasized in his eighteenth-century dictionary, "We *amend* a *bad*, but *improve* a *good* thing." To be perfect stemmed from the Latin *perfectus*: "[c]omplete; consummate; finished; neither defective nor redundant." Johnson quoted sixteenth-century English theologian Richard Hooker to further define the term: "We count those things *perfect*, which want nothing requisite for the end, whereto they were instituted."[2] In other words, to seek perfection was to first determine the proper end of a thing and then to continually improve the thing from good to better, or to amend the thing, removing its imperfections, until it could fully achieve that end for which it was instituted.

Blackstone and Jefferson adopted these Enlightenment-era concepts of improvement and perfection and adapted them to law and governance. Theoretically, they shared a belief in the "golden age" of Saxon liberty, finding simplicity and beauty in the ancient law codes. Both men advocated for progress, but it was a progress to be achieved by a return to first principles, whether through Blackstone's efforts to return to King Alfred as the founder of the common law and to include instruction in English law and jurisprudence at the university level or Jefferson's assertion that Anglo-Saxon political principles formed the foundation of governance for the new United States. Both men believed that those principles could be discovered through a combination of experimentation, observation, and inductive reasoning.

The Science of Improvement: Thomas Jefferson

Blackstone's emphasis on the improvement and perfection of the English common law has been discussed in full in part 1. That emphasis was evident, in theory and in practice, in the British colonies in North America as they became the new United States. The colonists carried forward a view of law and governance held by their English predecessors, who were described by their contemporaries as "think[ing] they have taken from the government of the Romans all that is best, *and corrected its faults.*" While the Americans adapted Enlightenment thinking to their own "particular intellectual style" and "domestic developments," the "substance of their ideas came from a handful of European thinkers."[3]

Thomas Jefferson provides a terrific example of one who sought to apply European principles—particularly those of Newtonian science—to the study of law and governance, as seen in his *Notes on the State of Virginia.* Jefferson's *Notes* were written between 1781 and 1782 and published in England in 1787, with this advertisement, which highlights Jefferson's sense of an ongoing—and perhaps never-ending—quest for knowledge:

> The following Notes were written in Virginia in the year 1781, and somewhat corrected and enlarged in the winter of 1782, in answer to Queries proposed to the Author, by a Foreigner of Distinction, then residing among us. The subjects are all treated imperfectly; some scarcely touched on. To apologize for this by developing the circumstances of the time and place of their composition, would be to open wounds which have already bled enough. To these circumstances some of their imperfections may with truth be ascribed; the great mass to the want of information and want of talents in the writer. He had a few copies printed, which he gave among his friends: and a translation of them has been lately published in France, but with such alterations as the laws of the press in that country rendered necessary. They are now offered to the public in their original form and language.[4]

The *Notes* then follow, as Jefferson forecast, through a series of twenty-three queries, ranging from the "Boundaries of Virginia" to "Climate" to "Counties and towns" to "Manufacturers" to "Histories, memorials, and state-papers." Each query is then followed by Jefferson's own detailed observations and conclusions. Jefferson believed his *Notes on the State of Virginia* were full of "imperfections," which he attributed both to the circumstances surrounding their writing and to his own shortcomings as an author.[5] He published them nevertheless, in the hopes that they would be of some benefit to the reader—and they are. Jefferson left us with a wealth of information not only about the physical, political, and economic landscape of Virginia, but also about his own thoughts on law and legal reform. There is a sense, in the *Notes* as a whole, and in the individual queries, of work to be improved upon, perfected, and finally completed.

Query 13, "Constitutions," is illuminating on this front. After providing an overview of the history of Virginia from 1584 forward, Jefferson claimed that Virginia's new state constitution "was formed when we were new and unexperienced in the science of government. It was the first too which was formed in the whole United States. No wonder then that time and trial have discovered very capital defects in it."[6] Jefferson's language here is telling. Like Adams, he sees himself as engaged in the "science of government." Like Adams, he believes in the power of experience and "time and trial" to illuminate defects and provide information that could be used for future amendments and improvements. We see Jefferson's practical outworking of these ideas in the text that follows, as he then detailed the "defects" of the Virginia state constitution and his recommendations for their improvement.

The defects, themselves, were revealed through time and trial—the time that had passed since the creation of the Virginia state constitution and the trial or opportunity to test out its principles, which that time had afforded. The defects revealed through that test, according to Jefferson, included lack of representation or unequal representation in the legislature, inadequate voting rights, an inappropriate homogeneity between the senate and the house of delegates, and a variety of concerns relating to an undue concentration of power in the legislative body.[7]

Jefferson discussed each defect in turn, utilizing Adams's and Blackstone's approach to the "science of government" throughout his discussion. And, like both John Adams and James Madison, Jefferson identified the principles of good governance by historical observation, through his own study of the successes or failures of other governments past and present, including the republic of Venice, the Roman Republic, the Roman Empire, Great Britain, and the other states of the Union, including Massachusetts, Rhode Island, New York, New Jersey, and Pennsylvania.[8] Jefferson then utilized comparison as a means of evaluating Virginia's adherence to those principles, thereby identifying where, and why, the Virginia Constitution had gone astray and where improvement was necessary.

It is evident throughout Query 13 that Jefferson believed improvement was possible, as he urged his countrymen to "apply, at a proper season, the proper remedy; which is a convention to fix the constitution, *to amend its defects*, to bind up the several branches of government by certain laws, which when they transgress their acts shall become nullities."[9] Jefferson's use of "proper" here reflects the idea of a "fit" solution that is appropriately adapted to the circumstances at hand. His emphasis on fixing and amending makes clear that he believed improvement of the Virginia Constitution was possible. Throughout Query 13, he supplied his countrymen with a scientific model of observation, comparison, and experimentation to direct them toward that end.

Jefferson's hopes for improvement in the realm of law were not limited to the Virginia Constitution. He also included in his *Notes* his own work on the revision of Virginia's criminal code. As we will soon see, in this work, and in his belief in the role of education in the improvement and perfection of the law, Jefferson practically applied the ideas of improvement and perfection—and the epistemological and jurisprudential methods by which improvement and perfection could occur—in ways that are remarkably similar to Blackstone's methodology for the improvement and perfection of the common law.

Education as a Means of Improvement and Perfection

As discussed previously, William Blackstone advocated for the teaching of English law in the universities precisely because he believed education in the first principles of the law was the primary method by which England could achieve accurate and lasting legal reform. Blackstone wished to see all university students trained in the law, so that they would then be equipped with the skills necessary to serve as judges, jurors, lawyers, members of Parliament, justices of the peace, or simply as landowners and citizens. The skill Blackstone believed to be most valuable for achieving this end was the ability to identify the first principles of the law and then apply those first principles in legal settings. He hoped that his students would later do just that—through their work on the bench, on juries, or in Parliament. This, then, would be the method by which the defects and corruptions of the English common law would be removed, and the common law would be improved and perfected over time.

Jefferson, likewise, tied education to legal reform. Where Blackstone focused on university legal education, Jefferson promoted a broader public education. Jefferson's views on education were integrally connected to his views on government; his concerns over the twin defects of inadequate representation and undue power in the Virginia legislature resulted from his belief in the necessity of self-governance, which required an educated citizenry.

In his *Notes on the State of Virginia*, Jefferson's discussion of education immediately follows his discussion of law reform. He proposed that talented students be selected for further education at the state's expense, claiming that of all of the reasons to support such a law, "none is more important, none more legitimate, than that of rendering the people the safe, as they are the ultimate, guardians of their own liberty." Jefferson argued that the minds of the people "must be improved to a certain degree" so that they can serve as the government's "safe depositories." Jefferson, like Blackstone, saw a vital connection between education, the pursuit of happiness, and justice, claiming that the goal of education ought to be as follows: "The first elements of morality too may be instilled into their minds; such as, when further developed as their judgments advance in strength, may teach them how to work out their own greatest happiness, by shewing them that it does not depend on the condition of life in which chance has placed them, but is always the result of good conscience, good health, occupation, and freedom in all just pursuits."[10]

Application to Criminal Law Reform

Blackstone and Jefferson ran parallel not only in their belief that the law could be, and ought to be, improved and perfected over time, and not only in the role that education had to play in that task, but also in the practical steps they took to improve the law in their own lifetimes. For Blackstone, one such practical step (of many) came in his revision of England's penal law, a work that he began in earnest in 1775–76 and successfully concluded in 1779.[11] Jefferson promoted a similar revision of the criminal code of Virginia from 1777 to 1779.

Blackstone biographer Wilfrid Prest has carefully detailed Blackstone's penal law reforms, which are summarized below.[12] What began with minor alterations to the then existing Transportation Act of 1719 resulted in much broader penal reforms, which were enacted in 1779. In advocating for these changes, Blackstone was influenced by the works of eighteenth-century jurist and philosopher Cesare Beccaria, an advocate for criminal law reform whose works influenced founders like Thomas Jefferson as well.[13] It is perhaps due to Beccaria's influence on Blackstone, and his *Commentaries*, and the confluence of Beccaria's proposals with Blackstone's and Jefferson's shared pursuit of improvement and perfection in the realm of law that Blackstone's plan is reflected in the plan that Jefferson would later promote.

Blackstone's reforms were passed in 1779 as the Penitentiary Act, and the full title of the legislation, "An Act to Explain and Amend the Laws Relating to the Transportation, Imprisonment, and Other Punishments, of Certain Offenders," emphasizes its effort at improvement. A key improvement advocated for by Blackstone appears in clause 5, where he deviated from the notion of merely altering the class of individuals to be sanctioned through transportation and, instead, offered alternatives to transportation, which he hoped would not only better deter individuals from committing crimes in the first place, but also better reform those individuals who had committed crimes, once convicted: "[I]f many Offenders, convicted of Crimes for which Transportation has been usually inflicted, were ordered to solitary Imprisonment, accompanied by well-regulated Labour, and religious Instruction, it might be the Means, under Providence, not only of deterring others from the Commission of the such like Crimes, but also of reforming the Individuals, and inuring them to Habits of Industry." This language provides insight into the history of the penal law and the legal philosophy implicit in its passage. In those places where transportation "had been usually inflicted," the act encourages, for "many Offenders," the alternative of "solitary Imprisonment" with "well-regulated Labour" and "religious Instruction." The stated purpose of these reforms is highlighted by the language as well, with the expressed hope not only that the reforms will achieve deterrence for future criminal conduct but also that the act will be used by Providence as the means "of reforming the Individuals, and inuring them to Habits of Industry." In this language, the act suggests a broad view of criminal law reform, considering not only improvements to the criminal law, by making it more just and efficacious, but also the improvement (or reform) of individuals convicted of crimes under that law. Blackstone described his intended setting for this reform as "experimental Houses of Confinement and Labour, which I would wish to call Penitentiary Houses."[14] "Experimental" highlights Blackstone's inductive legal philosophy. "Penitentiary" comes from the Latin "penitire," which is "to regret"; "repentance" is "to feel such regret for sins or crimes as produces amendment of life."[15] The idea that penitentiary houses could foster individual repentance was a reflection of Blackstone's Anglican religious beliefs. Blackstone remained committed to the "progress" being made in establishing such penitentiary houses even until his death.[16]

Perhaps the most interesting thing about the Penitentiary Act of 1779 is that its drafters sought not only to improve the penal law but also to improve the lives and habits of the individuals who were to be convicted under it—and all within an overarching framework of the workings of Providence. That the act was seen as an improvement on the existing penal law is evident from the response it received. It was described as "the most forward-looking English penal measure of its time," with Blackstone acknowledged as "the great promoter of the design."[17] Perhaps the most surprising praise came from Blackstone contemporary Jeremy Bentham. Bentham had despised Blackstone's *Commentaries* as an "antipathy to reformation."[18] Yet in spite of his quite critical view of Blackstone and the *Commentaries*, even Bentham recognized the improvements in law made possible by the Penitentiary Act of 1779, describing it as "a 'capital improvement . . . in penal legislation,'" although doing so while seemingly giving no credit to Blackstone as a drafter.[19]

Shortly after Blackstone began advocating for reform of the English penal law, Jefferson began work on the reform of Virginia's criminal code. In 1777 Jefferson was appointed to a committee of five individuals selected by the state of Virginia to revise the laws of that state. After debating the merits, and difficulties, of throwing out the existing law in its entirety and enacting a completely new Virginia code, the committee ultimately settled on revising the existing law. According to Jefferson, a wholesale rewriting of the law would have to be the work of a single author, to provide for both consistency and clarity in the text. This idea seemed unappealing to not a few of the committee members, as no one volunteered for the task. Furthermore, and this is where Jefferson's scientific thinking about law and epistemology shines through, Jefferson believed that to rewrite the law of Virginia would mean that the state would lose all of the benefits of trial and experimentation that had occurred from colonization forward. Indeed, Jefferson hypothesized, Virginia would have to begin those experiments anew, and he anticipated that decades or longer would pass before the language of the law would be fully tested and proved.[20]

After settling on revision, not wholesale rewriting, as an end goal, the committee, now reduced to three through death and attrition, divvied up the work and settled down to the task at hand. Jefferson took on "the common law and statutes to the 4. James I (when our separate legislatures were established)," George Wythe took on "the British statutes from that period to the present day," and Edmund Pendleton took on "the Virginia laws." The revisions continued for two years, with the committee reporting its suggestions to the general assembly on June 18, 1779.[21]

Jefferson's portion included revision of the Virginia criminal code, and he stated that "[o]n the subject of the Criminal Law, all were agreed that the punishment of death should be abolished, except for treason and murder; and that, for other felonies should be substituted hard labor in the public works, and in some cases, the Lex talionis."[22] What is fascinating about Jefferson's discussion here—apart from the reforms he proposed—is his inclusion of how the committee came to that agreement.

According to Jefferson, the committee looked to the law of the Anglo-Saxons, the Hebrews, the writings of criminologists such as Cesare Beccaria, and the experiments they had observed in neighboring states, such as Pennsylvania, as they considered reform of the Virginia criminal code. For example, Jefferson wrote that the committee had agreed that the *lex talionis*, or law of retaliation, would be an appropriate improvement to what was then the widespread use of the death penalty. Jefferson's later repudiation of that decision in his autobiography reveals not only his later thoughts on this proposed improvement but also the factors—primarily the Anglo-Saxon law and its possible Hebrew predecessor—that led to the selection of the *lex talionis* in the first place: "How this last revolting principle came to obtain our approbation, I do not remember. There remained indeed in our laws a vestige of it in a single case of a slave. It was the English law in the time of the Anglo-Saxons, copied probably from the Hebrew law of 'an eye for an eye, a tooth for a tooth,' and it was the law of several antient people. But the modern mind had left it far in the rear of it's advances."[23]

In terms of a broader framework for evaluating the death penalty, Jefferson referred to the writings of Beccaria and other jurists focused on criminal law. Jefferson's discussion of Beccaria highlights his reliance on evidence and reason as tools by which to discern the first principles of criminal justice and his commitment both to rightfulness (reflecting Blackstone's and Jefferson's previous adherence to fitness or rightness in relation to the law of nature) and to efficacy (which, for both Blackstone and Jefferson, would be evidence that a law is so rightly ordered). Jefferson stated, "Beccaria and other writers on crimes and punishments had satisfied the reasonable world of the unrightfulness and inefficacy of the punishment of crimes by death; and hard labor on roads, canals and other public works, had been suggested as a proper substitute."[24] The model for improvement that Jefferson described here calls to mind Blackstone's plan for the English Penitentiary Act of 1779, which included labor as a component.

In addition to citing Beccaria, Jefferson looked to the experiences of Pennsylvania, demonstrating a scientific belief in trial, experimentation, and observation as a means of gaining the knowledge necessary to determine the principles of good governance. Although reason, rightness, and efficacy had all worked to bring Jefferson to initially support Beccaria's promotion of "hard labor on roads, canals and other public works," the experience of Pennsylvania changed his mind. Noting the outworking of Beccaria's theories in Pennsylvania, Jefferson found that such hard labor in public degraded people instead of reforming them, causing a "prostration of character, . . . an abandonment of self-respect, as, instead of reform, plunged them into the most desperate & hardened depravity of morals and character."[25] Jefferson then used the information he gained from Pennsylvania's experiment with hard labor, and his own observation of that experiment, to adopt further changes, including the less publicly degrading proposal of solitary labor in prison versus hard labor in public. Like Blackstone, Jefferson was concerned not only with the improvement of the penal law but also with the improvement of the individuals who would be sentenced under it.

The final revision of the criminal code proposed to Virginia's general assembly provides a concrete example of the outworking of Jefferson's legal philosophy of improvement and perfection. First, instead of embarking on a wholesale rewrite, the revision sought to preserve the good that the committee believed was then present in the English common law, as adapted to Virginia. Jefferson's revision sought to better or improve on that good by utilizing principles of law he discovered through the lens of history; these improvements initially included the replacement of capital punishment in several instances with various forms of retaliation, which Jefferson and the committee approved at the time as an expression of the first principles articulated in the common law's Anglo-Saxon and presumably Hebrew predecessors. Jefferson's later claim that this law of retaliation, or *lex talionis*, had been repudiated by the modern mind is, itself, the outworking of Jefferson's scientific thinking on law as it displays his overarching belief that even presumed first principles established by custom and practice across history should be reexamined in terms of new knowledge about the larger principles of justice. If new insights gained through education or the inductive methods of observation and experimentation suggested that a law had ceased to be just or had become either "unrightful" or "inefficacious," that law should be amended.

We see Jefferson's legal philosophy of improvement most present in the final version of Jefferson's criminal law reform: hard labor, incorporated in response to Beccaria's reasoned arguments but modified by Jefferson's own observations of Pennsylvania's experiment. Thus, Jefferson's proposed improvements to the Virginia criminal code ultimately drew from first principles revealed by history and by observation. They included capital punishment, retained from the English common law, but greatly limited in its application; various forms of retaliation, drawn from the common law's Anglo-Saxon and presumed Hebrew predecessors; labor, proposed by Italian legal philosopher Cesare Beccaria and modified by Jefferson's observations of the Pennsylvania experiment; and the incorporation of mercy in response to "Excusable homicide," "Suicide," and "Apostacy. Heresy," each of which Jefferson claimed was "to be pitied not punished."[26] Although these reforms may seem exceedingly harsh to us today, they were a deliberate attempt to improve on the English law's heavy reliance on capital punishment. They highlight an interesting combination of first principles drawn from English law, legal theory and legal history, Christianity, and a Common Sense inductive epistemology and emphasis on knowledge to be gained by experience.

Intellectual Allies and Political Foes

Blackstone articulated a vision of improvement and perfection that was grounded in his understanding of English law and history, the intermingling of Christianity and science articulated by his latitudinarian Anglican faith, the Scottish Enlightenment's Common Sense school, and his response to what he viewed as the overly theoretical, abstract method of determining first principles of law advocated for by the Scholastics. The second section of the introduction to his *Commentaries*, and, indeed, his determined and ultimately successful push for a program of English legal education in the university system to rival the education in the Roman civil law that flourished on the Continent, evidences both his passion for the English common law and his discontent with the jumbled, inconsistent, and sometimes incoherent content of the English common law in his day. Blackstone's advocacy for a system of English legal education that would teach future judges, jurors, lawyers, MPs, and landowners not only the content of the law but also a clear and simple method for discovering and then applying the first principles of the law through the jurisprudence of the pursuit of happiness highlights his belief that the English common law could be, and should be, improved and perfected over time, bringing it ever more in harmony with, in his words, "the law of eternal justice," as revealed to man through the law of nature and the law of revelation.

Blackstone articulated a Common Sense epistemology in support of the idea that every man could identify the first principles of the law of eternal justice through his own pursuit of happiness. He expected his students first to pursue happiness and then, in their future work, to use the knowledge of first principles gained from that pursuit to improve the common law, bringing it ever more in harmony (more into perfection) with those first principles. His approach is scientific at the core. It involved experimentation (through a trying out of that which may make one happy), observation (through a reasoned consideration of results of that experiment, of whether happiness ensued), a conclusion (the determination, based on the evidence gained from the experiment, both of that which does or does not make one happy, as well as the first principles then highlighted by those results), and, finally, an application (the use of those principles to improve and perfect the English law).

Jefferson shared in Blackstone's two-part framework of education and first-principles methodology for the goal of improving and perfecting the common law. Like Blackstone, Jefferson articulated a Common Sense epistemology in support of the idea that man could identify the first principles of the laws of nature—which he described as the laws of nature and of nature's God—and then utilize those first principles toward the goal of improving and perfecting the law. But where Blackstone focused on reformation of the common law, and its application through statutes and court cases, Jefferson felt free to use knowledge of first principles to question—and reform—the entire framework of government. Thus, as seen in his *Notes on the State of Virginia*, Jefferson utilized this methodology not only in the area of criminal law reform, but also as he reassessed the entire Virginia Constitution, urging his fellow Virginians to question anew the framework of their new state government and to amend the constitutional text and pass laws as necessary to require Virginia's rulers to govern within those principles—or to forfeit the right to govern altogether.

Prior to that charge, Jefferson included in his *Notes* a discussion of Thomas Paine's *Common Sense*, deliberately referencing the same literature and first-principles arguments that the colonists had utilized against King George III and the framework of the English Constitution leading up to and during the American Revolution. It would be easy to miss the startling nature of that discussion. As Jefferson was writing his *Notes on the State of Virginia* in 1781–82, the ultimate success of the American Revolution, or even the new state of Virginia, was not a foregone conclusion. The new United States was only a precious few years beyond declaring its independence. The Articles of Confederation had only recently been ratified. The Constitution, stemming from the Articles' defects and failures, had yet to become.

It would seem a risky and premature time for promoting a revision of the entirety of Virginia's law and constitution. But Jefferson revealed a commitment to a scientific philosophy of law and focus on improvement that was at least as broad as Blackstone's and that, in some ways, allowed for even more freedom in reform. It is in this place that their legal and political philosophies diverged. Blackstone's hopes for the improvement of the English law focused on improvement of the common law through Parliament and the courts. Even for those laws that were manifestly unjust, Blackstone proclaimed that the remedy could come only through acts of Parliament, either to amend such laws or to declare them void.

In contrast, Jefferson seemed to believe that the knowledge gained through experiment and observation could be used not only for improvement of specific areas of Virginia law, but also for improvement of the Virginia Constitution as a whole. Blackstone articulated a methodology that would enable both the layperson and the lawyer to know and apply the first principles of the law in their private lives through the pursuit of happiness and then to carry out that methodology as a public duty through law reform. Jefferson trusted his fellow Virginians to carry out exactly that task not only in their individual lives and in potential law reform, but also in their public duty to continually reevaluate the framework of government and its ability to pursue its proper end of securing the happiness and safety to the people, a task befitting citizens who had consented to be governed. Thus, in his *Notes on the State of Virginia*, we see Jefferson take on criminal law reform in order to make the law more just, and we see him identify justice in this context through a combination of history, experimentation, observation, and reason. We also see him take on reform of the Virginia Constitution and do so with a focus on self-government and the first principles by which all governments must be bound. It is a task that has, at its foundation, the pursuit of happiness both as a private right and as a public duty.

It is the willingness of founders like Jefferson to question all things anew—to work toward improvement and perfection in every aspect of law, from the framing of the Constitution down to the details of state statutes—that led those on the Continent to look with enthusiasm on the new American experiment. Perhaps they felt the Americans had a freedom to conduct broadscale improvements—with the benefit of Enlightenment-era insights in the fields of philosophy, theology, law, and, science—in ways that they, themselves, did not feel so free. Enlightenment historian Peter Gay sums up these hopes very well: "The splendid conduct of the colonists, their brilliant victory, and their triumphant Founding of a republic were convincing evidence, to the philosophes at least, that men had some capacity for self-improvement and self-government, that progress might be a reality instead of a fantasy, and that reason and humanity might become governing rather than merely critical principles."[27]

It is a freedom that the Americans carried not only into the American Revolution but also into the new United States as they, in very short order, replaced the Articles of Confederation with the Constitution of the United States, which they believed would help them "to form a *more perfect* Union."[28] One of the first acts of Congress sought to support innovation and improvement through patents, and Jefferson served, as secretary of state, as head of the first patent office. Thomas Jefferson and Alexander Hamilton would later debate how best to support manufacturing in the new United States, taking the philosophy of improvement in a very practical direction as they sought to encourage innovation in trade, agriculture, and industry.[29] Virginia was not the only state to explore reform in criminal law, and other states followed suit as they sought to apply new understandings from a variety of disciplines to improve the laws that governed criminal justice. The new Americans followed this methodology of experimentation and observation in other areas as well and continued considering all things anew, as, throughout the 1800s, courts adapted the English common law to the circumstances of the developing United States, altering or overturning common-law precedent in foundational subfields such as water rights and property rights—all with an eye toward further encouraging a spirit of innovation and improvement in the new nation.

When writing the *Commentaries*, Blackstone viewed himself as furthering the development of an English common-law counterpart to the Roman civil law. Blackstone grounded his work in ancient English history, and he looked to the Anglo-Saxon kings Alfred the Great and Edward the Confessor as the ancient English progenitors of the common law's first principles. Thus, in his *Commentaries*, Blackstone told a story of English law that spanned from King Alfred's pursuit of wisdom and founding of the English common law to the restoration of the English common law by King Edward and finally to the incoherencies and inconsistencies that existed in the English common law of Blackstone's day. Although Jefferson opposed Blackstone's political views, he was enthralled by ancient

English history. Interestingly, Jefferson's love of Anglo-Saxon history, and his antipathy toward Blackstone as a "honeyed" Tory, both stemmed from Jefferson's larger understanding of a westward movement of liberty from ancient Greece and Rome to England and France and to the American colonies. Jefferson opposed Blackstone's Toryism as a tyrannical oppression of English liberty in the colonies even as he revered the Anglo-Saxon first principles upon which that English liberty had been built. When Jefferson included "the pursuit of happiness" in the Declaration of Independence, he did so within Blackstone's ancient, and eighteenth-century, understanding of the phrase.

Like Blackstone, Jefferson understood happiness as *eudaimonia*—the ancient Greek concept of human flourishing or well-being. Like Blackstone, Jefferson understood the pursuit of happiness as man's unalienable right to pursue the laws of nature and of nature's God as they pertained to man—the most sure and certain route to human flourishing or well-being. Like Blackstone, Jefferson believed that man's ability to pursue happiness was contingent upon his status as a free man, one who could exercise his free will, who was at liberty to choose to live in harmony with the law of nature as it applied to him. Like Blackstone, Jefferson believed that a man who chose to pursue happiness would therefore live a "fit," "virtuous," and "rightly-ordered" life.

Where Blackstone and Jefferson differed regarding the pursuit of happiness was in their purposes for including it in their works. Blackstone included the pursuit of happiness in the introduction to his *Commentaries* as part of his broader instruction to English university students on the first principles of English law. Blackstone believed that the eighteenth-century English common law suffered from inconsistencies and incoherencies because previous judges and MPs had neither known nor rightly applied the first principles on which the ancient English common law was based. Preparing English university students to correct those inconsistencies was Blackstone's primary goal in delivering the Oxford University lecture series that later became the *Commentaries*. In keeping with the teachings of the eighteenth-century English Enlightenment, Blackstone taught his students that the Creator governed the created world, and every living creature within it, according to the laws of nature, a set of first principles also known as the natural law. Knowledge gained by studying the natural law was one of two ways by which the Creator revealed the eternal law to humans (the other way being knowledge gained through study of the holy scriptures). Blackstone instructed his students that the Creator had "intimately connected, so inseparably interwoven the laws of eternal justice with the happiness of each individual." As a result, future lawyers, judges, and MPs could identify the law of eternal justice, and the corresponding first principles on which the English common law historically had been and, according to Blackstone, now ought to be based, by pursuing their own "real" and "substantial" happiness.[30]

Jefferson adopted Blackstone's definition of the pursuit of happiness, but not Blackstone's purpose or usage, when he included the phrase in the Declaration of Independence. Instead of including the phrase "pursuit of happiness" to further epistemology and jurisprudence, Jefferson included it in his affirmation of a select group of unalienable rights the Creator had endowed to all men. Blackstone's epistemological use of the pursuit of happiness emphasized the "happiness" portion of the phrase; by referring to their own "real" and "substantial" happiness, his students could know, and then rightly apply, the first principles of the law of nature as they applied to man. His epistemological purpose tied into his jurisprudential purpose, which also emphasized the "happiness" portion of the phrase: once Blackstone's students knew the first principles on which all positive law ought to be based, they could then work to improve and perfect the English common law so that it would more fully align with those first principles. In contrast to Blackstone, Jefferson emphasized the "pursuit" portion of the phrase when he included it as one of the three unalienable rights that he listed in his draft of the Declaration of Independence. For Jefferson, "life" was the threshold unalienable right, and it was swiftly followed by "liberty," defined in an eighteenth-century context as freedom from tyranny or freedom from slavery. Only when man had both life and liberty would he be able to exercise his third unalienable right: "the pursuit of Happiness."

Jefferson's emphasis on the "pursuit" portion of the phrase comes through in the choices he made in drafting the Declaration. Although he had access to the Virginia Declaration of Rights, which listed the right "to pursue *and obtain* happiness," Jefferson did not include the attainment of happiness as an unalienable right guaranteed to man by his Creator. Jefferson believed man had a right to the pursuit, but he did not guarantee—and did not seem to even believe in the possibility of—full attainment of happiness by man on earth. As he stated in his July 15, 1763, letter to John Page, "Perfect happiness I believe was never intended by the deity to be the lot of any one of his creatures in this world; but that he has very much put in our power the nearness of our approaches to it, is what I as stedfastly believe."

Jefferson's definition of the pursuit of happiness was that of Blackstone, but he was not the only founder at work on the Declaration. John Adams and Benjamin Franklin read Jefferson's draft of the Declaration and made significant edits to it before sending it on to the Continental Congress's full Committee of Five and then to the Continental Congress as a whole. The edits that Adams, Franklin, and Jefferson himself made to Jefferson's draft ranged from minor to substantive, and they were many, yet neither Adams and Franklin, nor the members of the Continental Congress who reviewed the draft after them, made a single change to the phrasing or placement of "the pursuit of happiness." That men as ideologically diverse as Jefferson, Adams, Franklin, and the members of the Continental Congress would all sign off on Jefferson's use and placement of "the pursuit of happiness" is evidence that four key strands of intellectual thought at the founding converged at the place where the pursuit of happiness found its meaning. It evoked a world governed by first principles, an idea that not only was a defining element of English law and legal theory, classical history and philosophy, Christianity, and the Scottish Enlightenment's emphasis on Newtonian Science and Common Sense epistemology, but also, as a result, would be both apparent and acceptable to Jefferson, Adams, and Franklin alike.

If Blackstone and Jefferson were foes, it was in their politics. And if they were allies, it was in their shared intellectual framework for seeking out the first principles that formed the foundations of the common law and working toward the improvement and perfection of that law over time. Ultimately, they would differ in how far, and in what directions, their visions of improvement and perfection would take them. But as their efforts at criminal law reform suggest, their shared jurisprudential foundation remained much the same.

CONCLUSION

FAR FROM BEING a glittering generality or a direct substitution for property, the pursuit of happiness had a distinct meaning to those who included it in two of the eighteenth-century's most influential legal documents: William Blackstone's *Commentaries on the Laws of England* (1765–69) and the Declaration of Independence (1776). That distinct meaning included a belief in first principles by which the created world is governed, the idea that these first principles were discoverable by man, and the belief that to pursue a life lived in accordance with those principles was to pursue a life of virtue, with the end result of happiness, best defined in the Greek sense of *eudaimonia*, or human flourishing. The pursuit of happiness is full of substance from Blackstone (and before) to the founders (and beyond). It was part of an English and Scottish Enlightenment understanding of epistemology and jurisprudence. It had meaning to those who wrote and spoke the phrase in eighteenth-century English and American legal contexts, and it had meaning to its listeners. The pursuit of happiness found its way into eighteenth-century English sermons and colonial-era speeches and writings on political tyranny. If the founders had intended to include in the Declaration a phrase that could serve as a synonymous or nonsubstantive substitution for Locke's unalienable right to property, "the pursuit of Happiness" would have been an odd phrase for them to have selected.

In Blackstone's *Commentaries*, the pursuit of happiness referred to a simple and certain science of jurisprudence from which laypersons, not only trained lawyers or philosophers, could engage in inductive reasoning to pass statutes and hand down judicial opinions that would be in harmony with the law of nature and the law of revelation, the Creator's two methods of communicating to man the great principles of his eternal law. The pursuit of happiness as an inductive science had its roots in latitudinarian Anglicanism and Scottish Common Sense philosophy, both of which drew heavily on the role that Isaac Newton's scientific discoveries played in the

131

Enlightenment. The pursuit of happiness, as used by Blackstone, had an earlier history even yet, as it reflected the pursuit of wisdom that King Alfred believed to be the duty of the king and the right of all subjects in the realm. It was also forward looking, as Blackstone believed that a jurisprudence based on the pursuit of happiness was the surest path to the improvement and perfection of the common law.

The pursuit of happiness in the Declaration of Independence has a similarly rich context. The three primary drafters of the Declaration, Thomas Jefferson, John Adams, and Benjamin Franklin, were immersed in an intellectual world that drew from the science of Newton, the law of England, the Stoicism and political philosophy of classical antiquity, and the providential theism and morality of the Bible. These three men, and their peers, drew from these bodies of knowledge in different ways. While Jefferson affirmed the classics and the Stoic philosophy of classical antiquity, he had grave reservations about Tory views of the English common law and the divine attributes of Jesus. He upheld a combination of reason and freedom of conscience with his founding of the University of Virginia and his drafting of the Virginia Statute on Religious Freedom and created a version of the Bible in which all references to the divinity of Christ were removed. He articulated a robust view of divine Providence and wrote frequently of an afterlife. In all areas, he governed his inquiries along an eighteenth-century inductive science of experiment, and this is nowhere more telling than in the reflections he compiled in his *Notes on the State of Virginia* and his efforts to improve the law of Virginia through careful, scientific, and historically grounded revision.

Adams also held to an unorthodox Christian faith and shared Jefferson's love for the classics. He had a particular affinity for Cicero, self-proclaimed upholder of the Roman Republic, and likely viewed himself as a modern-day Cicero as he engaged in an extensive and impressive scientific exploration of the first principles of governance. Adams was well versed in the common law and viewed his exploration as a means by which the common law could be perfected in the Constitution of the new American Republic. He believed in divine Providence and advocated for biblical morality.

Franklin had mixed views on Christianity—sometimes appearing more deist and sometimes evidencing support for a more particularly orthodox creed. Like Jefferson and Adams, he held a belief in divine Providence and upheld biblical morality. He spoke out against broad requirements for classical education, but encouraged—and read—the classics in translation.

He was self-taught on the study of English law and was heavily engaged with the key figures of the Scottish Enlightenment. His scientific work is a testament to his love for observation, experimentation, and the inductive method.

These men, all living in the same broad intellectual climate but each quite different from the others, approved of "the pursuit of happiness" as an unalienable right in the Declaration of Independence. The common theme among the four intellectual fields of their day was this shared idea of first principles by which the created world is governed and the Common Sense notion that these first principles were discoverable by man. That understanding is the heart of the meaning of the pursuit of happiness, not only for the founders but also for Blackstone and for those who engaged in inductive legal science in eighteenth-century England and eighteenth- and nineteenth-century America.

As mentioned previously, the first recorded reference of the phrase "pursuit of happiness" in a US Supreme Court case does not occur until 1823.[1] But what is perhaps more interesting than this articulation of the phrase nearly fifty years after the signing of the Declaration is the Court's articulation of first principles of law in earlier decisions. For example, in *Fletcher v. Peck* (1795), the US Supreme Court based its decision on "certain great principles of justice, whose authority is universally acknowledged," with the concurring opinion citing to "general principle . . . the reason and nature of things." In *Terrett v. Taylor* (1815), the Court based its holding on "the principles of natural justice, upon the fundamental laws of every free government."[2] A full understanding of the meaning of the pursuit of happiness in its historical context suggests that these phrases, too, are not glittering generalities but, instead, were intended to be articulations of the substantive legal principles that Blackstone and the founders believed the pursuit of happiness could enable man to identify. Their philosophy here was practical, as evidenced in their efforts to ascertain those first principles and then to apply those principles toward the improvement and perfection of the law over time.

If the pursuit of happiness seems empty, or too general, to us today, it is not because we, as a people, have lost the desire to pursue that which makes us happy but because the most common understanding of the word "happy" today aligns almost solely with what the eighteenth-century philosophers would have called a fleeting and temporal happiness versus a "real" and "substantial" happiness. The first is a happiness rooted in disposition, circumstance, and temperament; it is a temporary feeling of psychological pleasure. The second is happiness as *eudaimonia*—well-being or human flourishing. It includes a sense of psychological pleasure or feeling good but does so in a real or substantial sense. It is real in that it is genuine and true. It is substantial in that it pertains to the substance or essence of what it means to be fully human.[3]

The pursuit of happiness in this sense perhaps might include, as previous scholars have argued, the ownership of property, either in John Locke's narrower view of property as that which results from the application of man's labor or in his broader view of property as consisting of man's life, liberty, and estate. It could include the founders' understanding of property ownership as a precondition for the freeing of man's will, and therefore his ability to choose to live a life of virtue.[4] The pursuit of happiness could include the fulfillment to be found in private family life or the duty to live out a life of virtue in the public realm.[5] It could include the results of that pursuit, which John Adams identified as comfort, security, and ease. The end result of such a pursuit could be, in the words of *Black's Law Dictionary*, "the highest enjoyment, [the] increase [of] one's prosperity, or . . . the development of one's faculties."[6] It might even follow along the lines of *Black's Law Dictionary*'s *other* definition for the pursuit of happiness: "The principle— announced in the Declaration of Independence—that a person should be allowed to pursue the person's desires (esp. in regard to an occupation) without unjustified interference by the government"—although I suspect both Blackstone and the founders would have taken some pause at the verb "announced." But not one of these definitions fully encapsulates happiness or its pursuit in an eighteenth-century legal context; they are, instead, only pieces of the larger whole.

To recapture the eighteenth-century legal meaning of the pursuit of happiness is to limit the definition to one great thing—the pursuit of *eudaimonia*, or human flourishing. It is to evoke a private right to pursue a life lived in accordance with the laws of nature as they pertain to man and a public duty to govern in harmony with those laws. As contained in Blackstone's *Commentaries* and the Declaration of Independence, the pursuit of happiness is not a legal guarantee that one will attain happiness, even when happiness is defined within its eighteenth-century context. It is, instead, an articulation of the idea that, as humans, we were created to live, at liberty, with the unalienable right to engage in the pursuit.

Historiography of
William Blackstone and the *Commentaries*

For decades, scholars have attempted to make sense of the purpose and structure of Blackstone's *Commentaries on the Laws of England*. An overview of their arguments provides a framework not only for an exploration of Blackstone as a legal thinker and the *Commentaries* as a legal text, but also for an understanding of how previous studies of Blackstone both built upon and responded to one another and how their combined works might fill gaps in our understanding of both the man and the text.

Questions that scholars have considered include the following: Why did Blackstone write the *Commentaries* in the first place? What was his overarching purpose? Why did he structure the *Commentaries* as he did? What was the result of his efforts? Below, I conduct a chronological overview of the arguments of those authors whose works have been most prominent in the discourse that attempts to answer these questions.[1]

Previous Histories

Perhaps the most familiar historical stance taken on Blackstone's *Commentaries* is that of Blackstone contemporary Jeremy Bentham who, in his work *Fragment on Government* (1776), adamantly spoke out against both Blackstone and the *Commentaries*.

In the words of Blackstone biographer Wilfrid Prest, Bentham's work suggested "that the logical confusion and moral complacency which he detected in Blackstone's *Commentaries* were directly linked to their author's failings of character and intellect."[2] "Bentham and his followers" saw Blackstone as a "muddled reactionary at whom they sneered." Prest describes Bentham as "the most committed, ferocious, and influential" of Blackstone's critics.[3] Although Bentham was extremely vocal in his critique of Blackstone and the *Commentaries*, he was not necessarily accurate—a point on which several later reviewers of the *Commentaries* have agreed.

Daniel J. Boorstin is among those who disagree with Bentham's summary of Blackstone. In his 1941 work *The Mysterious Science of Law*, Boorstin

counters Bentham's argument by stating that Blackstone's *Commentaries* succeeded as a coherent summary of English law precisely because the *Commentaries* themselves were internally inconsistent. Specifically, Boorstin
argues that Blackstone created "a rational and apparently coherent statement of the legal system of his day" and did so by allowing "many contrary
ways of thinking" to coexist in the *Commentaries*. Boorstin states that the
document's "unity" and "coherence" came not from an "abstract system of
philosopher's logic" but, instead, from the work's status as "the product of
a man who believed in certain moral and social values, and who employed
all the ideas he found around him, to convince himself and to persuade his
readers that English law, embodying these values, was entitled to reverence
and support." As Boorstin puts it, "Blackstone was not a rigorous thinker,
and his work does not rank with the great books which demonstrate the
nicest intricacies of the mind of man." Yet according to Boorstin, "His
work had a unity which must have seemed to his readers to be due not to
any cold consistency of its logic, but rather to the meaning of its values for
society. The *Commentaries* sometimes lacked a philosopher's consistency, but
they had a sort of social consistency. It is this kind of consistency, certainly,
by which the work attained its vast significance in America, and by which
it ought finally to be judged."[4]

Duncan Kennedy, in his 1979 work "The Structure of Blackstone's *Commentaries*," argues against the very consistency and coherency that Boorstin
identifies and, in so doing, seems more in agreement with Bentham's earlier
critiques. Kennedy argues that Blackstone is "supremely unconvincing" and
that his *Commentaries* "cast as rational order what we see as something like
chaos." According to Kennedy, Blackstone's incoherence and inconsistency resulted from his political motivations: the *Commentaries* hide "political intentions beneath the surface of legal exposition." Thus, Blackstone
"set[s] out together, for the first time in English, all the themes that right to
the present day characterize attempts to legitimate the status quo through
doctrinal exegesis." In this way, Kennedy's Blackstone mirrors Bentham's
Blackstone as a man who operates primarily out of "a desire to legitimate
the legal status quo of the England of his day."[5]

In his 1983 article "Sir William Blackstone and His 'Commentaries on
the Laws of England' (1765–9): A Biographical Approach," I. G. Doolittle
takes a different approach and argues that Blackstone's *Commentaries* should
be analyzed not purely on the basis of its structure or content, but with
the aid of biographical and historical context. To conduct such an analysis,

Doolittle provides a time line of Blackstone's oral lectures on the laws of England and the publication of the *Commentaries*, which were Blackstone's written versions of those lectures. Doolittle argues that if Blackstone had conducted more substantial revisions in between the oral and written lectures, the *Commentaries* would have been saved from the "old-fashioned air which has puzzled and irritated future generations."[6] In his later biography of Blackstone, Doolittle revisits this point, arguing that substantial revisions to the *Commentaries* were prevented due to the limited time frame between the delivery of Blackstone's oral lectures and the production of the written *Commentaries*, a time frame that was likely shortened due to the unexpected arrival on the market of pirated versions of Blackstone's law lectures.[7] According to Doolittle, the haste to publish notwithstanding, Blackstone's *Commentaries* are much more cohesive and clear than they have been given credit for, and considering both Blackstone as a person and the time frame of his lectures on law in relation to the publications of his *Commentaries*, the coherence of the *Commentaries* becomes more clear.[8]

Like Doolittle, Alan Watson argues for a stronger coherence than the *Commentaries* had previously been granted. In his work, also entitled "The Structure of Blackstone's *Commentaries*," Watson attempts to bring coherence back to the *Commentaries* by drawing connections between the structure and theoretical framework of Blackstone's *Commentaries* and those of Justinian's *Institutes*, the well-respected and much-cited compilation of the Roman Civil Code that was completed by Emperor Justinian in AD 533. Specifically, Watson argues that Blackstone's *Commentaries* were influenced not only by Justinian's *Institutes*, but also by a tabulation of the *Institutes* created by Dionysius Gothofredus (1549–1622) and by Matthew Hale's *The Analysis of the Law* (1713), which Watson argues was influenced by Justinian's *Institutes* as well. Watson's key argument is that, although "Blackstone, Gothofredus, and Hale were constrained by the peculiarities of the structure Justinian created," Blackstone prevailed in "combining these elements each in its sphere to produce a structure satisfactory for the English law of his day."[9] In other words, according to Watson, Blackstone's key accomplishment was in his successful use of Justinian's *Institutes* as an organizing framework for English law.

Writing at about the same time as Watson, Michael Lobban adopts a position that lies somewhere between the logical "incoherency" arguments of Bentham, Boorstin, and Kennedy, on the one hand, and the chronological, social, and structural "coherency" arguments of Doolittle, Boorstin

(again), and Watson, on the other. Lobban argues that Blackstone was neither as logically "confused and contradictory" as Boorstin and Kennedy had
suggested nor as successful in "creating a new 'science of English law'" as
suggested by scholars like Watson. Instead, in his work "Blackstone and the
Science of the Law," Lobban argues that Blackstone followed in a long line
of eighteenth-century English legal scholars who had tried "to combine
two methodologies [of English Common Law and Roman Civil Law] by
looking at English law in a Roman way in order to prove that the English
law had a logical structure." Yet, Lobban argues, Blackstone differed from
his predecessors in a significant way: he tried "to use the Roman structure
on its own terms," not just as a "method of organization, but [as] a method
of analysis" that could actually explain the law as a deduction from first
principles.[10] Lobban concluded that this is where the inconsistency came
in: Blackstone failed in his attempt to reconcile the natural law deduction
of the civilian law with the analytical application of the common law and
therefore ultimately failed in adopting a consistent approach to the common
law through the *Commentaries*.

In his 1989 work *The Province of Legislation Determined: Legal Theory in
Eighteenth-Century Britain*, David Lieberman suggests that Blackstone may
have been more successful than either Boorstin or Lobban realized. Lieberman counters Lobban by arguing that Blackstone's primary purpose was not
solely to reconcile the English common law with a civilian-law deductive
system, but, instead, to create a body of English law that would educate
English lawyers, laypersons, university students, and future legislators in
the art of lawmaking. Blackstone's means to achieve this end was to create a
systematic understanding of the English common law within a natural law
framework.[11]

In his exploration of Blackstone and the *Commentaries*, Wilfrid Prest takes
the biographical approach to understanding the *Commentaries* that was first
encouraged by Doolittle.[12] In his work *William Blackstone: Law and Letters in
the Eighteenth Century* (2008) and in a chapter titled "Blackstone and Biography" in the edited compilation *Blackstone and His Commentaries: Biography,
Law, History* (2009), Prest, like Doolittle, highlights the important connections between Blackstone's life and the work he produced in the *Commentaries*. Prest argues that Blackstone was "the sort of writer who found it very
difficult to refrain from tinkering with his text," and, as a result, "the *Commentaries* was a work-in-progress, whose composition extended over more
than a quarter of a century." Prest argues that Blackstone was much more of

an innovator and improver than Bentham would allow and that a detailed look at the *Commentaries* shows not only an exposition of the common law as it then existed, but also Blackstone's own "criticisms and suggestions for improvement of current institutions and practices." In recognition of the coherence and intellectual acumen of both the text and its author, Prest argues that the *Commentaries* are reflective of the type of careful attention to word choice that characterized Blackstone himself.[13]

Finally, in her essay "A 'Model of the Old House': Architecture in Blackstone's Life and Commentaries," contained in *Blackstone and His Commentaries: Biography, Law, History* (2009), Carol Matthews also argues for Blackstone's love of order as evidenced in his *Commentaries*. To make this argument, Matthews draws on Blackstone's lifelong interest in architecture and the subsequent influence of that interest on the *Commentaries*. Like Prest and Doolittle, she takes a biographical approach, attempting to look at Blackstone's interests and activities beyond the law to uncover what he is doing in his *Commentaries*. Matthews succeeds in painting a fuller portrait of the man and his work. Of her own work, she states, "This essay has merely sketched the breadth, depth and intellectual ramifications of Blackstone's architectural activities, to suggest that they throw new light upon his life, religious views and jurisprudence. Many questions remain. Above all, it seems that Blackstone was studying architecture and the law simultaneously." She then urges future scholars of Blackstone to take a similar wide-lens biographical approach to his life and works.[14] That work has been ongoing, not only through the other essays included in *Blackstone and His "Commentaries"* but also in Wilfrid Prest's edited volume, *Re-interpreting Blackstone's "Commentaries": A Seminal Text in National and International Contexts* (2014).

Bentham, Boorstin, and Kennedy each seem to disagree with the content and purpose Blackstone outlined in the introduction to his *Commentaries*. Each scholar first sees the content of the *Commentaries* as incoherent in some way and then seeks to identify a motivating purpose that will explain the incoherent content. Bentham's explanation, in the words of Wilfred Prest, is that Blackstone was simply a "purblind defender of the unreformed Common Law."[15] Therefore, Blackstone was not concerned with the inconsistencies of the law as he portrayed it but, instead, was primarily concerned with promoting the existing common law, consistent or not. Kennedy offers a similar explanation, which is that Blackstone was politically motivated "to legitimate the legal status quo of the England of his day."[16] Thus,

Kennedy's Blackstone published the *Commentaries* in an unsuccessful attempt to demonstrate the rationality and acceptability of the then existing
English law.

Like Bentham and Kennedy, Boorstin argues that Blackstone was writing
to bring about "reverence and support" for the common law. Where Boorstin differs from Bentham and Kennedy is in his evaluation of the coherence
of the *Commentaries*. Specifically, Boorstin disagrees with Bentham's and
Kennedy's emphasis on logic as the basis for coherence and argues, instead,
for a coherence based on the "moral and social values" of Blackstone's time.
But Boorstin views even this type of coherence as a stretch, since it required
Blackstone "to convince himself and persuade his readers that English law,
embodying these values, was entitled to reverence and support."[17]

Although also troubled by perceived inconsistencies within the *Commentaries*, Lobban is persuasive in regard to Blackstone's purpose when he states
that, by his own words, Blackstone attempted to put into writing a system of English law that would rival the Roman civil-law system that had
swept the Continent. In this, Lobban offers a counter to Watson's claim that
Blackstone was trying to bring the *Commentaries* in line with the *Institutes*.
Instead, Blackstone was deliberately moving away from the civil law's structure, methods, and content, in order to work toward a robust and internally
coherent body of English law. Reaching this goal required Blackstone first
to acknowledge the natural law foundation of the civil law system and then
to explain to his reader that a natural law foundation similarly underlay the
English law. Lobban's argument for incoherence comes in at this point, with
his claim that Blackstone failed to reconcile the English common law with
the civilian deduction system and that he therefore failed to create a logical
system of English law. However, Blackstone did not desire to reconcile the
English common law with the Roman civil law. He did not envision the
Commentaries as the complete and fully consistent version of the common
law, as deduced from the natural law. Instead, Blackstone saw the *Commentaries* as a systematic attempt to compile the laws of England, as they then
existed, and to distinguish those laws from the Roman civil law, while
also acknowledging their shared natural law foundations. Thus, Blackstone
sought to make clear to his students that just as Justinian argued for natural
law principles in compiling the Roman civil law, so did natural law principles inform the English common law, even as those natural law principles
had been sometimes misapplied and even as the legal rules that had been
deduced from those principles differed. It is in Blackstone's frustration with

the Scholastic deductive method that he articulates the inductive method of the pursuit of happiness to take its place.

Blackstone's goal for his students is key to understanding his *Commentaries*, and it is Lieberman who has articulated Blackstone's educational purpose most clearly. According to Lieberman, Blackstone sought not only to explain the theory behind the English common-law system, but also to provide future lawyers, judges, and MPs with the methods they would need to properly enter into the practical art of lawmaking within that system. Blackstone's means to achieve this end was to summarize the English common law within a natural law framework. In this, Lieberman asserted, Blackstone succeeded, as his contemporaries found the *Commentaries* "to have furnished reason and erudition where confusion and technicality hitherto obtained."[18] Yet Lieberman's argument can be carried further still. A key point to understanding Blackstone's *Commentaries* is seeing not only where the *Commentaries* exhibit "reason and erudition" but also where they exhibit inconsistency.

Blackstone himself was fully aware of the inconsistencies in the English law, and although he abhorred their existence, he deliberately included them in his *Commentaries*. Blackstone believed that it was only by knowing and understanding the *then existing* inconsistencies and incoherencies of the English law that English lawyers, judges, and MPs could begin to do the work necessary to improve the English common law and bring it back to a place of harmony and order. The goal of the *Commentaries* was not to create logic and consistency in the English law where there was none but, instead, to compile the English law as it then was—inconsistencies and all—in a systematic format, acknowledging the law's debt to the natural law, and then to use that compilation, and its natural law foundation, as a basis from which to teach future lawmakers the art of lawmaking. In this, Blackstone looks much less like Bentham's "purblind defender of the unreformed Common Law" and much more like the "energetic innovator and tireless 'improver'" that recent biographical accounts of his life have shown him to be.[19]

Doolittle, Prest, and Matthews have emphasized such a biographical approach to the *Commentaries*, and rightly so. Viewing the *Commentaries* through a broader biographical lens overturns centuries-old misconceptions about Blackstone's *Commentaries* and the man himself. At the end of her essay on Blackstone and architecture, Matthews states that "if we are to understand both Blackstone the man and his *Commentaries* we must understand more deeply a consequent, and apparently fundamental, relationship in his thought between history, Christianity, architecture and the law."[20] I would add science and political philosophy as well.

The interplay in Blackstone's thought between "history, Christianity, architecture and the law," as well as science and political philosophy, is nowhere more evident than in his two-part goal of reforming legal education and legal analysis in England. When viewed in light of Blackstone's goals for legal education reform, the *Commentaries* become not a confusing or incoherent amalgamation of English common law, or a poor English counterpart to Justinian's *Institutes*, but, instead, an architectural blueprint of the then existing English law—"A Model of the Old House"[21]—inconsistencies and all. Blackstone believed that creating such a blueprint from which his students could be instructed in the English law, as opposed to the civil law, was an essential starting point for reforming English legal education.

Blackstone believed that the essential second step toward achieving these reforms was to provide students with a science of jurisprudence capable of assisting them in reading the blueprint and identifying the foundational principles upon which inconsistencies and incoherencies ("preposterous Additions" and "unskilful improvements") could be removed and an improved or perfected English law could be built. For Blackstone, the three main jurisprudential methods available for identifying the foundational principles were reason, revelation, and the pursuit of happiness.[22] In a departure from the Roman influence of Justinian and the Scholastic method of jurisprudence that had prevailed in the English universities, the jurisprudential method that Blackstone believed to have the greatest likelihood of success in reforming English law and lawmaking was also an inductive science of jurisprudence that was most particularly English and Anglican. That science of jurisprudence was the pursuit of happiness.

Historiography of

The Pursuit of Happiness in the Declaration of Independence

Four works stand out in their efforts to trace the drafting of the Decla-ration: John Hazelton, *The Declaration of Independence: Its History* (1906), Carl Becker, *The Declaration of Independence: A Study in the History of Political Ideas* (1922), Julian Boyd, *The Declaration of Independence: The Evolution of the Text as Shown in Facsimiles of Various Drafts by Its Author* (1945), and Pauline Maier, *American Scripture: Making the Declaration of Independence* (1997). Each work built on what came before, with Maier's reconstruction of the draft Declaration and the edits of the Continental Congress incorporating and updating the prior work of both Becker and Boyd. This reconstruction can be found in appendix C, pages 235–41, of her work, *American Scripture.*

In terms of the Declaration's historical context, Maier does a particularly nice job of situating the Declaration in the midst of other declarations of independence issued in 1776, while Barry Shain in his work *The Declaration of Independence in Historical Context: American State Papers, Petitions, Proclama-tions & Letters of the Delegates to the First National Congresses* (2014) explores the vast documentary history leading up to the Declaration.

In addition to exploring the Declaration's drafting, Becker and Maier each took a stance on the Declaration as a work of philosophy. Becker ar-gued that the Declaration embodied a natural rights philosophy that drew on classical philosophy and more recent conceptions of nature, but that this philosophy "could not survive the harsh realities of the [nineteenth-century] modern world."[1] Maier claimed that the Declaration prior to 1815 was largely a political document, not primarily a philosophical document, and that it only later came to stand "as a statement of basic principles for guidance of an established society."[2] These questions over the political phi-losophy of the Declaration of Independence—Is it a philosophical docu-ment? If so, what philosophy(ies) does it contain?—are ongoing and they are implicit in the exploration of the historical meaning of the pursuit of happiness.

A handful of scholars have focused more specifically on the phrase "the pursuit of Happiness" in the Declaration of Independence. As discussed previously, historians have argued that "the pursuit of Happiness" is a replacement phrase for "estate" or "property" in John Locke's writings, the happiness to be found in the increasing acquisition of material comfort in late-eighteenth-century Britain and America, the happiness to be found in family life, and an embodiment of the Scottish Enlightenment idea of public virtue. Each of these definitions has its merits, and each has its difficulties as well. The discussion below outlines these arguments more in depth, with an eye toward highlighting the significant contributions of these previous texts.

Pursuit of Happiness as
John Locke's Inherent Right to Property

In his *Two Treatises of Government* (1688), John Locke defines property as including "life, liberty, and estate." According to Locke's definition of estate (what we, today, would call property), God gave land to all men, and their use of it is limited to what they have altered with their labor and what they need to survive. In his 1977 work *In Pursuit of Happiness: American Conceptions of Property from the Seventeenth to the Twentieth Century*, William B. Scott argues that "pursuit of [h]appiness" is both a synonym for and a replacement of John Locke's third concept of property: estate.[3]

Scott claims that the founders adopted Locke's understanding of property as "all men's right to exclusive ownership of productive resources and to the fruits of their labor free from arbitrary governmental action."[4] In the Declaration, the founders asserted that Parliament's taxation had reduced them to slaves because their property was no longer their own. Thus, according to Scott, when the founders included "the pursuit of [h]appiness" as an unalienable right, they were actually invoking Locke's belief in property ownership, through improvement, as an inherent right—a right that the Parliament had no authority to take away through taxation.

Scott has done much to explicate the founders' understanding of property and how their views influenced their political philosophy. Yet the historical documents suggest two difficulties with Scott's argument that "pursuit of [h]appiness" is a synonymous replacement for Locke's "right to property." The first difficulty is that Jefferson, unlike Locke, did not believe owning property was an unalienable right.[5] Scott highlights this distinction and places it within its more specific historic context, arguing that Jefferson only spoke out against the natural right of property ownership while in

France because of the abuses in property ownership he saw there. Scott believed that Jefferson saw "ambiguities" even within the colonists' understandings of property ownership and, therefore, replaced "property" with "pursuit of [h]appiness" as a way to mitigate these differences. With this switch, Jefferson equated pursuit of happiness with property not to make owning property an unalienable right, but to ensure that the government would protect a person's right to seek happiness through the *opportunity* of owning property. Thus, Scott distinguishes an unalienable right to own property from an unalienable right to seek happiness through the opportunity of owning property. He then connects the latter to the pursuit of happiness, claiming that "the most pervasive and persistent conception of property has been that of *opportunity* or, as Jefferson so suggestively put it, the right to 'pursue happiness.'"[6]

Scott connects the opportunity to own property to the pursuit of happiness first by describing property ownership in terms of civic virtue, which he does through the writings of seventeenth-century English political philosopher James Harrington. Harrington believed "property was the decisive factor of politics" because it gave a landowner freedom and the ability to be "politically virtuous," since he did not need to depend on another for subsistence. Harrington thought property ownership "made possible disinterested 'civic virtue'" and that it was a decline in civic virtue that led to the English Civil War. Thus, in essence, Harrington promoted a seventeenth-century vision of an agrarian republic that helped shape the founders' vision of a pastoral republic, where a free, landowning citizenry would form the foundation of good government.[7]

Scott then ties Harrington to John Locke, whom he claims based his *Two Treatises of Government* "on Harrington's theory of political power." For Locke, property "included life, liberty, and estate" under a broader conception of "property" that was tied to "[s]elf-possession or liberty." Locke argued that men who were servants or slaves were "not self-possessed. Another person owned and controlled him. While a servile person retained his life, he had lost or given up his liberty." Thus, like Harrington, Locke believed that a man who was not in control of his property could not be free. According to Scott, "Many Americans accepted the ideas of Harrington and Locke and believed that only economically autonomous men were free."[8] The founders then built the Declaration on this assumption.

Scott's discussion of Harrington, Locke, and the idea of property ownership as a foundation for civic virtue and freedom is important. The founders accepted and promoted the ideal of "disinterested 'civic virtue'" exercised by free, property-holding males. However, there is a distinction to be made between property ownership as a necessary requirement for the exercise of civic virtue and the elevation of the opportunity for or act of property ownership itself to an unalienable right by merging the opportunity to acquire property with the meaning of the pursuit of happiness.

Scott combines the two in his argument that Jefferson "amended Locke's phrase" by changing "'life, liberty, and estate' to 'Life, Liberty, and the pursuit of [h]appiness'" in the Declaration. Scott believes Jefferson intended "pursuit of [h]appiness" to be a revitalized form of Locke's "estate," one that would guarantee landownership by the many and prevent the consolidation of large tracts by the few. However, in laying out the case for this change, Scott clarifies that "Jefferson never explained why he amended Locke's phrase to the 'pursuit of [h]appiness.'"[9] Thus, Scott uses Harrington and Locke to describe what Jefferson means by the pursuit of happiness, but he does so on the basis of a significant assumption: the assumption that Jefferson started with Locke's phrasing in the first place.

It is not an unfounded assumption. As discussed previously, Jefferson included Locke in his trinity of three great men and later was even accused of plagiarizing Locke when drafting the Declaration. Yet Jefferson's "pursuit of [h]appiness" might have had very little or nothing at all to do with Locke's concept of estate. The evidence shows this to be the case. While Scott claims that Jefferson looked to Locke and replaced "estate" with "pursuit of [h]appiness," Jefferson claims that he referred to "neither book nor pamphlet" while drafting the Declaration.[10] Jefferson was in Philadelphia at the Constitutional Convention at the time of the drafting. The only two documents Jefferson had by his side during the drafting process were a draft of the Virginia Declaration of Rights (1776), authored by George Mason, and Jefferson's own draft constitution for the state of Virginia.[11] What is fascinating about Mason's document is that, like Jefferson, Mason lists pursuit of happiness as an unalienable right, but he does so in addition to, not in replacement of, the idea of property as an unalienable right. Mason's "inherent rights" are grouped into four segments, as the brackets indicate below: "[1] the enjoyment of life [2] and liberty, [3] with the means of acquiring and possessing property, and [4] pursuing and obtaining happiness and safety."[12]

Mason's text, which is a more immediate resource to Jefferson than Locke both in time (as it was written just before the Declaration) and in location (as Jefferson had access to it during the drafting process), lists "acquiring and possessing property" and "pursuing and obtaining happiness and safety" as two separate and distinct inherent rights.[13] Furthermore, Locke himself defines the pursuit of happiness separately from property in his *Essay on Human Understanding*.[14] It is possible that Jefferson referred neither to Locke nor to Mason when drafting the Declaration. Indeed, Jefferson deviates from both Locke and Mason in his omission of property or estate. However, in the language that he retains, "life, liberty, and the pursuit of happiness," Jefferson's wording is more reflective of Mason's Virginia Declaration of Rights and Locke's *Essay on Human Understanding* than Locke's *Two Treatises*.[15] Thus, where Scott argues that Jefferson omitted Locke's "estate" and replaced it with the "pursuit of [h]appiness" as a synonym, other writings of the time demonstrate that the founders saw "estate" and "pursuit of [h]appiness" as two distinct unalienable rights and that Jefferson omitted the former from the Declaration while retaining the latter.

Pursuit of Happiness as Pursuit of Comfort in Eighteenth-Century Britain and America

In his work *The Invention of Comfort: Sensibilities and Design in Early Modern Britain and Early America* (2001), John E. Crowley argues that the pursuit of happiness relates to the increasing acquisition of material comfort in Britain and the colonies in the late eighteenth century. Crowley describes comfort as "an innovation of Anglo-American culture" in the eighteenth century that included a trend toward improving the existing "material culture," resulting in a corresponding "consumer revolution" to bring about those improvements.[16]

As Crowley demonstrates, although Britain and America experienced a consumer revolution during the eighteenth century, they were not of one mind in terms of this new focus on comfort. They alternatively linked increased consumption to man's "natural Right to enjoy the fruit of his own Labour" and to a decline in public virtue. To John Adams, an increased focus on comfort indicated a lifestyle devoted to "[l]uxury" and "[d]ebauchery." To British political economists, however, comfort became "a measure of the progress of civilization."[17]

Gradually, classical and Christian concerns about material comfort leading to luxury were transformed into humanitarian and social justice concerns for providing material comfort for the underprivileged. Crowley argues that Thomas Jefferson's "design and furnishing of Monticello epitomized the new obsession with comfort." Jefferson "criticized most Virginians' housing as '*uncomfortable*,'" and, at Monticello, he "sought to improve the heating, ventilation, illumination, privacy, and hygiene of conventional architecture." Jefferson embodied the idea of comfort as progress; he "used *comfort* in a new way, to anticipate a new world."[18]

According to Crowley, Adam Smith believed that comfort, otherwise known as "'the necessities and conveniences' of life," was related "to the material benefits of people's labor." Benjamin Franklin believed the necessities and conveniences highlighted by Smith led to man's happiness. In a letter to Lord Kames, Franklin stated his belief that "happiness consists more in small conveniences or pleasures that occur every day, than in great pieces of good fortune that happen but seldom to a man in the course of his life." Crowley states that it is for this reason that Jefferson continually renovated Monticello; he wished to make his life more comfortable and, therefore, to make himself more happy. As Crowley states: "Jefferson never elaborated on what he meant by 'the pursuit of happiness' . . . but given his lifelong obsession with the improvement of convenience and comfort, it seems reasonable to infer that he believed their successful pursuit would result in happiness."[19]

Crowley's work highlights the eighteenth century's philosophical and practical focus on progress and improvement. He may be right that Jefferson, like Franklin, believed increased material comfort would make him happier. And both men may have held this belief in a culture that, as Crowley suggests, increasingly regarded the acquisition of a certain level of "necessities and conveniences of life" to be a right. Thus, just as Locke would have men labor the land to acquire landed property, Smith would have men labor to acquire the "material benefits" of comfort—"'the necessities and conveniences' of life."[20] In this sense, Crowley's argument on material comfort is a more specific formulation of Scott's argument that pursuit of happiness provides the opportunity to acquire property, although the two differ in the types of property to be acquired and for what purpose. With the founders' distinction between pursuing and obtaining property and their additional distinction between fleeting and temporal versus real and substantial happiness, it does not seem that this conception of happiness is what they intended to embody in the Declaration's unalienable right.

Pursuit of Happiness as
Pursuit of a Quietly Enjoyed Family Life

In her work *The Pursuit of Happiness: Family and Values in Jefferson's Virginia* (1983), Jan Lewis states, "The phrase [pursuit of happiness] is in some measure a substitution for Locke's 'property,' but most historians agree that Jefferson intended something more inclusive and dynamic both." Thus,

Lewis agrees with Scott in part, but argues that Jefferson was moving away from the idea of happiness as found in propertied self-interest and toward "a more hopeful notion of social felicity, a secular substitution for the eternal reward." Lewis argues that pursuit of happiness refers to the pursuit of the social felicity to be found in family life.[21]

Lewis begins her discussion with a letter written by Jefferson's grandson Thomas Jefferson Randolph to his wife. After Jefferson's death, Randolph labored to save Monticello from Jefferson's creditors. In this tough time, he wrote to his wife, stating, "With you only I have known happiness." According to Lewis, Randolph equated happiness with family life: "Happiness for him was domestic and emotional; his pursuit took him home."[22]

Lewis sees Randolph's letter as indicative of the fact that, "[d]uring Thomas Jefferson's long life, Virginians came to define happiness in a new way, to pursue it in new arenas. . . . [T]he family became the focus of men's and women's deepest longings." Although Lewis begins her discussion in the eighteenth century, she places this shift in focus firmly within the nineteenth century, stating that "no eighteenth-century person would have so inflated the importance of family." Describing this change from eighteenth- to nineteenth-century views of family is the purpose of her book. While Lewis provides an important history of changes in how Americans viewed family life, her periodization of that change means that this definition of happiness could not apply to what pursuit of happiness meant at the time of the founding. Even if the meaning could apply then, Lewis is not certain that it does. She argues, instead, that Jefferson intended to "gloss over differences of aspiration [in the Revolutionary Era] with the lovely phrase 'pursuit of happiness'" and that "[n]o one knows precisely what Jefferson had in mind" by including the phrase as one of the Declaration's unalienable rights.[23]

In a later essay on "Happiness" in *The Blackwell Encyclopedia of the American Revolution* (1991), Lewis explores happiness more in depth. Having encountered Lewis's entry on happiness late in my research, I was interested to see that she, too, had hypothesized that the lack of debate surrounding the inclusion of "happiness" in the Declaration of Independence meant either "that the meaning of the concept was either so clear and commonly understood that no comment was required, or that its connotation was so vague and ambiguous that each could attach to it his own definition." In this piece, Lewis explores several possible influences on Jefferson, concluding that Jefferson merged an individualist notion of happiness as property with a "public or social happiness" along the lines of James Wilson, Jean Jacques Burlamaqui, and Francis Hutcheson. Lewis explores eighteenth-century understandings of happiness beyond mere property ownership, but ultimately seems to define happiness in Lockean property terms—a "human happiness [that] proceeds from the individual's enjoyment, improvement, and use of his possessions." She concludes that it was this more individualistic, property-oriented understanding of happiness that was in play by the time of the American Revolution.[24]

Pursuit of Happiness as a Scottish Enlightenment Notion of Public Virtue

When Lewis began considering the idea of pursuit of happiness in terms of social felicity, she was following the prior work of Garry Wills.[25] In his work *Inventing America: Jefferson's Declaration of Independence* (1978), Wills states, "When Jefferson spoke of pursuing happiness, he had nothing vague or private in mind. He meant a public happiness which is measurable."[26]

According to Wills, Jefferson "wanted to measure everything with Newton's pendulum" and believed that "all things work by the Laws of Nature and Nature's God." Indeed, Wills argues that, from the start, the Declaration "is Newtonian" and that it was intended to be so by Jefferson: "[H]e was never vague or 'idealistic' in his treatment of natural laws. Those laws state, for him, how things happen and why they could not happen any other way."[27]

Happiness works well within this Newtonian framework. In the eighteenth century, happiness was "inextricably linked with the effort to create a science of man based on numerical gauges for all his activity." According to Wills, pursuit of happiness "supplies us with the ground of human right and the goal of human virtue. It is the basic drive of the self, and the only means given for transcending the self." As Scottish Enlightenment thinker Francis Hutcheson stated, "The several rights of mankind are therefore first made known by the natural feelings of their hearts, and their natural desires pursuing such things as tend to the good of each individual or those dependent on him; and recommending to all certain virtuous offices." Wills argues that, like Hutcheson, Jefferson viewed rights in terms of duties; thus, the right to life was also "the duty to stay alive." Furthermore, Jefferson's ideals mirrored those of Adam Smith, who believed that "by acting according to the dictates of our moral faculties, we necessarily pursue the most effectual means for promoting the happiness of mankind."[28]

With these passages from Hutcheson and Smith, Wills does much to enhance our understanding of the pursuit of happiness as a public duty. Wills brought the Scottish Enlightenment's emphasis on Newtonian science to the forefront of founding-era political philosophy. He illustrates just how strongly Jefferson was influenced by Newtonian science. Furthermore, Wills demonstrates that the Scottish Enlightenment concept of public virtue was both present and influential at the time of the founding. His work here is insightful and engaging.

As Wills explains in his work, the idea of public virtue or public happiness suggests something of a communal duty. Specifically, public virtue at the time of the founding related to a duty toward virtue in the civic realm, with the understanding that public virtue provided the foundation for good government and, therefore, a foundation for the happiness of the governed. Wills argues that, by including the phrase "the pursuit of Happiness," in the Declaration, Jefferson "meant a public happiness which is measurable."[29] While Wills aptly highlights both public virtue and a measurable public happiness, the Declaration lists "the pursuit of Happiness" as an unalienable right (not a duty) endowed to man (as an individual, not communally) by his Creator.

As Wills explains, men like Hutcheson believed rights implied duties. Wills is right to emphasize "the law of man's nature as his right."[30] He does much to demonstrate that the founders' concept of virtue is key to understanding what they meant by "the pursuit of Happiness." In fact, of all of the previous histories, Wills comes closest to identifying what the founders meant by the phrase. But his discussion is incomplete in that it does not fully explore the individual, unalienable-right implications of the phrase.

A review of the historiography reveals that scholars have carefully and thoughtfully debated the meaning of the pursuit of happiness for years, with each work making a contribution to our understanding of founding-era thought. Yet each of the previous accounts had a tendency to define the pursuit of happiness too narrowly, missing a piece of its larger context and meaning. Apart from Wills, the historiography has tended to follow two trends: the idea that the work in the phrase "the pursuit of Happiness" is done by "Happiness," not "pursuit," and the idea that to pursue happiness means to pursue one thing (such as property ownership) and, therefore, does not mean the pursuit of another (such as family life).

In their definitions of pursuit of happiness, Scott, Crowley, and Lewis follow these trends: by focusing on the end result of happiness, they emphasize a specific thing people might pursue (property, material comfort, a family life) in order to make themselves happy. The Declaration, however, has a different focus. The Declaration's right to *pursue* happiness is very different from the right to *obtain* happiness, a distinction that preceded the drafting of the Declaration, going back to thinkers like Aristotle. In other words, happiness as an end was a different thing altogether from the pursuit of that end. As stated previously, George Mason included a list of inherent rights in his 1776 Virginia Declaration of Rights: "the enjoyment of life and liberty, with the means of acquiring and possessing property, and pursuing and obtaining happiness and safety."[31] Jefferson not only omitted "acquiring and possessing property" (as discussed above), but also omitted the "obtaining" portion of the inherent right to pursue happiness. Thus, while Jefferson believed man had an unalienable right to pursue happiness, he did not believe he had an unalienable right to obtain it. Scott comes closest to this view, in his argument that with the phrase "pursuit of Happiness," the founders intended the government to protect man's right to an opportunity to own property and not man's right to actually own property. Crowley and Lewis are more removed, as they seem to focus not on the *pursuit* of happiness but on the *acquisition* of that which will bring about happiness and the idea that one can acquire certain things (material comfort, a family life, property) that will then make one happy. The distinction is small, but it is important.

The previous historiography also reflects a tendency of founding-era scholarship to focus on a single strand of late-eighteenth-century thought. As a result, previous histories have done much to broaden our understanding of individual thinkers such as John Locke, Francis Hutchison, Adam Smith, and Isaac Newton, but with the result of narrowing the meaning of "the pursuit of Happiness" to definitions that are—to varying degress—at odds with the context and content of the Declaration. Wills does the most to step outside of this trend. In her later piece, Lewis does so as well.

As used in the Declaration of Independence, "the pursuit of Happiness" evoked man's unalienable right to choose to live in harmony with the laws of nature and of nature's God as they pertained to man. It was a phrase that met with continued and consistent approval as the Declaration was drafted, even as so many other words and phrases were omitted and altered. The "pursuit of happiness" remained, unaltered (but for the later capitalization of "happiness"), not because it was so general as to have no meaning but because its meaning was found in the synthesis of thought articulated by Blackstone in his *Commentaries*—the same synthesis of thought that was to be found at the place where four key strands of founding-era thought converged. It was this meaning of the phrase that the founders intended to evoke when they affirmed the pursuit of happiness as an unalienable right.

Blackstone's *Commentaries*, Introduction, Section the Second,
Of the Nature of Laws in General, pp. 38–44

Author's Note

The first London edition of Blackstone's *Commentaries* was published by
Oxford's Clarendon Press from 1765 to 1769. Between 1765 and Blackstone's death in 1780, the *Commentaries* were edited and republished eight
times, with a ninth London edition, published posthumously, containing
additional edits believed to have been made by Blackstone in his lifetime.[1]

The first American edition was published by Robert Bell in Philadelphia
from 1771 to 1772.[2] Library records suggest that both John Adams and
Thomas Jefferson owned copies of the Bell edition.[3] It is not clear which
London edition of the *Commentaries* Bell reprinted in his first edition.[4] The
first Bell edition contains at least one substantive alteration that has been
identified as occurring in the second London edition, as indicated in note
14. The first Bell edition also misspells "vegitable" for "vegetable" on page
38, changes "it's due" to "his due" on page 40, and makes a variety of small
punctuation changes—a common one being the replacement of semicolons
with colons—throughout this portion of Blackstone's text.[5]

For the purposes of this work, the most interesting changes are those that
occur with Blackstone's discussion of the pursuit of happiness. In the first
London edition, Blackstone describes "this one paternal precept" as "that
man should "pursue his own happiness."[6] According to W. G. Hammond,
that wording and punctuation remained unchanged in the first seven London editions of the *Commentaries*.[7] If Hammond is correct, then it was this
language that the founders would have read, either in one of these early London editions or in an American reprint, prior to drafting the Declaration.

For the eighth edition, published in 1778, Blackstone changed this language from the awkwardly punctuated "that man should "pursue his own
happiness" to "that man should pursue his own true and substantial happiness."[8] The addition of "true" and "substantial" appear to be for purposes of clarification only. Both words align with Blackstone's description of

happiness as "real" and "substantial" in this section of the *Commentaries*.[9] That descriptive language had been present from the first edition of the *Commentaries* forward.[10]

Notes that were included by Blackstone in the first edition of his *Commentaries* have been marked with symbols and included as footnotes in this Appendix to show where they were originally included in the text.

Notes that highlight editorial changes that W. G. Hammond identified across the first nine editions of the *Commentaries* have been marked numerically and included in the endnotes to this Appendix.

Page numbers have been inserted in brackets to show the original page breaks from the first edition of the *Commentaries*.

William Blackstone, *Commentaries on the Laws of England*, volume 1, introduction, pages 38–44 (ending just before "Municipal law, thus understood . . ." on page 44)

[38] *Section the Second, Of the Nature of Laws in General*

Law, in it's most general and comprehensive sense, signifies a rule of action; and is applied indiscriminately to all kinds of action, whether animate, or inanimate, rational or irrational. Thus we say, the laws of motion, of gravitation, of optics, or mechanics, as well as the laws of nature and of nations. And it is that rule of action, which is prescribed by some superior, and which the inferior is bound to obey.

Thus when the supreme being formed the universe, and created matter out of nothing, he impressed certain principles upon that matter, from which it can never depart, and without which it would cease to be. When he put that matter into motion, he established certain laws of motion, to which all moveable bodies must conform. And, to descend from the greatest operations to the smallest, when a workman forms a clock, or other piece of mechanism, he establishes at his own pleasure certain arbitrary laws for it's direction; as that the hand shall describe a given space in a given time; to which law as long as the work conforms, so long it continues in perfection, and answers the end of it's formation.

If we farther advance, from mere inactive matter to vegetable and animal life, we shall find them still governed by laws; more numerous indeed, but equally fixed and invariable. The whole progress of plants, from the seed to the root, and from thence to the seed again; —— the method of animal nutrition, digestion, [39] secretion, and all other branches of vital oeconomy; —— are not left to chance, or the will of the creature itself, but are performed in a wondrous involuntary manner, and guided by unerring rules laid down by the great creator.

This then is the general signification of law, a rule of action dictated by some superior being; and in those creatures that have neither the power to think, nor to will, such laws must be invariably obeyed, so long as the creature itself subsists, for it's existence depends on that obedience. But laws, in their more confined sense, and in which it is our present business to consider them, denote the rules, not of action in general, but of *human* action or conduct: that is the precepts by which man, the noblest of all sublunary beings, a creature endowed with both reason and freewill, is commanded to make use of those faculties in the general regulation of his behaviour.

Man, considered as a creature, must necessarily be subject to the laws of his creator, for he is entirely a dependent being. A being, independent of any other, has no rule to pursue, but such as he prescribes to himself; but a state of dependence will inevitably oblige the inferior to take the will of him, on whom he depends, as the rule of his conduct: not indeed in every particular, but in all those points wherein his dependance consists. This principle therefore has more or less extent and effect, in proportion as the superiority of the one and the dependence of the other is greater or less, absolute or limited. And consequently as man depends absolutely upon his maker for every thing, it is necessary that he should in all points conform to his maker's will.

This will of his maker is called the law of nature. For as God, when he created matter, and endued it with a principle of mobility, established certain rules for the perpetual direction of that motion; so, when he created man, and endued him with freewill to conduct himself in all parts of life, he laid down cer-[40]tain immutable laws of human nature, whereby that freewill is in some degree regulated and restrained, and gave him also the faculty of reason to discover the purport of those laws.

Considering the creator only as a being of infinite *power*, he was able unquestionably to have prescribed whatever laws he pleased to his creature, man, however unjust or severe. But as he is also a being of infinite *wisdom*, he has laid down only such laws as were founded in those relations of justice, that existed in the nature of things antecedent to any positive precept.

These are the eternal, immutable laws of good and evil, to which the creator himself in all his dispensations conforms; and which he has enabled human reason to discover, so far as they are necessary for the conduct of human actions. Such among others are these principles: that we should live honestly, should hurt nobody, and should render to every one it's due; to which three general precepts Justinian* has reduced the whole doctrine of law.

But if the discovery of these first principles of the law of nature depended only upon the due exertion of right reason, and could not otherwise be attained[11] than by a chain of metaphysical disquisitions, mankind would have wanted some inducement to have quickened their inquiries, and the greater part of the world would have rested content in mental indolence, and ignorance it's inseparable companion. As, therefore, the creator is a being not only of infinite *power*, and *wisdom*, but also of infinite *goodness*, he has been pleased so to contrive the constitution and frame of humanity, that we should want no other prompter to enquire after and pursue the rule of right, but only our own self-love, that universal principle of action. For he has so intimately connected, so inseparably interwoven the laws of eternal justice with the happiness of each individual, that the latter cannot be attained but by observing the former; and, if the former be punctually obeyed, it cannot but induce the latter. In consequence of which mutual connection of justice and human felicity, he has not per-[41]plexed the law of nature with a multitude of abstracted rules and precepts, referring merely to the fitness or unfitness of things, as some have vainly surmised; but has graciously reduced the rule of obedience to this one paternal precept, "that man should "pursue his own happiness."[12] This is the foundation of what we call ethics, or natural law. For the several articles into which it is branched in our systems, amount to no more than demonstrating, that this or that action tends to man's real happiness, and therefore very justly concluding that the performance of it is a part of the law of nature; or, on the other hand, that this or that action is destructive of man's real happiness, and therefore that the law of nature forbids it.

This law of nature, being co-eval with mankind and dictated by God himself, is of course superior in obligation to any other. It is binding over all the globe, in all countries, and at all times: no human laws are of any validity, if contrary to this; and such of them as are valid derive all their force, and all their authority, mediately or immediately, from this original.

---

* *Juris praecepta sunt haec, honeste vivere, alterum non laedere, suum cuique tribuere. Inst.* 1.1.3.

But in order to apply this to the particular exigencies of each individual, it is still necessary to have recourse to reason; whose office it is to discover, as was before observed, what the law of nature directs in every circumstance of life; by considering, what method will tend the most effectually to our own substantial happiness. And if our reason were always, as in our first ancestor before his transgression, clear and perfect, unruffled by passions, unclouded by prejudice, unimpaired by disease or intemperance, the task would be pleasant and easy; we should need no other guide but this. But every man now finds the contrary in his own experience; that his reason is corrupt, and his understanding full of ignorance and error.

This has given manifold occasion for the benign interposition of divine providence; which, in compassion to the frailty, the imperfection, and the blindness of human reason, hath been [42] pleased, at sundry times and in divers manners, to discover and enforce it's laws by an immediate and direct revelation. The doctrines thus delivered we call the revealed or divine law, and they are to be found in the holy scriptures. These precepts, when revealed, are found upon comparison to be really a part of the original law of nature, as they tend in all their consequences to man's felicity. But we are not from thence to conclude that the knowledge of these truths was attainable by reason, in it's present corrupted state; since we find that, until they were revealed, they were hid from the wisdom of the ages. As then the moral precepts of this law are indeed of the same original with those of the law of nature, so their intrinsic obligation is of equal strength and perpetuity. Yet undoubtedly the revealed law is (humanly speaking)[13] of infinitely more authority than what we generally call the natural law.[14] Because one is the law of nature, expressly declared so to be by God himself; the other is only what, by the assistance of human reason, we imagine to be that law. If we could be as certain of the latter as we are of the former, both would have an equal authority; but, till then, they can never be put in any competition together.

Upon these two foundations, the law of nature and the law of revelation, depend all human laws; that is to say, no human laws should be suffered to contradict these. There is, it is true, a great number of indifferent points, in which both the divine law and the natural leave a man at his own liberty; but which are found necessary for the benefit of society to be restrained within certain limits. And herein it is that human laws have their greatest force and efficacy; for, with regard to such points as are not indifferent, human laws are only declaratory of, and act in subordination to, the former. To instance in the case of murder: this is expressly forbidden by the divine, and demonstrably by the natural law; and from these prohibitions arises the true unlawfulness of this crime. Those human laws, that annex a punishment to it, do not at all increase it's moral guilt, or superadd any fresh obligation *in foro conscientiae* to abstain from [43] its perpetration. Nay, if any human law should allow or injoin us to commit it, we are bound to transgress that human law, or else we must offend both the natural and the divine. But with regard to matters that are in themselves indifferent, and are not commanded or forbidden by those superior laws; such, for instance, as exporting of wool into foreign countries; here the inferior legislature has scope and opportunity to interpose, and to make that action unlawful which before was not so.

If man were to live in a state of nature, unconnected with other individuals, there would be no occasion for any other laws, than the law of nature, and the law of God. Neither could any other law possibly exist; for a law always supposes some superior who is to make it; and in a state of nature we are all equal, without any other superior but him who is the author of our being. But man was formed for society; and, as is demonstrated by the writers on this subject,* is neither capable of living alone, nor indeed has the courage to do it. However, as it is impossible for the whole race of mankind to be united in one great society, they must necessarily divide into many; and form separate states, commonwealths, and nations; entirely independent of each other, and yet liable to a mutual intercourse. Hence arises a third kind of law to regulate this mutual intercourse, called "the law of "nations;" which, as none of these states will acknowledge a superiority in the other, cannot be dictated by either;[15] but depends entirely upon the rules of natural law, or upon mutual compacts, treaties, leagues, and agreements between these several communities: in the construction also of which compacts we have no other rule to resort to, but the law of nature; being the only one to which both† very justly observes, that *quod naturalis ratio inter omnes homines constituit, vocatur jus gentium.*

Thus much I thought it necessary to premise concerning the law of nature, the revealed law, and the law of nations, before [44] I proceeded to treat more fully of the principle subject of this section, municipal or civil law; that is, the rule by which particular districts, communities, or nations

---

   * Puffendorf, *l.7.c.1.*, compared with Barbeyrac's commentary.
   † *Ff.* 1.1.9.

are governed; being thus defined by Justinian,* "*jus civile est quod quisque sibi populus constituit.*" I call it *municipal* law, in compliance with common speech; for, tho' strictly that expression denotes the particular customs of one single *municipium* or free town, yet it may with sufficient propriety be applied to any one state or nation, which is governed by the same laws and customs.

---

* *Inst.* 1.2.1.

Jefferson's "original Rough draught" of the Declaration of Independence with Thomas Jefferson's, John Adams's, and Benjamin Franklin's Edits Included, as Reconstructed by Carl Becker

THE FOLLOWING VERSION of the Declaration of Independence is a reconstruction completed by Carl Becker in 1922. Becker states that this reconstruction represents the Declaration "as it probably read when Jefferson made the 'fair copy' which was presented to Congress as the report of the Committee of Five."[1] This reconstruction is helpful for viewing the changes that Jefferson, Adams, and Franklin made to Jefferson's original draft of the Declaration prior to its submission to the Continental Congress by the Committee of Five. Becker's reconstruction is reproduced in full here, with his explanatory notations included.

THE ROUGH DRAFT

as it probably read when Jefferson

made the 'fair copy' which was pre-

sented to Congress as the report of

the Committee of Five.

A DECLARATION BY THE REPRESENTATIVES OF THE

UNITED STATES OF AMERICA, IN GENERAL

CONGRESS ASSEMBLED.

When in the course of human events it becomes neces-
one   *dissolve the political bands which have con-*
sary for a‸people to‸advance from that subordination in
nected them with another, and to
which they have hitherto remained, & to assume among
                    separate and equal
the powers of the earth the‸equal & independent station

to which the laws of nature & of nature's god entitle them,

a decent respect to the opinions of mankind requires that
                              the sep-
they should declare the causes which impel them to the
aration

163

Drafting the Declaration   161

self-evident;

We hold these truths to be ~~sacred & undeniable~~; that

  they are endowed by their

all men are created equal ~~& independent~~; that ~~from that~~

creator with equal rights, some of which are   *rights; that*

~~equal creation they derive in rights~~ inherent & inalienable

              these

among ~~which~~ are ~~the preservation of~~ life, ~~&~~ liberty, &

                                            rights

the pursuit of happiness; that to secure these ~~ends,~~

governments are instituted among men, deriving their

just powers from the consent of the governed; that

whenever any form of government shall become*s* de-

structive of these ends, it is the right of the people to

alter or to abolish it, & to institute new government,

laying it's foundation on such principles & organizing

it's powers in such form, as to them shall seem most likely

to effect their safety & happiness.   prudence indeed will

dictate that governments long established should not be

changed for light & transient causes: and accordingly all

experience hath shewn that mankind are more disposed to

suffer while evils are sufferable, than to right themselves

by abolishing the forms to which they are accustomed.

but when a long train of abuses & usurpations, begun

at a distinguished period, & pursuing invariably the

same object, evinces a design to ~~subject~~ reduce them

* *under absolute Despotism*

~~to arbitrary power~~, it is their right, it is their duty, to

* Dr. Franklin's handwriting

162   *The Declaration of Independence*

throw off such government & to provide new guards

for their future security. such has been the patient

sufferance of these colonies; & such is now the necessity

which constrains them to expunge their former systems

of government. the history of ~~his~~ present ~~majesty~~ is a
<small>*the   king of Great Britain*</small>

history of unremitting injuries and usurpations, among
<small>*appears no solitary fact*</small>
which ~~no one fact stands single or solitary~~ to contradict

the uniform tenor of the rest, all ~~of which~~ have in
<small>*but all*</small>

direct object the establishment of an absolute tyranny

over these states. to prove this, let facts be submitted

to a candid world, for the truth of which we pledge

a faith yet unsullied by falsehood.

he has refused his assent to laws the most wholesome and

  necessary for the public good:

he has forbidden his governors to pass laws of immediate

  & pressing importance, unless suspended in their opera-

  tion till his assent should be obtained; and when so

  suspended, he has neglected utterly[1] to attend to them.

he has refused to pass other laws for the accomodation

  * Mr. Adams' handwriting

[1] The Rough Draft reads, "he has neglected ~~utterly~~." The copy
<small>*utterly*</small>
in the "Notes" reads "utterly neglected." My belief is that this was
one of the corrections made by Congress which Jefferson neglected to
indicate as he commonly did such corrections, by bracketing the
omitted word.

Drafting the Declaration 163

of large districts of people unless those people would
relinquish the right of representation ^{in the legislature}, a right inestimable to them & formidable to tyrants only:

he has called together legislative bodies at places unusual,
uncomfortable & distant from the depository of their
public records for the sole purpose of fatiguing them into
compliance with his measures:

he has dissolved, Representative houses repeatedly & continually, for opposing with manly firmness his invasions
on the rights of the people:

~~he has dissolved~~ he has refused for a long ~~space of time~~ ^{* time after such dissolutions}
to cause others to be elected, whereby the legislative
powers, incapable of annihilation, have returned to the
people at large for their exercise, the state remaining in
the meantime exposed to all the dangers of invasion
from without, & convulsions within:

he has endeavored to prevent the population of these
states; for that purpose obstructing the laws for naturalization of foreigners; refusing to pass others to encourage their migrations hither; & raising the conditions
of new appropriations of lands:

he has suffered the administration of justice totally to

* Mr. Adams

164   *The Declaration of Independence*

states
cease in some of these ~~colonies,~~ refusing his assent to
laws for establishing judiciary powers:

he has made our judges dependent on his will alone,
† *the*   *and payment*
for the tenure of their offices, and ⋏amount ⋏of their
salaries:

he has erected a multitude of new offices by a self-
assumed power, & sent hither swarms of officers to
harrass our people & eat out their substance:
–without our consent·
he has kept among us in times of peace ⋏standing armies &
the
without our consent. of our legislatures
ships of war :

he has effected to render the military, independent of &
superior to the civil power:

he has combined with others to subject us to a jurisdiction
foreign to our constitutions and unacknoleged by our
acts of
laws; giving his assent to their pretended ~~acts of~~ legislation,

for quartering large bodies of armed troops among
us;

for protecting them by a mock-trial from punish-
which
ment for any murders they should commit on
the inhabitants of these states;

† Dr. Franklin

Drafting the Declaration   165

for cutting off our trade with all parts of the world;

for imposing taxes on us without our consent;

for depriving us of the benefits of trial by jury;

for transporting us beyond seas to be tried for pretended offenses;

for abolishing the free system of English laws in a neighboring province, establishing therein an arbitrary government, and enlarging it's boundaries so as to render it at once an example & fit instrument for introducing the same absolute rule into these ~~colonies~~ states;

valuable
* abolishing our most ~~important~~ laws

for taking away our charters, & altering fundamentally the forms of our governments;

for suspending our own legislatures & declaring themselves invested with power to legislate for us in all cases whatsoever:

he has abdicated government here, withdrawing his governors, & declaring us out of his allegiance & protection:

he has plundered our seas, ravaged our coasts, burnt our towns & destroyed the lives of our people:

he is at this time transporting large armies of foreign mercenaries to compleat the works of death, desolation & tyranny, already begun with circumstances of cruelty

* Dr. Franklin

166   *The Declaration of Independence*

& perfidy unworthy the head of a civilized nation:

he has endeavored to bring on the inhabitants of our
   frontiers the merciless Indian savages, whose known
   rule of warfare is an undistinguished destruction of
   all ages, sexes, & conditions of existence:

he has incited [1] treasonable insurrections of our fellow-
   citizens, with the allurements of forfeiture & confisca-
   tion of our property:

he has constrained others[2] *~~fallin~~ ̭ ~~into his hands~~, on the*
taken captives

high seas to bear arms against their country ~~& to destroy~~

·~~& be destroyed by the brethren whom they love~~, to become

the executioners of their friends & brethren, or to fall

themselves by their hands.

he has waged cruel war against human nature itself,
   violating it's most sacred rights of life & liberty in the
   persons of a distant people who never offended him,
   captivating & carrying them into slavery in another

---

[1] The copy in the "Notes" reads "excited."

[2] The copy in the "Notes" reads "our fellow citizens" in place of
"others." This is the reading of the text as adopted by Congress;
but as the change does not appear on the Rough Draft, I have assumed
that this was a change made by Congress. The paragraph is written
in the Rough Draft as here shown, following the paragraph beginning,
"he has incited." Congress changed the order, placing the paragraph
beginning "he has constrained" immediately following the one beginning "he is at this time transporting." The copy in the "Notes" follows
the order adopted by Congress.

Drafting the Declaration   167

hemisphere, or to incur miserable death in their transportation thither. this piratical warfare, the opprobrium of *infidel* powers, is the warfare of the *Christian* king of Great Britain. *determined to keep open a market where MEN should be bought & sold,* he has prostituted his negative for suppressing every legislative attempt to prohibit or to restrain this execrable ~~determining to keep open a market where MEN should be bought & sold~~ commerce and that this assemblage of horrors might want no fact of distinguished die, he is now exciting those very people to rise in arms among us, and to purchase that liberty of which *he* has deprived them, by murdering the people upon whom *he* also obtruded them; thus paying off former crimes committed against the *liberties* of one people, with crimes which he urges them to commit against the *lives* of another.
in every stage of these oppressions we have petitioned for redress in the most humble terms; our repeated petitions have been answered *only* by repeated injury.[1] a prince whose character is thus marked by every act which may define a tyrant, is unfit to be the ruler of a people who mean to be free. future ages will scarce believe that the hardiness

* Dr. Franklin
[1] The Rough Draft reads "injuries." See above, p. 148, note 1.

168   *The Declaration of Independence*

of one man, adventured within the short compass of

to ~~lay~~ *a foundation¹ so broad & undisguised for tyranny*   [over "to lay": *build*]

twelve years only, ~~on so many acts of tyranny without~~

~~a mask,~~ over a people fostered & fixed in principles of

~~liberty.~~ *freedom.*

Nor have we been wanting in attentions to our British

brethren. we have warned them from time to time of

attempts by their legislature to extend a jurisdiction over

these our states. we have reminded them of the cir-

cumstances of our emigration & settlement here, no one

of which could warrant so strange a pretension: that

these were effected at the expence of our own blood &

treasure, unassisted by the wealth or the strength of

Great Britain: that in constituting indeed our several

forms of government, we had adopted one common king,

thereby laying a foundation for perpetual league & amity

with them: but that submission to their parliament was

no part of our constitution, nor ever in idea if history may

be credited: and we appealed to their native justice &

magnanimity as well as to the ties of our common kindred

to disavow these usurpations which were likely to interrupt

connection &

our correspondence ~~& connection.~~ they too have been

¹ The copy in the "Notes" reads "to lay a foundation."

Drafting the Declaration   169

deaf to the voice of justice & of consanguinity, & when occasions have been given them, by the regular course of their laws, of removing from their councils the disturbers of our harmony, they have by their free election re-established them in power. at this very time too they are permitting their chief magistrate to send over not only soldiers of our common blood, but Scotch & foreign

* destroy us

mercenaries to invade & deluge us in blood. these facts have given the last stab to agonizing affection, and manly spirit bids us to renounce forever these unfeeling brethren. we must endeavor to forget our former love for them, and to hold them as we hold the rest of mankind, enemies in war, in peace friends. we might have been a free & a great people together; but a communication of grandeur & of freedom it seems is below their dignity. be it so,

& to glory

since they will have it: the road to glory & happiness

apart from them

is open to us too; we will climb it in a separately state,

---

* Dr. Franklin

' The Rough Draft reads,
  -must- tread apart from them
  "we will climb it ⋀ in a separately state."

The text as adopted by Congress reads "we will climb it apart from them." The copy in the "Notes" is the only one which gives the reading "we will tread it apart from them." If the change from "climb" to "tread" was made before the Committee of Five submitted its

170 *The Declaration of Independence*

and acquiesce in the necessity which ~~pronounces~~ ^{de} our

everlasting adieu! eternal separation!

We therefore the representatives of the United States of America in General Congress assembled do, in the name & by authority of the good people of these states, reject and renounce all allegiance & subjection to the kings of Great Britain & all others who may hereafter claim by, through, or under them; we utterly dissolve & ~~break off~~ all political connection which may ~~have~~ ^{have} heretofore subsisted between us & the people or parliament of Great Britain; and finally we do assert and declare[1] these colonies to be free and independent states, and that as free & independent states they ~~shall hereafter~~ have ^{full}

report, we must suppose that Jefferson made an error in the Lee copy and that Congress changed the "tread" back to "climb." This seems improbable. See below, pp. 199–201.

[1] Here I have followed the Rough Draft instead of the Lee copy. The Lee copy reads, "parliament or people . . . we do assert these colonies." There is no indication on the Rough Draft that 'people or parliament' was at any time changed to 'parliament or people,' nor is there any indication that 'and declare' was at any time omitted. Furthermore, the text adopted by Congress reads "publish and declare," which seems to indicate that the words 'and declare' were in the report of the Committee of Five. I assume therefore that the different reading of the Lee copy is the result of an error in copying. The copy which Jefferson incorporated in his "Notes" follows the reading of the Rough Draft; on the other hand, two other copies made by Jefferson, probably at the same time he made the Lee copy, follow the reading of the Lee copy. Cf. Hazelton, *op. cit.*, 177, 340.

Drafting the Declaration 171

power to levy war, conclude peace, contract alliances, establish commerce, & to do all other acts and things which independent states may of right do. And for the support of this declaration we mutually pledge to each other our lives, our fortunes, & our sacred honour.

The Declaration of Independence with Edits by the
Continental Congress Marked, as Reconstructed by Carl Becker

The following version of the Declaration of Independence is Becker's reconstruction of the Declaration of Independence as it was sent to Congress
by the Committee of Five, with Congress's edits marked.[1] This version is
helpful for seeing the changes that were made specifically by Congress.
Becker's reconstruction is reproduced here in full, along with his explanatory notations.

THE DECLARATION OF INDEPENDENCE

*(as it reads in the Lee copy, which is probably
the same as the report of the Committee of Five,
with parts omitted by Congress crossed out and
the parts added interlined in italics.)*

A DECLARATION BY THE REPRESENTATIVES OF THE
UNITED STATES OF AMERICA IN GENERAL
CONGRESS ASSEMBLED.

When in the course of human events it becomes necessary for one people to dissolve the political bands which
have connected them with another, and to assume among

Drafting the Declaration   175

the powers of the earth the separate and equal station
to which the laws of nature and of nature's god entitle
them, a decent respect to the opinions of mankind requires that they should declare the causes which impel
them to the separation.

We hold these truths to be self-evident; that all men
are created equal; that they are endowed by their
Creator with ~~inherent and~~ *certain un*inalienable[1] rights; that
among these are life, liberty, and the pursuit of happiness;
that to secure these rights, governments are instituted
among men, deriving their just powers from the consent
of the governed; that whenever any form of government
becomes destructive of these ends, it is the right of the
people to alter or to abolish it, and to institute new government, laying it's foundation on such principles, and organizing it's powers in such form as to them shall seem most
likely to effect their safety and happiness.   prudence

[1] The Rough Draft reads "[inherent &] *certain*inalienable." There is
no indication that Congress changed "inalienable" to "unalienable";
but the latter form appears in the text in the rough Journal, in the
corrected Journal, and in the parchment copy. John Adams, in making
his copy of the Rough Draft, wrote "unalienable." See above, p. 142,
note 2. Adams was one of the committee which supervised the printing
of the text adopted by Congress, and it may have been at his suggestion
that the change was made in printing. "Unalienable" may have been
the more customary form in the eighteenth century.

176   *The Declaration of Independence*

indeed will dictate that governments long established should not be changed for light & transient causes. and accordingly all experience hath shewn that mankind are more disposed to suffer, while evils are sufferable, than to right themselves by abolishing the forms to which they are accustomed. but when a long train of abuses and usurpations, ~~begun at a distinguished period &~~ pursuing invariably the same object, evinces a design to reduce them under absolute despotism, it is their right, it is their duty, to throw off such government, & to provide new guards for their future security. such has been the patient sufferance of these colonies, & such is now the necessity
                                 alter
which constrains them to ~~expunge~~ their former systems of government. the history of the present king of Great
                                      repeated
Britain is a history of ~~unremitting~~ injuries and usurpations, ~~among which appears no solitary fact to contradict the uniform tenor of the rest, but~~ all ~~have~~
                                      having
direct object the establishment of an absolute tyranny over these states. to prove this let facts be submitted to a candid world, ~~for the truth of which we pledge a faith yet unsullied by falsehood.~~

He has refused his assent to laws the most wholesome and
   necessary for the public good.

Drafting the Declaration   **177**

he has forbidden his governors to pass laws of immediate
& pressing importance, unless suspended in their operation till his assent should be obtained; and when so
suspended, he has *utterly* neglected ~~utterly~~ to attend to them.

he has refused to pass other laws for the accomodation of
large districts of people, unless those people would
relinquish the right of representation in the legislature;
a right inestimable to them, & formidable to tyrants
only.

he has called together legislative bodies at places unusual,
uncomfortable, & distant from the depository of their
public records, for the sole purpose of fatiguing them
into compliance with his measures.

he has dissolved Representative houses repeatedly & ~~con-~~
~~tinually~~, for opposing with manly firmness his invasions
on the rights of the people.

he has refused for a long time after such dissolutions to
cause others to be elected whereby the legislative
powers, incapable of annihilation, have returned to
the people at large for their exercise, the state remaining in the meantime exposed to all the dangers of invasion from without, & convulsions within.

he has endeavored to prevent the population of these

178 *The Declaration of Independence*

states; for that purpose obstructing the laws for naturalization of foreigners; refusing to pass others to
encourage their migrations hither; & raising the
conditions of new appropriations of lands.

       obstructed
he has ~~suffered~~ the administration of justice ~~totally to~~
                         by
~~cease in some of these states,~~ refusing his assent to
laws for establishing judiciary powers.

he has made ~~our~~ judges dependent on his will alone, for
the tenure of their offices, and the amount & paiment
of their salaries.

he has erected a multitude of new offices ~~by a self assumed~~
~~power,~~ & sent hither swarms of officers to harrass our
people, and eat out their substance.

he has kept among us, in times of peace, standing armies
~~and ships of war,~~ without the consent of our legislatures.

he has affected to render the military independent of, &
superior to, the civil power.

he has combined with others to subject us to a jurisdiction
foreign to our ~~constitutions~~ and unacknoleged by
our laws; giving his assent to their acts of pretended
legislation for quartering large bodies of armed troops[1]
among us;

   [1] The text in the corrected Journal reads "bodies of troops."

Drafting the Declaration   179

for protecting them by a mock-trial from punishment
for any murders which they should commit on the
inhabitants of these states;

for cutting off our trade with all parts of the world;

for imposing taxes on us without our consent;

for depriving us *in many cases* of the benefits of trial by jury;

for transporting us beyond seas to be tried for pretended offenses;

for abolishing the free system of English laws in a
neighboring province, establishing therein an arbitrary government, and enlarging it's boundaries so
as to render it at once an example & fit instrument
for introducing the same absolute rule into these
states;

for taking away our charters, abolishing our most
valuable laws, and altering fundamentally the forms
of our governments;

for suspending our own legislatures, & declaring themselves invested with power to legislate for us in all
cases whatsoever.

he has abdicated government here, ~~withdrawing his~~
by
~~governors~~, &∧declaring us out of ~~his allegiance and~~
and waging war against us
protection .

180   *The Declaration of Independence*

he has plundered our seas, ravaged our coasts, burnt our

towns, & destroyed the lives of our people.

he is at this time transporting large armies of foreign

mercenaries, to compleat the works of death, desola-

tion & tyranny, already begun with circumstances of
scarcely paralleled in the most barbarous ages and totally
cruelty & perfidy unworthy the head of a civilized

nation.
excited domestic insurrection amongst us and has
he has endeavored to bring on the inhabitants of our

frontiers the merciless Indian savages, whose known

rule of warfare is an undistinguished destruction of

all ages, sexes, & conditions of existence.

he has incited treasonable insurrections of our fellow

-citizens, with the allurements of forfeiture & con-

fiscation of property.
our fellow citizens
he has constrained others, taken captives on the high

seas to bear arms against their country, to become the

executioners of their friends & brethren, or to fall

themselves by their hands.

he has waged cruel war against human nature itself,

violating it's most sacred rights of life & liberty in the

persons of a distant people, who never offended him,

captivating and carrying them into slavery in another

hemisphere, or to incur miserable death in their trans-

~~portation thither.—this piratical warfare, the opprobrium of *infidel* powers, is the warfare of the *Christian*
king of Great Britain.—determined to keep open a
market where~~ MEN ~~should be bought & sold, he has
prostituted his negative for suppressing every legislative attempt to prohibit or to restrain this execrable
commerce:—and that this assemblage of horrors might
want no fact of distinguished die, he is now exciting
those very people to rise in arms among us, and to
purchase that liberty of which *he* has deprived them,
by murdering the people upon whom *he* also obtruded
them:—thus—paying—off former crimes committed
against—the *liberties*—of—one—people,—with—crimes
which he urges them to commit against the *lives* of
another.~~

In every stage of these oppressions, we have petitioned for
redress in the most humble terms; our repeated petitions
have been answered only by repeated injury. a prince
whose character is thus marked by every act which may
define a tyrant, is unfit to be the ruler of a *free* people ~~who
mean to be free.~~—future ages will scarce believe that the
hardiness of one man adventured within the short compass
of twelve years only to build a foundation, so broad and

182   *The Declaration of Independence*

~~undisguised, for tyranny over~~ a people ~~fostered and fixed~~

~~in principles of freedom.~~

Nor have we been wanting in attentions to our British

brethren. we have warned them from time to time of
                                              an unwarrantable
attempts by their legislature to extend ~~a~~ jurisdiction
        us.
over these ~~our states.~~ we have reminded them of the

circumstances of our emigration and settlement here, ~~no~~

~~one of which could warrant so strange a pretension:~~

~~that these were effected at the expence of our own blood~~

~~and treasure, unassisted by the wealth or the strength~~

~~of Great Britain: that in constituting indeed our several~~

~~forms of government, we had adopted one common king,~~

~~thereby laying a foundation for perpetual league and amity~~

~~with them: but that submission to their parliament was~~

~~no part of our constitution, nor ever in idea, if history~~
                           have
~~may be credited:~~ and we appealed to their native justice
                              and we have conjured them by
& magnanimity, ~~as well as to~~ the tyes of our common

kindred, to disavow these usurpations, which ~~were likely~~
        would inevitably   *s*
~~to~~ interrupt our connection & correspondence. they too

have been deaf to the voice of justice and of consan-

guinity[1]; ~~and when occasions have been given them,~~

~~by the regular course of their laws, of removing from their~~

[1] The text in the corrected Journal reads "and consanguinity."

Drafting the Declaration   183

~~councils the disturbers of our harmony, they have by~~
~~their free election re-established them in power. at this~~
~~very time too, they are permitting their chief magistrate~~
to send ~~over not only soldiers of our common blood, but~~
~~Scotch and foreign mercenaries to invade and destroy~~
~~us. these facts have given the last stab to agonizing~~
~~affection; and manly spirit bids us to renounce forever~~
therefore
~~these unfeeling brethren.~~ we must endeavor ~~to forget our~~
~~former love for them, and to hold them~~ as we hold the
~~rest of mankind, enemies in war, in peace friends. we~~
~~might have been a free & a great people together; but~~
~~a communication of grandeur and of freedom, it seems, is~~
~~below their dignity. be it so, since they will have it.~~
~~the road to happiness and to glory is open to us too;~~
~~we will climb it apart from them, and~~ acquiesce in the
and hold them, as we hold the rest
necessity which denounces our ~~eternal~~ separation !
of mankind, enemies in war, in peace friends.
We therefore the Representatives of the United states
appealing to the supreme judge of the world for the rectitude of our intentions
of America in General Congress assembled, ∧do, in the
colonies, solemnly
name & by authority of the good people of these∧states,
publish and declare, that these united colonies are and of right ought
~~reject and renounce all allegiance and subjection to the~~
to be free and independent states; that they are absolved from all allegi-
~~kings of Great Britain, & all others who may hereafter~~
ance to the British Crown, and that
~~claim by, through, or under them; we utterly dissolve~~

184   *The Declaration of Independence*

all political connection ~~which~~ ~~may~~ ~~heretofore~~ ~~have~~ sub-
        them   *state*
sisted between ~~us~~∧and the∧people ~~or~~ ~~parliament~~ of Great
is & ought to be totally dissolved;
Britain ; ~~and~~ ~~finally~~ ~~we~~ ~~do~~ ~~assert~~ ~~and~~ ~~declare¹~~ ~~these~~

~~colonies~~ ~~to~~ ~~be~~ ~~free~~ ~~and~~ ~~independent~~ ~~states,~~ & that as

free & independent states, they have full power to levy

war, conclude peace, contract alliances, establish com-

merce, & to do all other acts and things which independent

states may of right do.   And for the support of this dec-
with a firm reliance on the protection of divine providence,
laration, we mutually pledge to each other our lives,

our fortunes, and our sacred honor.

¹ The reading here is not precisely that of the Lee copy. See p. 170,
note 1.

The Declaration of Independence,
A Transcript from the National Archives

Author's Note

The text that is included on the following pages follows the National Archives' transcription of the Declaration of Independence, which is available at https://www.archives.gov/founding-docs/declaration-transcript.

In Congress, July 4, 1776.
The unanimous Declaration of the thirteen united States of America,
When in the Course of human events, it becomes necessary for one people to dissolve the political bands which have connected them with another, and to assume among the powers of the earth, the separate and equal station to which the Laws of Nature and of Nature's God entitle them, a decent respect to the opinions of mankind requires that they should declare the causes which impel them to the separation.

We hold these truths to be self-evident, that all men are created equal, that they are endowed by their Creator with certain unalienable Rights, that among these are Life, Liberty and the pursuit of Happiness.--That to secure these rights, Governments are instituted among Men, deriving their just powers from the consent of the governed, --That whenever any Form of Government becomes destructive of these ends, it is the Right of the People to alter or to abolish it, and to institute new Government, laying its foundation on such principles and organizing its powers in such form, as to them shall seem most likely to effect their Safety and Happiness. Prudence, indeed, will dictate that Governments long established should not be changed for light and transient causes; and accordingly all experience hath shewn, that mankind are more disposed to suffer, while evils are sufferable, than to right themselves by abolishing the forms to which they are accustomed. But when a long train of abuses and usurpations, pursuing invariably the same Object evinces a design to reduce them under absolute Despotism, it is their right, it is their duty, to throw off such Government, and to provide new Guards for their future security.--Such has been the patient sufferance of these Colonies; and such is now the necessity which constrains them to alter their former Systems of Government. The history of the present King of Great Britain is a history of repeated injuries and usurpations, all having in direct object the establishment of an absolute Tyranny over these States. To prove this, let Facts be submitted to a candid world.

He has refused his Assent to Laws, the most wholesome and necessary for the public good.

He has forbidden his Governors to pass Laws of immediate and pressing importance, unless suspended in their operation till his Assent should be obtained; and when so suspended, he has utterly neglected to attend to them.

He has refused to pass other Laws for the accommodation of large districts of people, unless those people would relinquish the right of Representation in the Legislature, a right inestimable to them and formidable to tyrants only.

He has called together legislative bodies at places unusual, uncomfortable, and distant from the depository of their public Records, for the sole purpose of fatiguing them into compliance with his measures.

He has dissolved Representative Houses repeatedly, for opposing with manly firmness his invasions on the rights of the people.

He has refused for a long time, after such dissolutions, to cause others to be elected; whereby the Legislative powers, incapable of Annihilation, have returned to the People at large for their exercise; the State remaining in the mean time exposed to all the dangers of invasion from without, and convulsions within.

He has endeavoured to prevent the population of these States; for that purpose obstructing the Laws for Naturalization of Foreigners; refusing to pass others to encourage their migrations hither, and raising the conditions of new Appropriations of Lands.

He has obstructed the Administration of Justice, by refusing his Assent to Laws for establishing Judiciary powers.

He has made Judges dependent on his Will alone, for the tenure of their offices, and the amount and payment of their salaries.

He has erected a multitude of New Offices, and sent hither swarms of Officers to harrass our people, and eat out their substance.

He has kept among us, in times of peace, Standing Armies without the Consent of our legislatures.

He has affected to render the Military independent of and superior to the Civil power.

He has combined with others to subject us to a jurisdiction foreign to our constitution, and unacknowledged by our laws; giving his Assent to their Acts of pretended Legislation:

For Quartering large bodies of armed troops among us:

For protecting them, by a mock Trial, from punishment for any Murders which they should commit on the Inhabitants of these States:

For cutting off our Trade with all parts of the world:

For imposing Taxes on us without our Consent:

For depriving us in many cases, of the benefits of Trial by Jury:

For transporting us beyond Seas to be tried for pretended offences

For abolishing the free System of English Laws in a neighbouring Province, establishing therein an Arbitrary government, and enlarging its Boundaries so as to render it at once an example and fit instrument for introducing the same absolute rule into these Colonies:

For taking away our Charters, abolishing our most valuable Laws, and altering fundamentally the Forms of our Governments:

For suspending our own Legislatures, and declaring themselves invested with power to legislate for us in all cases whatsoever.

He has abdicated Government here, by declaring us out of his Protection and waging War against us.

He has plundered our seas, ravaged our Coasts, burnt our towns, and destroyed the lives of our people.

He is at this time transporting large Armies of foreign Mercenaries to compleat the works of death, desolation and tyranny, already begun with circumstances of Cruelty & perfidy scarcely paralleled in the most barbarous ages, and totally unworthy the Head of a civilized nation.

He has constrained our fellow Citizens taken Captive on the high Seas to bear Arms against their Country, to become the executioners of their friends and Brethren, or to fall themselves by their Hands.

He has excited domestic insurrections amongst us, and has endeavoured to bring on the inhabitants of our frontiers, the merciless Indian Savages, whose known rule of warfare, is an undistinguished destruction of all ages, sexes and conditions.

In every stage of these Oppressions We have Petitioned for Redress in the most humble terms: Our repeated Petitions have been answered only by repeated injury. A Prince whose character is thus marked by every act which may define a Tyrant, is unfit to be the ruler of a free people.

Nor have We been wanting in attentions to our Brittish brethren. We have warned them from time to time of attempts by their legislature to extend an unwarrantable jurisdiction over us. We have reminded them of the circumstances of our emigration and settlement here. We have appealed to their native justice and magnanimity, and we have conjured them by the ties of our common kindred to disavow these usurpations, which, would inevitably interrupt our connections and correspondence. They too have been deaf to the voice of justice and of consanguinity. We must, therefore, acquiesce in the necessity, which denounces our Separation, and hold them, as we hold the rest of mankind, Enemies in War, in Peace Friends.

We, therefore, the Representatives of the United States of America, in General Congress, Assembled, appealing to the Supreme Judge of the world for the rectitude of our intentions, do, in the Name, and by Authority of the good People of these Colonies, solemnly publish and declare, That these United Colonies are, and of Right ought to be Free and Independent States; that they are Absolved from all Allegiance to the British Crown, and that all political connection between them and the State of Great Britain, is and ought to be totally dissolved; and that as Free and Independent States, they have full Power to levy War, conclude Peace, contract Alliances, establish Commerce, and to do all other Acts and Things which Independent States may of right do. And for the support of this Declaration, with a firm reliance on the protection of divine Providence, we mutually pledge to each other our Lives, our Fortunes and our sacred Honor.

Georgia
Button Gwinnett
Lyman Hall
George Walton

North Carolina
William Hooper
Joseph Hewes
John Penn

South Carolina
Edward Rutledge
Thomas Heyward, Jr.
Thomas Lynch, Jr.
Arthur Middleton

Maryland
Samuel Chase
William Paca
Thomas Stone
Charles Carroll of
Carrollton

Virginia
George Wythe
Richard Henry Lee
Thomas Jefferson
Benjamin Harrison
Thomas Nelson, Jr.
Francis Lightfoot Lee
Carter Braxton

Delaware
Caesar Rodney
George Read
Thomas McKean

New York
William Floyd
Philip Livingston
Francis Lewis
Lewis Morris

New Jersey
Richard Stockton
John Witherspoon
Francis Hopkinson
John Hart
Abraham Clark

Massachusetts
Samuel Adams
John Adams
Robert Treat Paine
Elbridge Gerry

Rhode Island
Stephen Hopkins
William Ellery

Connecticut
Roger Sherman
Samuel Huntington
William Williams
Oliver Wolcott

Massachusetts	Pennsylvania	New Hampshire	New Hampshire
John Hancock	Robert Morris	Josiah Bartlett	Matthew Thornton
	Benjamin Rush	William Whipple	
	Benjamin Franklin		
	John Morton		
	George Clymer		
	James Smith		
	George Taylor		
	James Wilson		
	George Ross		

NOTES

Introduction

1. As determined by a search for the phrase "pursuit of happiness" in US Supreme Court cases through Westlaw. Unless stated otherwise, the text of the Declaration to which I will refer is a transcription of the Declaration that is on display in the National Archives, as listed in the bibliography. The National Archives notes that "the spelling and punctuation reflects the original." This final version differs only in capitalization (such as "Life, Liberty, and the pursuit of Happiness" instead of "life, liberty & the pursuit of happiness"), minor punctuation, and some spelling (such as "unalienable rights" instead of the original version's "inalienable rights") from the draft approved by the Continental Congress. Key changes that occurred during the drafting of the Declaration will be discussed in part 2. For reconstructions of the Declaration throughout the drafting process, see appendixes 4–5.

2. Brian A. Garner, ed., *Black's Law Dictionary*, s.v. "happiness, right to pursue." The contrast between this definition and the definition of "pursuit of happiness" will be discussed in part 3.

3. See Paul E. Sigmund, ed., *The Selected Political Writings of John Locke*, chap. 5, "Of Property," section 27; and chap. 7, "Of Political or Civil Society," section 87.

4. Ibid., xi, xxiv.

5. William B. Scott argues that Jefferson likely "amended Locke's phrase to the 'pursuit of Happiness,'" as a result of Jefferson's own "serious doubts concerning the moral justification of certain forms of property." Scott suggests that Jefferson inserted "pursuit of happiness" "in an effort to restore the old moral content to the concept of individual property." Scott is summarizing Jefferson's concerns about newer forms of property ownership, generally, in contrast to Locke's "natural property." William B. Scott, *In Pursuit of Happiness: American Conceptions of Property from the Seventeenth to the Twentieth Century*, 41–42. In 1775 Jefferson wrote against Great Britain's treatment of the colonists, a treatment that he compared to enslavement and expressed incredulity that "the divine Author of our existence intended a part of the human race to hold an absolute property in, and an unbounded power over others." *A Declaration by the Representatives of the United Colonies of North-America, Now Met in Congress at Philadelphia, Setting Forth the Causes and Necessity of Their Taking Up Arms*. For a vigorous argument that Jefferson's concerns about property ownership did *not* extend to property ownership in slaves and that rhetoric such as that quoted above was for political purposes only, see Paul Finkelman, "Jefferson

and Slavery: 'Treason against the Hopes of the World,'" 181. For a contrasting discussion of Jefferson's views on slavery, see Lucia C. Stanton, "'Those Who Labor
for My Happiness': Thomas Jefferson and His Slaves," 147.

6. Scott, *In Pursuit of Happiness*, 41–42; John E. Crowley, *The Invention of Comfort: Sensibilities & Design in Early Modern Britain & Early America*, 142–43, 200; Jan
Lewis, *The Pursuit of Happiness: Family and Values in Jefferson's Virginia*, xii–xiv, 200.
Lewis argues that this understanding of the pursuit of happiness did not develop
until the nineteenth century and would be anachronistic if applied to the Declaration. See Garry Wills, *Inventing America: Jefferson's Declaration of Independence*,
240–55 (discussing both pursuit and happiness).

7. As will be discussed in part 2, the Virginia Declaration of Rights, which
Jefferson had with him as he drafted the Declaration of Independence, lists the
inherent rights of "the enjoyment of life and liberty, with the means of acquiring
and possessing property, and pursuing and obtaining happiness and safety." See also
John Locke, *Two Treatises of Government* (for life, liberty, and property) and *Essay on
Human Understanding* (for the pursuit of happiness).

8. Carl Becker included, and in part disagreed with, Rufus Choate's description
of the Declaration's "glittering and sounding generalities of natural right," with
Becker stating that the few generalities contained in the Declaration were "'glitter-
ing and sounding' . . . in their substance and not in their form." Carl Becker, *The
Declaration of Independence: A Study in the History of Political Ideas*, 201–2. See also
Pauline Maier, *American Scripture: Making the Declaration of Independence*, 134.

9. Unless stated otherwise, the version of Blackstone's *Commentaries* utilized for
this work is a reprint of the original first edition that was published by Clarendon
Press, Oxford, from 1765 to 1769. See William Blackstone, *Commentaries on the
Laws of England*. For a reconstruction of the portion of Blackstone's *Commentaries*
that is central to this work, with Blackstone's edits from the first through eight
editions marked, please see appendix 3.

10. Ibid., 1:38–39, 42.

11. Samuel Johnson, *A Dictionary of the English Language*, s.v. "fit, adj., 2."

12. Blackstone, *Commentaries*, 1:41.

13. "Real" is a synonym for "substantial," which is defined as "real; actually
existing." "Substance" is defined as "the essential part." "Essential" refers to the
essential nature of a thing. Johnson, *Dictionary of the English Language*, s.v. "real,"
"substance," and "essential."

14. This change in language is noted in the William G. Hammond edition of
Blackstone's *Commentaries*, which incorporated all changes made throughout the
first eight editions of the work along with notations regarding the edition in which
each change was made. See William G. Hammond, ed., *"Commentaries on the Laws
of England" by Sir William Blackstone, KT., One of the Justices of His Majesty's Court
of Common Pleas. From the Author's Eighth Edition, 1778. Edited for American Lawyers*,
69 (noted as p. 41 of the original). For more on Blackstone's tendency to edit each
new edition of the *Commentaries*, see Wilfrid Prest, "Blackstone and Biography,"
9. Blackstone's edits "continued to affect all eight editions of the Commentaries

published during Blackstone's lifetime, as well as the first posthumous edition of 1783, which purports to include his final manuscript revisions."

15. Letter from Jefferson to Madison (February 17, 1826), in Adrienne Koch and William Peden, eds., *The Life and Selected Writings of Thomas Jefferson*, 726, discussed in Gerald T. Dunne, "American Blackstone," 321, 326.

16. See Blackstone, *Commentaries*, 1:38–43.

17. G. Edward White, "Recovering the World of the Marshall Court," 781, 819–20. In an effort to reflect White's methodology, this work focuses specifically on the legal meaning of the pursuit of happiness, as understood by Blackstone and the founders. For a broad intellectual history of the idea of happiness in Western thought, see Darrin M. McMahon, *Happiness: A History*.

18. G. E. White, "Recovering the World of the Marshall Court," 819–20.

19. Ibid., 820–21.

20. Eighteenth-century understandings of the laws of nature, the law of nature, and natural law; the law of revelation, the divine law, and the law of God; and nature's God will be described more fully in parts 1–2.

Chapter 1

1. Blackstone, *Commentaries*, 1:3. This series of lectures provided the foundation for Blackstone's four-volume work titled *Commentaries on the Laws of England*, which was published between 1765 and 1769. David Lieberman, *The Province of Legislation Determined: Legal Theory in Eighteenth-Century Britain*, 31.

2. Lieberman, *Province of Legislation Determined*, 34 (quoting Sir William Jones).

3. Ibid., 34 (quoting William Jones, *An Essay on the Law of Bailments* [London: J. Nichols, 1781], 123; and Edward Wynne, *Eunomus* [London: B. White, 1785], 1:6–7, 2:52–57).

4. Blackstone, *Commentaries*, 1:32.

5. Ibid., 27 (emphasis in the original). Blackstone's use of italics in his reference to Aristotle suggests that he includes the philosopher's argument as a way to address counterarguments by those who uphold Aristotle's teachings but would disagree with Blackstone on the study of law. It is a shrewd use of Aristotle and a good demonstration of the fact that, as will be discussed, Blackstone disagreed with the more abstract of Aristotle's methods, but not his overall purpose. This passage remains unchanged in the Hammond version, which incorporated all of Blackstone's edits through the eighth edition of the *Commentaries*, with the exception of "it's" changed to "its" where appropriate. Hammond, "*Commentaries*," 29–30.

6. Samuel Johnson selected the Watts quotation to accompany his third definition of "system." Johnson, *Dictionary of the English Language*, s.v. "system."

7. Blackstone, *Commentaries*, 1:4.

8. Ibid., 3–6.

9. Ibid., 5–6.

10. Ibid., 7–10.

11. Ibid., 9–11. Lieberman has argued well for this guiding purpose behind the *Commentaries*. See Lieberman, *Province of Legislation Determined*, 34.

12. Robert Anderson, *British Universities Past and Present*, 22. Anderson cites John Gascoigne, *Cambridge in the Age of the Enlightenment: Science, Religion and Politics from the Restoration to the French Revolution* (Cambridge: Cambridge University Press, 1989), 19; John Cannon, *Aristocratic Century: The Peerage of Eighteenth-Century England* (New York: Cambridge University Press, 1984), 47; and M. G. Brock and M. C. Curthoys, eds., *The History of the University of Oxford*, vol. 6, *Nineteenth-Century Oxford, Part 1* (Oxford: Clarendon Press, 1997), 478–79.

13. Blackstone, *Commentaries*, 1:11–13.

14. John W. Barker, *Justinian and the Later Roman Empire*, 65, 67, 203.

15. Craig A. Stern, "Justinian: Lieutenant of Christ, Legislator for Christendom," 157.

16. Barker, *Justinian and the Later Roman Empire*, 168.

17. Ibid., 168, 170.

18. Peter Stein, *Roman Law in European History*, 33–34.

19. Barker, *Justinian and the Later Roman Empire*, 170; Stein, *Roman Law in European History*, 34–35; Stern, "Justinian," 159.

20. Barker, *Justinian and the Later Roman Empire*, 170–71; Stein, *Roman Law in European History*, 34. The *Corpus Juris Civilis* is alternately spelled as the *Corpus Iuris Civilis*.

21. Stern, "Justinian," 159–60 (citing Justinian, *The Institutes of Justinian*, trans. J. A. C. Thomas [New York: Elsevier Science, 1975], 1–3).

22. As quoted in Stern, "Justinian," 158–59.

23. Stern, "Justinian," 163–64, quoting Justinian, *The Institutes of Justinian*, 3.

24. Stein, *Roman Law in European History*, 35.

25. P. N. Ure, *Justinian and His Age*, 139; Stern, "Justinian," 162.

26. Stein, *Roman Law in European History*, 43.

27. Dr. Joseph Fornieri helped refine my thinking on the Scholastic tradition with his comments on a previous draft of this work at the Lehrman American Studies Institute at Princeton in June 2012.

28. Blackstone, *Commentaries*, 1:40–41. The awkward use of quotation marks before "that," before "pursue," and then after "happiness" occurs in the first London edition, published by Oxford's Clarendon Press from 1765 to 1769 and in the first American edition, published by Robert Bell in Philadelphia from 1771 to 1772. Library records suggest that both John Adams and Thomas Jefferson had the Bell edition in their libraries. The first Bell edition purports to be a reprint of the first London edition, but at least one substantive alteration in the Bell edition has been identified by G. W. Hammond as occurring in the second London edition, which is the replacement of the sentence "Yet undoubtedly the revealed law is (humanly speaking) of infinitely more authority than what we generally call the natural law" with this sentence: "Yet undoubtedly the revealed law is of infinitely more authenticity than that moral system, which is framed by ethical writers, and denominated the natural law." See Hammond, *"Commentaries,"* 70 (from WB P. 42); Bell, 42; and appendix 3 to this work. The Bell edition also switches "vegitable" for "vegetable" on p. 38, changes "it's due" to "his due" on p. 40, and makes a variety of small

punctuation changes. Nevertheless, the Bell edition includes the above passage exactly as it was included in the original London edition. For information on the first Bell edition and Adams's and Jefferson's ownership of it, see Lisa Gold, "Books the Founders Read: *Blackstone's Commentaries on the Laws of England*"; and, for Adams, see Wilfrid Prest and Michael Widener, "250 Years of Blackstone's *Commentaries*: An Exhibition/Curated by Wilfrid Prest, Michael Widener." Blackstone heavily revised the eighth London edition of the *Commentaries*, the final edition printed before his death, and changed this "one paternal precept" to "that man should pursue his own true and substantial happiness." These adjectives appear to be a simple clarification, as they align with Blackstone's description of happiness as real and substantial throughout this section of his *Commentaries*. Hammond, *"Commentaries,"* 69 (noted as p. 41 of the original). For Blackstone's use of "real" and "substantial" to describe happiness, see Blackstone, *Commentaries*, 1:41.

29. Wilfrid R. Prest, *William Blackstone: Law and Letters*, 32–33.

30. J. W. Tubbs, *The Common Law Mind: Medieval and Early Modern Conceptions*, 171–72 (quoting Aristotle [see nn90–95]). Tubbs believes that this type of reasoning is inapplicable to law, but Blackstone would disagree.

31. Anderson, *British Universities Past and Present*, 1–2.

32. Ibid., 23; Michael J. Hofstetter, *The Romantic Idea of a University: England and Germany, 1770–1850*, 3.

33. Anderson, *British Universities Past and Present*, 5 (citing "chapters by J. McConica and J. M. Fletcher," in *The History of the University of Oxford*, ed. J. McConica, vol. 3, *The Collegiate University* [Oxford: Clarendon Press, 1986]).

34. Anderson, *British Universities Past and Present*, 5, 7.

35. Hofstetter, *Romantic Idea of a University*, 11–12 (citing Edward Gibbon, *Autobiographies*, ed. John Murray [London: John Murray, 1896], 70 [quoting Edward Gibbon; emphasis added]).

36. Anderson, *British Universities Past and Present*, 24, 7.

37. Daniel R. Coquillette, *The Anglo-American Legal Heritage*, 437. See also Anderson, *British Universities Past and Present*, 7.

38. Coquillette, *Anglo-American Legal Heritage*, 437.

39. As will be discussed, Blackstone's overview of the law in the introduction to the *Commentaries* largely mirrors Christopher St. Germain's discussion, with some notable differences that highlight Blackstone's more Protestant views, including Blackstone's distrust of both the infallibility of the prince or the infallible judgment of rulers and the primacy Blackstone placed on scripture. Blackstone claimed that Sir Matthew Hale's *Analysis of the Law* (1713) was the "most natural and scientifical of any, as well as the most comprehensive." Carol Matthews, "A 'Model of the Old House': Architecture in Blackstone's Life and *Commentaries*," 31. Matthews quotes Blackstone and cites W. Blackstone, *An Analysis of the Laws of England* (Oxford: Clarendon Press, 1756), vii.

40. Blackstone, *Commentaries*, 1:32.

41. Ibid., 30.

42. Ibid., 38.

43. I. Bernard Cohen, *Science and the Founding Fathers: Science in the Political Thought of Jefferson, Franklin, Adams and Madison*, 114–21; Blackstone, *Commentaries*, 1:38–42.

44. Richard Hooker, *Of the Lawes of the Ecclesiastical Politie* (1594–97), bk. 1.

45. See also Christopher St. Germain, who describes the "law of reason as the law of nature as it pertains to reasonable creatures." Christopher St. Germain, *The Doctor and Student* (1518). For Blackstone's use of natural law, see Blackstone, *Commentaries*, 1:42.

46. Blackstone, *Commentaries*, 1:38–39.

47. Ibid.

48. Ibid., 39–40.

49. Ibid., 38–39 (emphasis in the original).

50. For a discussion of the Greek concept of *eudaimonia* and how it differs from current English-language conceptions of happiness, see William J. Prior, *Virtue and Knowledge: An Introduction to Ancient Greek Ethics*, 148–55.

51. Aristotle, *The Nichomachean Ethics of Aristotle*, 1.7.15.

52. Blackstone, *Commentaries*, 1:41.

53. Ibid., 40.

54. Aristotle, *Nichomachean Ethics of Aristotle*, 1.7.15, 1.8.4.

55. Blackstone, *Commentaries*, 1:40, 36, 40. In his work "The Structure of Blackstone's *Commentaries*," Alan Watson has argued for the structural influence of Justinian's *Institutes* on Blackstone's *Commentaries*. Although I disagree with some of Watson's larger conclusions, I do think Blackstone agreed with Justinian's focus on immutable principles. See Watson, "Structure of Blackstone's *Commentaries*," 795.

Chapter 2

1. Blackstone's work reflected the earlier work of Christopher St. Germain while also expressing more Anglican and Scottish Enlightenment views.

2. Anderson, *British Universities Past and Present*, 5.

3. Prest, *William Blackstone*, 309; David A. Lockmiller, *Sir William Blackstone*, 70n43 (citing William Connor Sydney, *England and the English in the Eighteenth Century: Chapters in the Social History of the Times*, 2nd ed. [1891]). For an excellent article that explores this interrelationship while also exploring the historiography, see James R. Jacob and Margaret C. Jacob, "The Anglican Origins of Modern Science: The Metaphysical Foundations of the Whig Constitution."

4. Alan Charles Kors, "The Pursuit of Happiness." I attended Dr. Kors's talk on Bishop Butler's understanding of pursuit of happiness in the midst of conducting my research. I am indebted to Dr. Kors for pointing me to Bishop Butler and for the time he spent talking with me about my own conclusions regarding Blackstone's and the founders' understandings of pursuit of happiness. The ideas shared in Kors's lecture have provided a framework for the following discussion of Butler's understanding of the pursuit of happiness.

5. David E. White, ed., *The Works of Bishop Butler*, 4; Ernest Campbell Mossner, *Bishop Butler and the Age of Reason: A Study in the History of Thought*; William Archibald Spooner, *Bishop Butler*, 12.

6. Terrence Penelhum, *Butler*, 1.

7. Christopher Cunliffe, ed., *Joseph Butler's Moral and Religious Thought: Tercentenary Essays*, 48.

8. D. White, *Works of Bishop Butler*, 4; Mossner, *Bishop Butler*, 3; Cunliffe, *Butler's Moral and Religious Thought*, 48.

9. May, *The Enlightenment in America*, 17 (quoting John Tillotson, "The Precepts of Christianity not Grievous," in *The Works of the Most Reverend Dr. John Tillotson, Late Lord Archbishop of Canterbury, in Ten Volumes* [London: n.p., 1820], 1:468–69).

10. Raymond D. Tumbleson, "'Reason and Religion': The Science of Anglicanism," 131, 134.

11. Butler and Blackstone were drawing on a shared learned culture composed of ideas that, in many cases, harked back to antiquity. For example, Blackstone's discussion of pursuit of happiness reflects that of Butler, and both men are voicing ideas previously expressed in John Locke, *An Essay Concerning Human Understanding* and the philosophy of classical antiquity.

12. Kors, "The Pursuit of Happiness"; Blackstone, *Commentaries*, 1:40.

13. Blackstone, *Commentaries*, 1:39–41; Kors, "The Pursuit of Happiness."

14. Jacob and Jacob, "Anglican Origins," 264.

15. Tumbleson, "'Reason and Religion,'" 150 (bracketed portions added).

16. Jacob and Jacob, "Anglican Origins," 258.

17. Ibid.

18. Johnson, *Dictionary of the English Language*, s.v. "real." "Real" is a synonym for "substantial," which is defined as "real; actually existing."

19. "Substance" is defined as "the essential part." Ibid., s.v. "substance"; *Oxford English Dictionary*, s.v. "substance" and "substantial." This same definition appears in the etymology for "Substance" (ca. 1330) in the *Oxford English Dictionary*.

20. Charles L. Barzun, "Common Sense and Legal Science," 1051, 1054. Barzun argues for the development of inductive legal science in early America. As demonstrated in the discussion that follows, the same common sense legal science he sees in the Scottish Enlightenment's Common Sense school and nineteenth-century early America is reflected in Blackstone's *Commentaries*. Later, I will demonstrate that this understanding of legal science was present in "the pursuit of Happiness" in the Declaration of Independence as well.

21. Ibid., 1055.

22. Ibid., 1062–65. See also Alexander Broadie, *A History of Scottish Philosophy*, 246–51.

23. Barzun, "Common Sense and Legal Science," 1062–63, 1065; Broadie, *History of Scottish Philosophy*, 246–51, 274–75.

24. Barzun, "Common Sense and Legal Science," 1066.

25. Ibid., 1055.

26. Ibid., 1066.

27. Ibid., 1066–67.

28. Blackstone, *Commentaries*, 1:27.

29. This Enlightenment idea of improvement and progress was held by Thomas Jefferson as well. Peter S. Onuf, "Ancients, Moderns, and the Progress of Mankind: Thomas Jefferson's Classical World," 36–37.

Chapter 3

1. Ronald S. Crane, "Anglican Apologetics and the Idea of Progress, 1699–1745 (Concluded)," 365.

2. Ibid., 365, 367.

3. Ronald S. Crane, "Anglican Apologetics and the Idea of Progress, 1699–1745," 280.

4. Prest, "Blackstone and Biography," 10.

5. Crane, "Anglican Apologetics (Concluded)," 365.

6. Crane, "Anglican Apologetics," 305.

7. See Blackstone, *Commentaries*, 1:5–6.

8. James Campbell, ed., *The Anglo-Saxons*, 241–42; David Horspool, *King Alfred: Burnt Cakes and Other Legends*, 171. Horspool points out, however, that others saw Alfred as "a paragon of unquestionable royal authority" (ibid.).

9. Coquillette, *Anglo-American Legal Heritage*, 38, 41.

10. Kurt von S. Kynell, *Saxon and Medieval Antecedents of the English Common Law*, 27–28; Campbell, *The Anglo-Saxons*, 242.

11. Blackstone, *Commentaries*, 4:405.

12. Kynell, *Saxon and Medieval Antecedents*, 213.

13. Frank Barlow, *Edward the Confessor*, 178.

14. For an argument that Edward's work in law is more legend than history, see Theodore F. T. Plucknett, *A Concise History of the Common Law*, 256.

15. Blackstone, *Commentaries*, 1:23; Kynell, *Saxon and Medieval Antecedents*, 212.

16. Simon Keynes and Michael Lapidge, trans., *Alfred the Great: Asser's Life of King Alfred and Other Contemporary Sources*, 92, 99, 107. For a discussion of Alfred's program of literacy and how Alfred may have intended it to help forge a common English identity, see Horspool, *King Alfred*, 179–80.

17. Leslie Webster and Janet Backhouse, eds., *The Making of England: Anglo-Saxon Art and Culture, AD 600–900*, 254. Webster and Backhouse explore artistic and cultural evidence for confirmation or contradiction of the legend of Alfred as a ruler.

18. Campbell, *The Anglo-Saxons*, 132.

19. Webster and Backhouse, *Making of England*, 254.

20. Campbell, *The Anglo-Saxons*, 157. David Horspool supports this connection, claiming that "[t]o Alfred a personal interest in wisdom was a facet of true Christian kingship." Horspool, *King Alfred*, 128.

21. Horspool, *King Alfred*, 131.

22. *Webster's New Universal Unabridged Dictionary*, s.v. "wisdom."

23. Samuel Johnson traces the word "wisdom" back to Saxon roots, defining it as "Sapience; the power of judging rightly." Johnson, *Dictionary of the English Language*, s.v. "wisdom." The *Oxford English Dictionary* defines wisdom as the "capacity of judging rightly in matters relating to life and conduct" and dates it to Old Saxon, as early as 888. The *Oxford English Dictionary* also defines wisdom as "one of the manifestations of the divine nature in Jesus Christ."

24. Campbell, *The Anglo-Saxons*, 157.

25. Horspool, *King Alfred*, 134–35. For Alfred's translation of Gregory the Great's *Book of Pastoral Rule*, see Campbell, *The Anglo-Saxons*, 156.

26. Campbell, *The Anglo-Saxons*, 157.

27. Ibid.

28. On the English common-law principles of divergence and nonrepugnancy, see Mary Sarah Bilder, *The Transatlantic Constitution: Colonial Legal Culture and the Empire*, 1–4.

29. Bilder, *Transatlantic Constitution*, 1–4. Bilder's discussion of colonial law and common law mirrors William Blackstone's argument that inferior laws could not be in contradiction to superior laws. In particular, Blackstone argued that human law could differ at the level of municipal law, but that, nevertheless, "no human laws" could "contradict" the "two foundations" of the English common law, which were "the law of nature and the law of revelation." Blackstone, *Commentaries*, 1:42.

30. Blackstone, *Commentaries*, 1:5, 10.

31. For an excellent discussion of architecture in Blackstone's *Commentaries*, as well as his other works, see Matthews, "'Model of the Old House,'" 15–34; and Prest, *William Blackstone*, 44–48, 67–68, 77–79.

32. Blackstone, *Commentaries*, 1:35, 42.

33. Peter Gay, *The Enlightenment*, 2:24–25.

34. Crane, "Anglican Apologetics (Concluded)," 375.

35. Blackstone, *Commentaries*, 4:403–4.

36. Kynell, *Saxon and Medieval Antecedents*, 84.

37. Blackstone, *Commentaries*, 42 (emphasis added).

38. Matthews, "'Model of the Old House,'" 15–34.

39. Ibid., 29 (quoting Blackstone, *Letters*, 4).

40. Ibid., 29–30 (quoting Blackstone, *Commentaries*, 1:10, "Introduction," which was first published as *A Discourse on the Study of the Law* [Oxford, 1758]).

41. Johnson, *Dictionary of the English Language*, s.v. "modern, 1" and "modern, 2."

42. Douglas Harper, ed., *Online Etymology Dictionary* (2001–17), s.v. "improve." Entries in the *Online Etymology Dictionary* are compiled from *The Oxford English Dictionary* (2nd ed.), the *Barnhart Dictionary of Etymology* (1988), Weekley's *Etymological Dictionary of Modern English* (1921), and Ernest Klein's *Comprehensive Etymological Dictionary of the English Language* (1971), with additional information drawn from sources listed in the editor's note on sources and methods.

43. Johnson, *Dictionary of the English Language*, s.v. "improvement."

44. Garner, *Black's Law Dictionary*, s.v. "happiness, right to pursue."

45. Matthews, "'Model of the Old House,'" 30 (citing Blackstone, *Commentaries*, 4:436).

46. Samuel Johnson describes simplicity as plain or artless, without deceit. Johnson, *Dictionary of the English Language*, s.v. "simplicity."

47. Note that definition 6 is the only definition whose usage examples include the phrase "more curious," mirroring Blackstone's use here. Johnson, *Dictionary of the English Language*, s.v. "curious, 6" and "refinement, 1 and 2."

48. Definition of voluntary improvement is from *Black's Law Dictionary*, s.v. "improvement, voluntary improvement"; Johnson, *Dictionary of the English Language*, s.v. "art."

49. Matthews, "'Model of the Old House,'" 29 (emphasis added) (citing Blackstone, *Letters*, 4).

50. Ibid., 30 (citing Blackstone, *Commentaries*, 4:436).

51. Prest, *William Blackstone*, 59.

52. Johnson, *Dictionary of the English Language*, s.v. "sage" and "pedant." Johnson specifically tied pedantry back to university education, including with his definition of pedantry this quotation from Jonathan Swift: "From the universities the young nobility are sent for fear of contracting any airs of pedantry by a college education."

53. Prest, *William Blackstone*, 59.

54. Ibid.

55. Wilfrid Prest, whose work pointed me to these passages from Blackstone's poetry, comes to some similar conclusions as he considers this passage along with an unprinted couplet. To distinguish my conclusions, above, I have included his conclusions here: "'And thence the genuine Maxims draw | Of unsophisticated Law!' Here 'unsophisticated' is synonymous with original and unadulterated. In chronological terms the reference is to Anglo-Saxon England, as witness the invocation of 'mighty Alfred,' king of the West Saxons, no less celebrated in the role of law-giver than for his military exploits against the Danes, or his supposed foundation of Oxford University. That the Saxon 'ancient constitution' was the bedrock of English justice and liberties, notwithstanding subsequent Norman innovations overlaying and subverting its original purity, had long been a staple of legal and political discourse. But in Blackstone's verses the concept derives an added element from the late seventeenth-century Newtonian revolution in natural philosophy. Human law is depicted as a complex mechanism of 'countless wheels,' whose diverse ('mix'd, yet uniform') components mesh harmoniously together to achieve the same objective, of right, or justice, as laid down by their original human creator. For Alfred's spiritual presence continues to imbue and oversee their operation, just as the dependence of the entire natural universe on various physical laws determined and still regulated by God was demonstrated by Isaac Newton. Perhaps the young William Blackstone already saw himself as the Common Law's Newton, transforming darkness into light, as Alexander Pope famously depicted the great natural philosopher. His poem does set out an extremely ambitious agenda of discovery and reform, since the law's true animating principles and genuine maxims, once

properly understood, must supersede the 'mystic, dark, discordant lore' currently on offer." Ibid., 59–60 (citing "Ms. Middle of page 76" in a description of "Select Poems and Translations" provided by Vernon L. Smith, law librarian of the Boalt Hall Law School, University of California at Berkeley [letter on file there], writing to David A. Lockmiller, January 11, 1955).

Chapter 4

1. Jefferson, "Autobiography," 17.
2. Ibid., 13–17. For additional discussion of the Declaration's drafting, see Becker, *Declaration of Independence*, 135–93; and John Hazelton, *The Declaration of Independence: Its History*, 141–93.
3. Jefferson, "Autobiography," 17.
4. Jefferson claims in his autobiography that the committee selected him to write the first draft. John Adams disagrees, stating that Adams and Jefferson were appointed to write it together, that Jefferson encouraged Adams to write it alone, but that Adams then convinced Jefferson to be the one to draft it. See ibid.; and Becker, *Declaration of Independence*, 135–36.
5. "From Thomas Jefferson to James Madison, 30 August 1823."
6. Becker, *Declaration of Independence*, 151–71. See also Jefferson's letter to Madison stating that Adams's and Franklin's alterations "were two or three only, and merely verbal." "From Thomas Jefferson to James Madison, 30 August 1823."
7. John Adams, "Autobiography, Part 1, through 1776," sheet 24 of 53.
8. Thomas Jefferson to James Madison, August 30, 1823.
9. Becker, *Declaration of Independence*, 139n1.
10. An image of what Jefferson later claimed to be the "original Rough draught" of the Declaration, with the edits of Jefferson, Adams, and Benjamin Franklin marked, can be viewed at the Library of Congress exhibition "Declaring Independence: Drafting the Documents," "Jefferson's 'original Rough draught' of the Declaration of Independence," https://www.loc.gov/exhibits/declara/ruffdrft.html.

For an idea of what the "original Rough draught" of the Declaration might have looked like "before it was revised by the other members of the Committee of Five and by Congress," see Julian P. Boyd, ed., *The Papers of Thomas Jefferson*, 243–47.

After reviewing Jefferson's "original Rough draught," the Committee of Five submitted a clean or "fair copy" to the Continental Congress. This "fair copy" has been preserved through Thomas Jefferson's July 8, 1776, letter to Richard Henry Lee, where he included the "fair copy" with the changes of the Continental Congress highlighted and in Jefferson's autobiography, where he includes "the form of the declaration as originally reported [to the Continental Congress]. The parts struck out by Congress shall be distinguished by a black line drawn under them; & those inserted by them shall be placed in the margin or in a concurrent column." Thomas Jefferson, "Autobiography," 18–24. Becker included the "fair copy" Jefferson sent to Lee, with the alterations of the Continental Congress marked, in his work *Declaration of Independence*, 174–84.

Pauline Maier incorporated and updated the prior work of both Becker and Boyd and considered Jefferson's own errors in the copies he preserved in her reconstruction of the Declaration as delivered to, and then edited by, the Continental Congress. Maier's work is especially detailed and precise, carefully noting points of difference with previous efforts to reconstruct these texts. Maier, *American Scripture*, 235–41.

11. For the full account of Becker's analysis on this point, see *Declaration of Independence*, 151–53.

12. Ibid., 139n1, 137–61.

13. Ibid., 151–52, 157.

14. Jefferson, "Autobiography," 17.

15. Thomas Jefferson, "Jefferson's 'original Rough draught.'"

16. Quoted in Becker, *Declaration of Independence*, 207–9. For an image of the final copy as recorded on parchment paper, see "The Declaration of Independence" in Founding Documents at the National Archives. For a transcript of the original parchment paper version of the Declaration, see "Declaration of Independence: A Transcription" in Founding Documents at the National Archives.

17. Becker, *Declaration of Independence*, 207–9. The story, included in Jefferson's writings and recounted by Becker, is as follows: "I was sitting by Dr. Franklin, who perceived that I was not insensible to these mutilations. 'I have made it a rule,' said he, 'whenever in my power, to avoid becoming the draughtsman of papers to be reviewed by a public body. I took my lesson from an incident which I will relate to you. When I was a journeyman printer, one of my companions, an apprentice Hatter, having served out his time was about to open shop for himself. His first concern was to have a handsome signboard, with a proper inscription. He composed it in these words: 'John Thompson, Hatter, makes and sells hats for ready money,' with a figure of a hat subjoined. But he thought he would submit it to his friends for their amendments. The first he shewed it to thought the word 'hatter' tautologous, because followed by the words 'makes hats' which shew he was a hatter. It was struck out. The next observed that the word 'makes' might as well be omitted, because his customers would not care who made the hats. If good and to their mind, they would buy, by whomsoever made. He struck it out. A third said he thought the words 'for ready money' were useless as it was not the custom of the place to sell on credit. Every one who purchased expected to pay. They were parted with, and the inscription now stood 'John Thompson sells hats.' '*Sells* hats' says his next friend? Why nobody will expect you to give them away. What then is the use of that word? It was stricken out, and 'hats' followed it, the rather, as there was one painted on the board. So his inscription was reduced ultimately to 'John Thompson' with the figure of a hat subjoined." Becker, *Declaration of Independence*, 208–9.

18. Maier, *American Scripture*, 237; for the most complete and nuanced record of these changes, see 235–41. Jefferson seems to charge King George III not only with refusing to assent to laws that would "prohibit or restrain" slavery, but also with "the piratical warfare" of "captivating and carrying [men] into slavery" in North America. The full passage is as follows: "[H]e has waged cruel war against

human nature itself, violating it's most sacred rights of life & liberty in the persons of a distant people who never offended him, captivating & carrying them into slavery in another hemisphere, or to incur miserable death in their transportation thither. this piratical warfare, the opprobrium of infidel powers, is the warfare of the CHRISTIAN king of Great Britain. determined to keep open a market where MEN should be bought & sold, he has prostituted his negative for suppressing every legislative attempt to prohibit or to restrain this execrable commerce: and that this assemblage of horrors might want no fact of distinguished die, he is now exciting those very people to rise in arms among us, and to purchase that liberty of which he has deprived them, & murdering the people upon whom he also obtruded them; thus paying off former crimes committed against the liberties of one people, with crimes which he urges them to commit against the lives of another." Maier, *American Scripture*, 239.

19. For a more structural account, see ibid.

20. Adams, "Autobiography." For Jefferson disputing this account, see Jefferson, "From Thomas Jefferson to James Madison, 30 August 1823."

21. Jefferson, "From Thomas Jefferson to Henry Lee, May 8, 1825," 1500–1501.

22. James Otis, *Against Writs of Assistance*. The portion included above is the portion of Otis's speech that was summarized in the notes of John Adams.

23. Thomas Jefferson, "A Summary View of the Rights of British America," 105–22. Pauline Maier has also noted the connection between Jefferson's work here and his charges of tyranny against King George III in the Declaration. Maier claims that "A Summary View" is the "first sustained piece of American political writing that subjected the King's conduct to direct and pointed criticism." Maier, *American Scripture*, 112–23.

24. Jefferson, "Summary View," 105, 120–21, 110.

25. Maier, *American Scripture*, 239.

26. Ibid., 121, 122 (quoting an 1822 letter from John Adams to Timothy Pickering).

27. Cohen, *Science and the Founding Fathers*.

28. Blackstone, *Commentaries*, 1:38, 39–40.

29. Jefferson, "Summary View."

30. Kody W. Cooper and Justin Buckley Dyer, "Thomas Jefferson, Nature's God, and the Theological Foundations of Natural-Rights Republicanism," 23–24.

31. Becker, *Declaration of Independence*, 142.

32. Jefferson, "From Thomas Jefferson to Henry Lee, May 8, 1825," 1500–1501.

Chapter 5

1. John Adams, "Letter from John Adams to Timothy Pickering, August 6, 1822," Founders Online, National Archives, https://founders.archives.gov/documents/Adams/99-02-02-7674.

2. "From Thomas Jefferson to James Madison, 30 August 1823," Founders Online, National Archives, http://founders.archives.gov/documents/Jefferson/98-01-02-3728.

3. Thomas Jefferson, "From Thomas Jefferson to Henry Lee, May 8, 1825," 1500–1501.

4. Carl J. Richard argues well for an intermingling of these ideas at the founding in *The Founders and the Classics: Greece, Rome, and the American Enlightenment.* Richard's work provides a jumping-off point for my exploration of key ideas that influenced Jefferson, Adams, and Franklin, in general, and their thinking on the pursuit of happiness, in particular. Where Richard emphasizes the intermingling of the four strands, I argue for a point of convergence that cuts across all four strands and is instrumental to understanding both the pursuit of happiness and the Declaration as a whole. Bernard Bailyn similarly discusses founding-era ideas as "a blend of ideas and beliefs" (*The Ideological Origins of the American Revolution*, v), while Gordon Wood uses like terms to argue for "a general pattern of beliefs about the social process—a set of common assumptions about history, society, and politics that connected and made significant seemingly discrete and unrelated ideas." Gordon Wood, *The Creation of the American Republic, 1776–1787*, viii.

5. See Blackstone, *Commentaries*, 42; and Becker, *Declaration of Independence*, 26–27.

6. Kermit L. Hall, William Wiecek, and Paul Finkelman, *American Legal History: Cases and Materials*, 7–8.

7. James C. Spalding, "Loyalist as Royalist, Patriot as Puritan: The American Revolution as a Repetition of the English Civil Wars," 329–30.

8. Hall, Wiecek, and Finkelman, *American Legal History*, 7–8. As Garry Wills has noted, Carl Becker asserted the Declaration's debt to John Locke. Wills counters Becker and the literature that has adhered to Becker by claiming that the founders were more indebted to the Scottish Enlightenment than to John Locke. See Wills, *Inventing America.*

9. Hall, Wiecek, and Finkelman, *American Legal History*, 8.

10. This history is summarized well ibid. and in Stephen B. Presser and Jamil S. Zainaldin, *Law and Jurisprudence in American History.*

11. Otis, *Against Writs of Assistance.*

12. Hall, Wiecek, and Finkelman, *American Legal History*, 6–7, 27–29.

13. Presser and Zainaldin, *Law and Jurisprudence*, 68.

14. Otis, *Against Writs of Assistance.*

15. Presser and Zainaldin, *Law and Jurisprudence*, 69; Allen D. Boyer, ed., *Law, Liberty, and Parliament: Selected Essays on the Writings of Sir Edward Coke*, 176–77.

16. Presser and Zainaldin, *Law and Jurisprudence*, 69.

17. Boyer, *Law, Liberty, and Parliament*, 66.

18. Presser and Zainaldin, *Law and Jurisprudence*, 69.

19. Hall, Wiecek, and Finkelman, *American Legal History*, 23–24.

20. Otis, *Against Writs of Assistance.* The portion included above is the portion of Otis's speech that was summarized in the notes of John Adams.

21. Hall, Wiecek, and Finkelman, *American Legal History*, 60–61.

22. Jefferson, "Summary View."

23. Hall, Wiecek, and Finkelman, *American Legal History*, 63–64, 69–70.

24. Maier, *American Scripture.*

25. Merrill D. Peterson, *Thomas Jefferson and the New Nation: A Biography,* 16–19.

26. Maier, *American Scripture,* 125–26.

27. Ibid.

28. Julius S. Waterman, "Thomas Jefferson and Blackstone's *Commentaries,*" 451–54.

29. See Richard, *Founders and the Classics*; and Gay, *The Enlightenment,* 1:39.

30. See Richard, *Founders and the Classics.*

31. Ibid., 125–26, 132–39; Polybius, *The Histories,* bk. 6, pp. 1–12.

32. Richard, *Founders and the Classics,* 132, 125–26.

33. Marcus Tullius Cicero, "On the State."

34. Richard, *Founders and the Classics,* 132.

35. Ibid., 133.

36. John E. Paynter, "The Rhetorical Design of John Adams's 'Defence of the Constitutions of . . . America,'" 532.

37. Richard, *Founders and the Classics,* 133.

38. Polybius, *The Histories,* bk. 6, pp. 3–5, 10–13; Marcus Tullius Cicero, "On Laws," 192–220.

39. Paynter, "Rhetorical Design," 533.

40. Richard, *Founders and the Classics,* 134.

41. Marcus Tullius Cicero, "Pro Archia ('For Archias')," vii, 120.

42. Trevor Colbourn, ed., *Fame and the Founding Fathers: Essays by Douglass Adair,* 17–29; Cicero, "Pro Archia ('For Archias')," 120.

43. Richard, *Founders and the Classics,* 53–54, 59–61, 63.

44. Farrell, "Young John Adams," 373, 376, 373.

45. For evaluation based on ancient standards, see Richard, *Founders and the Classics,* 53–83.

46. Susan Suavé Meyer, *Ancient Ethics: A Critical Introduction,* 140.

47. Raymond J. Devettere, *Introduction to Virtue Ethics: Insights of the Ancient Greeks,* 126–27; Richard, *Founders and the Classics,* 170, 217–18. To live virtuously was to live in accord with the natural law: there is a "prescriptive force of the divine reason that all human beings must follow if they are to achieve excellence and happiness." Meyer, *Ancient Ethics,* 140. The Stoic notion of virtue comports well with Aristotle's understanding of happiness (*eudaimonia*) as "living well." Prior, *Virtue and Knowledge,* 149–50.

48. For an overview of these key aspects of Stoicism, see Simon Hornblower and Anthony Spawforth, eds., *The Oxford Classical Dictionary,* s.v. "Stoicism." Greek philosopher Aristotle believed that to be happy was to live well and that this was the ultimate end goal of man, "for both the common run of people and cultivated men call [this "ultimate end of all human activity"] happiness, and understand by 'being happy' the same as 'living well' and 'doing well.'" Prior, *Virtue and Knowledge,* 149. The Greek word for this conception of happiness is *eudaimonia,* which is to be distinguished from English understandings of happiness: "[T]he English word 'happiness' suggests a state of psychological contentment, pleasure or joy and,

though this subjective component is not absent from the Greek *eudaimonia*, it is not its primary connotation. . . . [Aristotle states that] people understand by *eudaimonia* 'living well' and 'doing well.'" Ibid., 149–50.

49. Gay, *The Enlightenment*, 1:164.

50. Richard, *Founders and the Classics*, 170.

51. Meyer, *Ancient Ethics*, 140.

52. Richard, *Founders and the Classics*, 170.

53. Prior, *Virtue and Knowledge*, 217–18.

54. Hornblower and Spawforth, *The Oxford Classical Dictionary*, s.v. "Stoicism."

55. Richard, *Founders and the Classics*, 170. "The Stoic norm 'live according to nature' means that human beings should act according to their rational nature and deliberate about what they should do," thus, ". . . virtuous living in Stoicism is a matter of discovering and conforming to the *a priori* norms embedded in nature." Devettere, *Introduction to Virtue Ethics*, 127–28. See also Meyer, *Ancient Ethics*, 138.

56. For more on Marcus Aurelius and Epictetus as followers of Stoicism, see Meyer, *Ancient Ethics*, 134; and Prior, *Virtue and Knowledge*, 208. "Marcus Aurelius' *Meditations* and Epictetus' *Discourses* and *Manual* . . . were more practically oriented than their predecessors: their major contribution to Stoicism lay in presenting its moral philosophy in popular form, rather than in developing its metaphysics and epistemology." Prior, *Virtue and Knowledge*, 208. Both Marcus Aurelius and Epictetus furthered "the reorientation toward practical ethics." Gay, *The Enlightenment*, 1:165. For Jefferson's appreciation of Epictetus, see Onuf, "Ancients, Moderns, and the Progress of Mankind," 35.

57. Meyer, *Ancient Ethics*, 171–73.

58. Prior, *Virtue and Knowledge*, 208; Meyer, *Ancient Ethics*, 175.

59. Quoted in Meyer, *Ancient Ethics*, 171.

60. "The first law of nature was self-preservation." Peter S. Onuf, *Jefferson's Empire: The Language of American Nationhood*, 94.

61. Hornblower and Spawforth, *The Oxford Classical Dictionary*, s.v. "Libertas." See also the discussion of "classical Latin *lîbertât-*, *lîbertâs*" in the etymology of liberty in *The Oxford English Dictionary*, s.v. "liberty, n. 1."

62. Maier, *American Scripture*, 121.

63. Richard, *Founders and the Classics*, 120.

64. See listing of court cases, petitions, and declarations of rights in Presser and Zainaldin, *Law and Jurisprudence*, 308. See also Hall, Wiecek, and Finkelman, *American Legal History*, 304.

65. Gay, *The Enlightenment*, 1:374–75.

66. Blackstone, *Commentaries*, 1:38.

67. Ibid., 41–42.

68. Richard, *Founders and the Classics*, 173–75.

69. See *The Westminster Confession of Faith*; and *The Book of Common Prayer* (1559 and 1662 versions).

70. Richard, *Founders and the Classics*, 20.

71. *Westminster Confession of Faith*, chap. 5.

72. Daniel Dreisbach, *Reading the Bible with the Founding Fathers*, 88–89.

73. Carl J. Richard, *The Founders and the Bible*, 2, 11–62; Dreisbach, *Reading the Bible with the Founding Fathers*, 15–19, 23–48.

74. Richard, *Founders and the Classics*, 19 (for college entrance requirements); Dreisbach, *Reading the Bible with the Founding Fathers*, 56–57 (for reading the Bible in its original language).

75. Col. 1:15–17 (NIV). The King James Version reads as follows: "[Christ] is the image of the invisible God, the firstborn of every creature: For by him were all things created, that are in heaven, and that are in earth, visible and invisible, whether they be thrones, or dominions, or principalities, or powers: all things were created by him, and for him: And he is before all things, and by him all things consist."

76. Rom. 1:20 (NIV). The King James Version reads as follows: "For the invisible things of him from the creation of the world are clearly seen, being understood by the things that are made, even his eternal power and Godhead."

77. Richard, *Founders and the Classics*, 19.

78. John 1:1–4 (NIV). The King James Version reads as follows: "In the beginning was the Word, and the Word was with God, and the Word was God. The same was in the beginning with God. All things were made by him; and without him was not any thing made that was made. In him was life; and the life was the light of men."

79. For commentary on John 1:1–17, see Spiros Zodhiates, ed., *Hebrew-Greek Key Word Study Bible: New International Version*, 1238.

80. Rom. 2:15 (KJV).

81. Acts 17:16–23 (NIV). The language from the King James Version reads as follows: "Whom therefore ye ignorantly worship, him declare I unto you."

82. Acts 17:24–28 (NIV). The language from the King James Version reads as follows: "God that made the world and all things therein, seeing that he is Lord of heaven and earth, dwelleth not in temples made with hands; Neither is worshipped with men's hands, as though he needed any thing, seeing he giveth to all life, and breath, and all things; And hath made of one blood all nations of men for to dwell on all the face of the earth, and hath determined the times before appointed, and the bounds of their habitation; That they should seek the Lord, if haply they might feel after him, and find him, though he be not far from every one of us: For in him we live, and move, and have our being; as certain also of your own poets have said, For we are also his offspring."

83. Richard, *Founders and the Classics*, 5, 173, 174–75 (quoting Charles Secondat de Montesquieu, *The Spirit of the Laws*, trans. Thomas Nugent [New York: Colonial Press, 1899], 1:1, 3).

84. Richard, *Founders and the Bible*, 100.

85. Jean-Jacques Burlamaqui, *The Principles of Natural and Politic Law* (1747), pt. 2, "Of the Law of Nature," chap. 1, sec. 12–13; and pt. 2, "Of the Law of Nature," chap. 2, sec. 6.

86. Richard, *Founders and the Bible*, 100, 99. See also Dreisbach, *Reading the Bible with the Founding Fathers*, 12 ("Almost all [of the founders] agreed that there was a Supreme Being who intervened in the affairs of men and nations"), 86–88.

87. Richard, *Founders and the Bible*, 99–103; Dreisbach, *Reading the Bible with the Founding Fathers*, 90–91.

88. Richard, *Founders and the Classics*, 7. For more on Christianity, the Bible, and civic virtue, see Dreisbach, *Reading the Bible with the Founding Fathers*, 66–70.

89. Richard, *Founders and the Classics*, 175.

90. Otis, *Against Writs of Assistance*. The portion here is from John Adams's notes on Otis's speech. The "law written on his heart" is taken from the Holy Bible, Romans 2:15 (KJV).

91. Richard, *Founders and the Bible*, 1, 7, 61. See also Dreisbach, *Reading the Bible with the Founding Fathers*, 66–70.

92. Richard, *Founders and the Classics*, 175.

93. See Garry Wills on the pursuit of happiness and public virtue and Isaac Kramnick's essay differentiating Scottish Enlightenment thinking from "Lockean liberalism or neo-classical republicanism." Wills, *Inventing America*; Isaac Kramnick, "Ideological Background," 90.

94. In addition to Wills, *Inventing America*, see Jan Lewis, "Happiness"; Kramnick, "Ideological Background," 90; and Arthur Herman, "'That Great Design': Scots in America," chap. 9 in *The Scottish Enlightenment: The Scots' Invention of the Modern World*, 219–54.

95. Richard, *Founders and the Classics*, 182.

96. I. Bernard Cohen and Richard S. Westfall, eds., *Newton: A Norton Critical Edition*, xiii.

97. Peterson, *Jefferson and the New Nation*, 386. See also Gay, *The Enlightenment*, 2:559–60.

98. Gay, *The Enlightenment*, 1:11–12, 2:155.

99. Tumbleson, "'Reason and Religion,'" 134–35. See Jacob and Jacob, "Anglican Origins," 258.

100. John Locke, *Essays on the Law of Nature*, 111.

101. Crane, "Anglican Apologetics (Concluded)," 363.

102. Jacob and Jacob, "Anglican Origins," 264.

103. Peterson, *Jefferson and the New Nation*, 47, 48.

104. Cohen and Westfall, *Newton*, 360; Richard S. Westfall, "Newton and Christianity," 356–57.

105. Cohen and Westfall, *Newton*, 358–60.

106. Peterson, *Jefferson and the New Nation*, 47.

107. Edward Dolnick, *The Clockwork Universe: Isaac Newton, the Royal Society & the Birth of the Modern World*, 316.

108. Gay, *The Enlightenment*, 2:129–30; Wills, *Inventing America*, 365–66.

109. Peterson, *Jefferson and the New Nation*, 47.

110. For a discussion of John Adams's application of Newton's scientific methods to the field of political science, see Paynter, "Rhetorical Design," 531.

111. John Adams, *A Defence of the Constitutions of the United States*.

112. Colbourn, *Fame and the Founding Fathers*, 158–60, 191–92. See also Cohen, *Science and the Founding Fathers*, 227–30, 237–38, 257–62.

113. Herman, *Scottish Enlightenment*, 250.

Chapter 6

1. Gay, *The Enlightenment*, 2:555–58.

2. Ibid., 558–59.

3. Richard, *Founders and the Classics*, 81–83; Gay, *The Enlightenment*, 2:561. For Common Sense philosophy, see Barzun, "Common Sense and Legal Science."

4. Gay, *The Enlightenment*, 2:561.

5. For John's description of Christ as logos, see Zodhiates, *Hebrew-Greek Key Word Study Bible*, 1238. For Paul's claims in Acts, see Acts 17:16–28.

6. Gay, *The Enlightenment*, 2:562–63.

7. Stephen Miller, "The Strange Career of Joseph Addison," 650–51; Christine Dunn Henderson and Mark E. Yellin, eds., *Cato, a Tragedy, and Selected Essays*, xxii.

8. Miller, "Strange Career of Joseph Addison," 650–51.

9. Henderson and Yellin, *Cato*, xvi; Miller, "Strange Career of Joseph Addison," 652.

10. Henderson and Yellin, *Cato*, xvi.

11. Gay, *The Enlightenment*, 1:41.

12. Henderson and Yellin, *Cato*, xix.

13. Franklin, *Autobiography*, Part 9.

14. For a description of *Cato* and its impact on George Washington and the founders, see Richard, *Founders and the Classics*, 57–60. See also Henderson and Yellin, *Cato*, xxii.

15. Richard, *Founders and the Classics*, 57–58; Colbourn, *Fame and the Founding Fathers*, 17, 404, 404n.

16. Waterman, "Jefferson and Blackstone's *Commentaries*," 454 (quoting Plucknett, *Concise History*, 207).

17. Ibid. (citing 1 Hammond, "Blackstone" (1890), ix). Interestingly enough, in the late revolutionary and early founding eras, founders like Thomas Jefferson and John Adams began to laud the benefits of Justinian's civil code and to promote it both as the foundation of the English common law and as a system more fully based on reason and, therefore, more fully reflective of natural law principles. See Richard, *Founders and the Classics*, 181–83.

18. Becker, *Declaration of Independence*, 107, 109.

19. Trevor Colbourn, *The Lamp of Experience: Whig History and the Intellectual Origins of the American Revolution*, 227.

20. Horspool, *King Alfred*, 171, 140, 170.

21. The following discussion builds on a brief intellectual history of John Adams, Benjamin Franklin, and Thomas Jefferson in Richard, *Founders and the Classics*, 169–95.

22. Maier, *American Scripture*, 125.

23. Peterson, *Jefferson and the New Nation*, 15–18.

24. Gay, *The Enlightenment*, 2:559.

25. Horspool, *King Alfred*, 170; Colbourn, *Lamp of Experience*, 208–9 (quoting letter from John Adams to Abigail Adams, August 14, 1776, in *Familiar Letters of John Adams*, edited by Charles Francis Adams [1876], 211).

26. Horspool, *King Alfred*, 170.

27. Gay, *The Enlightenment*, 1:55; Peterson, *Jefferson and the New Nation*, 13; Richard, *Founders and the Classics*, 22, 36.

28. Richard, *Founders and the Classics*, 181. For Epictetus, see Onuf, "Ancients, Moderns, and the Progress of Mankind," 35.

29. Herman, *Scottish Enlightenment*, 251.

30. Peterson, *Jefferson and the New Nation*, 15.

31. Richard, *Founders and the Bible*, 1, 243–44, 248; Dreisbach, *Reading the Bible with the Founding Fathers*, 62–64. Dreisbach notes this title as "The Life and Morals of Jesus of Nazareth" and states it is one of two texts Jefferson compiled on the life and morals of Jesus.

32. Richard, *Founders and the Bible*, 1, 243–44, 3, 61, 244 (quoting Jefferson's letter to F. A. Van der Kemp, April 25, 1816, as included in Bergh and Lipscomb, *Writings of Thomas Jefferson*, 15:3).

33. Cooper and Dyer, "Thomas Jefferson, Nature's God, and the Theological Foundations of Natural-Rights Republicanism," 4.

34. Onuf, "Ancients, Moderns, and the Progress of Mankind," 47–48; Richard, *Founders and the Bible*, 102.

35. Thomas Jefferson, "Letter from Thomas Jefferson to William Short (October 31, 1819)," Founders Online, National Archives, https://founders.archives.gov /?q=Recipient%3A%22Short%2C%20William%22&s=1111311111&r=324. For a full discussion of Thomas Jefferson's study of both Epicurus and Jesus, see Onuf, "Ancients, Moderns, and the Progress of Mankind," 47–49.

36. Richard, *Founders and the Bible*, 215–18.

37. Ibid., 1, 24, 43–44. As Dreisbach notes, Adams continued "extensive and serious" study of the Bible during his lifetime. Dreisbach, *Reading the Bible with the Founding Fathers*, 60.

38. Richard, *Founders and the Bible*, 102–3, 111; Dreisbach, *Reading the Bible with the Founding Fathers*, 151.

39. Richard, *Founders and the Classics*, 30–31, 194, 132–33.

40. Farrell, "Young John Adams," 377–78, 388.

41. Gordon Wood, *The Americanization of Benjamin Franklin*, 165.

42. Gay, *The Enlightenment*, 2:559.

43. Richard, *Founders and the Bible*, 78, 4, 66–67; Dreisbach, *Reading the Bible with the Founding Fathers*, 86–91.

44. See especially Adams's discussion of mixed government and its perfection as it moves from Rome to Great Britain to the constitutions of the new United States in John Adams, "Part XXX: Ancient Republics, and Opinions of Philosophers."

45. John Adams, *Notes for an Oration at Braintree*, in *Diary and Autobiography*, 2:57–60 (1772), quoted in Wood, *Americanization of Benjamin Franklin*, 165.

46. For a discussion of John Adams's application of Newton's scientific methods to the field of political science, see Paynter, "Rhetorical Design."

47. Ibid., 558.

48. Duncan Kennedy, "The Structure of Blackstone's *Commentaries*," 236; Marcus Tullius Cicero, *De Inventione*, 31–32. For natural principles, see Marcus Tullius

Cicero, "In Defence of Titus Annius Milo," 215–78, esp. 266; and Cicero, "On the State," 172–74, 183. For more on the Stoic idea of natural principles or exceptionless laws, see Hornblower and Spawforth, *The Oxford Classical Dictionary*, s.v. "Stoicism."

49. Richard, *Founders and the Bible*, 66–67 (quoting L. H. Butterfield, ed., *The Adams Family Correspondence* [Cambridge, MA: Harvard University Press, 1963], John to Abigail Adams, May 17, 1776, 1:410].

50. Gay, *The Enlightenment*, 1:14. For David Hume's appreciation of Franklin, see Gay, *The Enlightenment*, 2:558–59.

51. Gay, *The Enlightenment*, 2:559.

52. Wills, *Inventing America*, 99–100; Herman, *Scottish Enlightenment*, 182, 231–30; Michael Atiyah, "Benjamin Franklin and the Edinburgh Enlightenment," 591, 596–97, 600.

53. Wood, *Americanization of Benjamin Franklin*, 164–66, 215–16, 172 (citing Alfred Owen Aldridge, *Franklin and His French Contemporaries* 26 [1957], 260).

54. Wood, *Americanization of Benjamin Franklin*, 18–19, 56.

55. Richard, *Founders and the Classics*, 196–98, 203–4, 219–20.

56. Gay, *The Enlightenment*, 1:40.

57. Richard, *Founders and the Classics*, 194; Richard, *Founders and the Bible*, 52; Dreisbach, *Reading the Bible with the Founding Fathers*, 54 (on Christ's moral teachings).

58. Richard, *Founders and the Bible*, 71–72, 100–101. See also Dreisbach, *Reading the Bible with the Founding Fathers*, 91–92, 137–44. Dreisbach leaves open the possibility that Franklin's belief in divine Providence might not have been as strong as Franklin's language suggests.

59. Wood, *Americanization of Benjamin Franklin*, 225 (quoting *The Autobiography of Benjamin Franklin* [Leonard Labaree et al., eds., 1964], 161–62), 229 (quoting Franklin's response to Ezra Stiles's letter of March 1790).

Chapter 7

1. Waterman, "Jefferson and Blackstone's *Commentaries*," 451–57 (quoting Wickersham, "Presentation Address of Blackstone Memorial," *American Bar Association Journal* 10 [1924]: 576–78).

2. Ibid., 479, 478 (citing Haines, "Revival of Natural Law Concepts" 54, 56 [1930]; and Wilson, "Works," 3:206 [1804]).

3. Letter from Thomas Jefferson to James Madison (1826) included in Waterman, "Jefferson and Blackstone's *Commentaries*," 459 (quoting from a letter in Thomas Jefferson, *The Works of Thomas Jefferson*, edited by Paul Leicester Ford [1930], 456).

4. Onuf, *Jefferson's Empire*, 94; Hornblower and Spawforth, *The Oxford Classical Dictionary*, s.v. "Libertas." See also the discussion of "classical Latin *lībertāt-*, *lībertās*" in the etymology of liberty in *The Oxford English Dictionary*, s.v. "liberty, n.1."

5. For the influence of Newton at the founding, see Cohen, *Science and the Founding Fathers*; Wills, *Inventing America*; Howard Mumford Jones, *The Pursuit of Happiness*; and Richard, *Founders and the Classics*. For the debate over the founders' and

framers' references to classical antiquity, see Bailyn, *Ideological Origins of the American Revolution*; Onuf, "Ancients, Moderns, and the Progress of Mankind"; Jones, *The Pursuit of Happiness*; Michael Meckler, ed., *Classical Antiquity and the Politics of America: From George Washington to George W. Bush*; and Richard, *Founders and the Classics*. For the influence of the Bible on the founders, see Richard, *Founders and the Bible*; and Dreisbach, *Reading the Bible with the Founding Fathers*.

6. John Adams, "Adams's Resolution Authorizes the Colonies to Establish Legitimate and Independent Governments"; "The Constitution of the Commonwealth of Massachusetts (1780)."

7. Safety as security or safeguard comes from the Old French *sauvete*. Harper, *Online Etymology Dictionary*, s.v. "safety (n.)."

8. Becker, *Declaration of Independence*, 149–50.

9. For a discussion of "glory" and "fame" at the founding, see Douglass Adair, "Fame and the Founding Fathers"; and Colbourn, *Fame and the Founding Fathers*, 17–29.

10. For a discussion of the author of this change, see Becker, *Declaration of Independence*, 139–52.

Chapter 8

1. John Kersey, *A New English Dictionary*, s.v. "happy"; Johnson, *Dictionary of the English Language*, s.v. "happy"; James Buchanan, *A New English Dictionary*, s.v. "happy"; John Walker, *A Critical Pronouncing Dictionary and Expositor of the English Language*, s.v. "happy"; Caleb Alexander, *The Columbian Dictionary of the English Language*, s.v. "happy."

2. Harper, *Online Etymology Dictionary*, s.v. "happy."

3. John Kersey defines "to bless" as "to make happy." Kersey, *A New English Dictionary*, s.v. "happy" and "to bless." See also Buchanan, *A New English Dictionary*, s.v. "happy" and "bless."

4. Francis Bacon, "Of Goodness and Goodness of Nature," 45–48.

5. David Hume, "Essay III: That Politics May Be Reduced to a Science," 18.

6. Francis Hutcheson, "Section III: The Senses of Virtue, and the Various Opinions about It, Reducible to One General Foundation. The Manner of Computing the Morality of Actions," 11:148.

7. John Locke, "Of the Beginning of Political Societies," chap. 8 of *Two Treatises of Government*; John Locke, *An Essay Concerning Human Understanding*, bk. 1, chap. 2, "Neither Principles nor Ideas Are Innate," and bk. 1, chap. 3, "No Innate Practical Principles."

8. Locke, *Essay Concerning Human Understanding*, bk. 1, chap. 2, "Neither Principles nor Ideas Are Innate"; bk. 1, chap. 3, "No Innate Practical Principles"; bk. 2, chap. 1, "Of Ideas"; bk. 2, chap. 21, "Of Power," sec. 52, "The Necessity of Pursuing True Happiness the Foundation of Liberty."

9. Gay, *The Enlightenment*, 1:376–77; Kors, "The Pursuit of Happiness."

10. Jacob and Jacob, "Anglican Origins," 264.

11. Henry Campbell Black, *A Dictionary of Law* (1891 reprint), 692 (citing Edmund Wingate's *Maximes of Reason; or, The Reason of the Common Law of England* [London, 1658] and Henry Finch's volume on law, *Finch's Law* [London, 1627, 1759]).

12. Blackstone, *Commentaries*, 2:7–8.

13. "Resolutions of the Continental Congress, October 19, 1765."

14. *Declaration and Resolves of the First Continental Congress, October 14, 1774.*

15. *A Declaration by the Representatives of the United Colonies of North-America, Now Met in Congress at Philadelphia, Setting Forth the Causes and Necessity of Their Taking Up Arms* (1775).

16. "Virginia Declaration of Rights (June 12, 1776, Virginia Convention of Delegates, Drafted by George Mason)."

17. John Bigelow, ed., *The Works of Benjamin Franklin*, 7–8, 10.

18. Benjamin Franklin, "Speech in the Convention on the Constitution (Unpublished) (Sept. 17, 1787)."

19. John Adams, "'U' to the *Boston Gazette* (Aug. 29, 1763)."

20. John Adams, "'U' to the *Boston Gazette* (Sept. 5, 1763)."

21. John Adams, "Thoughts on Government," 4:86–93.

22. John Adams, "Letter from John Adams to United States Congress (Nov. 22, 1800)," Adams Papers, http://founders.archives.gov/documents/Adams/99-02-02-4691.

23. Jefferson, "Summary View."

24. Thomas Jefferson, "Virginia Nonimportation Resolutions (June 22, 1770)."

25. See also Thomas Jefferson, "First Inaugural Address (Mar. 4, 1801)," "Third Annual Message to Congress (Oct. 17, 1803)," "Eighth Annual Message to Congress (Nov. 8, 1808)," "Second Annual Message to Congress (Dec. 15, 1802)," and "Second Inaugural Address (Mar. 4, 1805)."

26. Jefferson, "Letter from Thomas Jefferson to John Adams (April 25, 1794)," Jefferson Papers, http://founders.archives.gov/documents/Jefferson/01-28-02-0055; "Letter from Thomas Jefferson to John Adams (Dec. 28, 1796)," Jefferson Papers, http://founders.archives.gov/documents/Jefferson/01-29-02-0190-0002.

27. Benjamin Franklin, "A Man of Sense (February 11, 1735)."

28. Benjamin Franklin, "Articles of Belief and Acts of Religion (Nov. 20, 1728)."

28. Benjamin Franklin, "Autobiography, Part 9."

30. Ibid.

31. Aristotle, *The Nichomachean Ethics of Aristotle*, 2.1.1–3.

32. Franklin, "Autobiography, Part 9."

33. Ibid.

34. Ibid.

35. Benjamin Franklin, "Autobiography, Part 7"; Joseph Breintall, "Library Company to John Penn (May 31, 1735)." Benjamin Franklin was one of four men appointed to write this letter from the Library Company to John Penn. The letter is signed by Joseph Breintall, secretary and one of the four men appointed to write the letter.

36. John Adams, "Letter from John Adams to Abigail Adams (Oct. 29, 1775)," Adams Family Papers: An Electronic Archive, http://www.masshist.org/digital adams/archive/doc?id=L17751029ja&bc=%2Fdigitaladams%2Farchive%2F-browse%2Fletters_1774_1777.php.

37. John Adams, *Inaugural Address in the City of Philadelphia* (March 4, 1797).

38. John Adams, "The Massachusetts Constitution of 1780, Part the Second. The Frame of Government., Chapter V. The University at Cambridge, and Encouragement of Literature, etc., Section II. The Encouragement of Literature, etc."

38. John Adams, "Diary 1: 8 November 1755–29 August 1756."

40. Thomas Jefferson, "Letter from Thomas Jefferson to William Short (October 31, 1819)," Founders Online, National Archives, https://founders.archives .gov/?q=Recipient%3A%22Short%2C%20William%22&s=1111311111&r=324.

41. Thomas Jefferson, "Notes on the Doctrine of Epicurus (ca. 1799)"; Thomas Jefferson, "Letter from Thomas Jefferson to José Corrêa da Serra (Apr. 19, 1814)," Jefferson Papers, http://founders.archives.gov/documents/Jefferson/03-07-02-0216.

42. Thomas Jefferson, "Letter from Thomas Jefferson to Amos J. Cook (21 January 1816)," Founders Online, National Archives, https://founders.archives .gov/?q=Project%3A%22Jefferson%20Papers%22%20Author%3A%22Jeffer son%2C%20Thomas%22%20Recipient%3A%22Cook%2C%20Amos%20 J.%22&s=1511311111&r=1&sr=cook.

Chapter 9

1. For an excellent discussion of the philosophy of improvement through the related concept of amelioration of slavery, see Christa Dierksheide, *Amelioration and Empire: Progress and Slavery in the Plantation Americas*.

2. Johnson, *Dictionary of the English Language*, s.v. "improve" and "perfect."

3. Gay, *The Enlightenment*, 1:41 (quoting Marquis D'Argenson: *Considérations sur le gouvernement ancient et présent de la France* [1764, edn. 1765], 23 [emphasis added]), 2:558–59.

4. Thomas Jefferson, "Notes on the State of Virginia," 124.

5. Ibid., 125, 124.

6. Ibid., 243.

7. Ibid., 243–55.

8. Ibid.

9. Ibid., 255.

10. Ibid., 125, 274, 273.

11. Prest, *William Blackstone*, 297.

12. Ibid., 296–301; Prest, "Blackstone and Biography," 10–11.

13. Prest, *William Blackstone*, 296–97.

14. Ibid., 297, 300. 19 George III, c. 74, "An Act to explain and amend the Laws relating to the Transportation, Imprisonment, and other Punishments of certain Offenders," included ibid., 296–97, 299.

15. Harper, *Online Etymology Dictionary*, s.v. "repent," "penitenance," and "penitentiary."

16. Prest, *William Blackstone*, 309, 299.

17. Ibid., 297 (quoting S. Devereaux, "The Making of the Penitentiary Act, 1775–1779," *Historical Journal* 42 [1999]: 405; and J. Aiken, *A View of the Character and Public Services of John Howard Esq.* [1792], 107).

18. Prest, "Blackstone and Biography," 10 (quoting Jeremy Bentham, *A Fragment on Government*, edited by R. Harrison [Cambridge, 1988], 4).

19. Prest, *William Blackstone*, 298; Prest, "Blackstone and Biography," 10–11.

20. Jefferson, "Autobiography," 37–40, 263ff.

21. Ibid., 37–38.

22. Ibid.

23. Ibid., 39.

24. Ibid., 40.

25. Ibid., 41.

26. Jefferson, "Notes on the State of Virginia," 270–71.

27. Gay, *The Enlightenment*, 2:555.

28. Constitution of the United States of America (emphasis added).

29. Carson Holloway, "Securing American Independence: Hamilton's Report on Manufactures," chap. 7 of *Hamilton versus Jefferson in the Washington Administration: Completing the Founding or Betraying the Founding?*, 113–37.

30. Blackstone, *Commentaries*, 1:40, 41.

Conclusion

1. *Green v. Biddle*, 21 U.S. 1, 63 (1823).

2. G. Edward White, "Volumes III–IV: The Marshall Court and Cultural Change, 1815–35," 604–5 (citing *Fletcher v. Peck*, 10 U.S. 87, 133, 143 [1795]), 608–9 (citing *Terrett v. Taylor*, 13 U.S. 43, 52 [1815]).

3. "Substance" is defined as "the essential part." Johnson, *Dictionary of the English Language*, s.v. "substance."

4. G. E. White, "Volumes III–IV," 2.

5. Lewis, *Pursuit of Happiness*; Wills, *Inventing America*.

6. Garner, *Black's Law Dictionary*, s.v. "pursuit."

Appendix I

1. This overview does not attempt to discuss the works on Blackstone that are more biographical in nature, but, instead, addresses those works that have been most dominant in seeking to identify the purpose, content, and value of Blackstone's *Commentaries*. For an excellent discussion of the history and quality of the biographies on William Blackstone, see Prest, "Blackstone and Biography."

2. Prest, "Blackstone and Biography," 6 (citing E. Foss, *The Judges of England* [London, 1848–64], 8:250).

3. Prest, "Blackstone and Biography," 6, 10.

4. Boorstin, *Mysterious Science of the Law*, 187–90.

5. Kennedy, "Structure of Blackstone's *Commentaries*," 210–11.

6. I. G. Doolittle, "Sir William Blackstone and His 'Commentaries on the Laws of England' (1765–9): A Biographical Approach," 111, 112.

7. I. G. Doolittle, *William Blackstone: A Biography*, 46–47, 82–83.

8. Doolittle, "Sir William Blackstone," 111–12.

9. Watson, "Structure of Blackstone's *Commentaries*," 795–96, 806, 811.

10. Michael Lobban, "Blackstone and the Science of the Law," 311, 321.

11. Lieberman, *Province of Legislation Determined*, 56–57, 66–67, 36–37.

12. See Prest, "Blackstone and Biography" and *William Blackstone*.

13. Prest, "Blackstone and Biography," 9–11.

14. Matthews, "'Model of the Old House,'" 34.

15. Prest, "Blackstone and Biography," 10.

16. Kennedy, "Structure of Blackstone's *Commentaries*," 211.

17. Boorstin, *Mysterious Science of the Law*, 187–88.

18. Lieberman, *Province of Legislation Determined*, 56–57, 66–67, 32–37.

19. Prest, "Blackstone and Biography," 10.

20. Matthews, "'Model of the Old House,'" 34.

21. Ibid., 15–34.

22. Ibid., 29 (quoting Blackstone, *Letters*, 4), 30 (citing Blackstone, *Commentaries*, 4:436); Blackstone, *Commentaries*, 1:38–43.

Appendix II

1. Becker, *Declaration of Independence*, 278–79, 237, 247.

2. Maier, *American Scripture*, xix, 125–26.

3. Scott, *In Pursuit of Happiness*, 29, chaps. 2–3.

4. Ibid., 5.

5. Peterson, *Jefferson and the New Nation*, 94–95.

6. Scott, *In Pursuit of Happiness*, 40–43, x (emphasis added).

7. Ibid., 24–26, 47, 35.

8. Ibid., 29–30, 36–37.

9. Ibid., 41–42.

10. The full quotation from Jefferson is included in Jefferson's August 30, 1823, letter to James Madison. Jefferson stated: "Rich Lee charged it as copied from Locke's treatise on government. Otis's pamphlet I never saw, & whether I gathered my ideas from reading or reflection I do not know. Know only that I turned to neither book or pamphlet while writing it. I did not consider it as any part of my charge to invent new ideas altogether & to offer no sentiment which had ever been expressed before." Hazelton, *Declaration of Independence*, 143–44.

11. Maier, *American Scripture*, 125–26.

12. Hall, Wiecek, and Finkelman, *American Legal History*, 69.

13. Ibid., 69.

14. Locke, *Essay on Human Understanding*.

15. Indeed, Maier argues that Jefferson's pursuit of happiness is a more succinct version of Mason's language in the Virginia Declaration of Rights and that Jefferson "meant to say more economically and movingly what Mason stated with some

awkwardness and at considerably greater length." Maier, *American Scripture*, 134. Maier argues that the phrase "no doubt demanded safety or security, and probably also included 'the means of acquiring and possessing property,' but not the ownership of specific things since property can be sold and is therefore alienable." Thus, Maier believes that Jefferson's language is simply a "rewriting of Mason" to create "a more memorable statement of the same content." Maier, *American Scripture*, 134. However, like Scott she does not address the distinction between the right to property and the right to the pursuit of happiness. Neither does she provide evidence that Jefferson (or Mason) intended the pursuit of happiness to represent a general sense of "safety and security" in society.

16. Crowley, *Invention of Comfort*, 142–43, 200.

17. Ibid., 142–43, 159–60.

18. Ibid., 143, 149, 198, 142.

19. Ibid., 165 (quoting Adam Smith, *Wealth of Nations*), 174 (quoting letter from Benjamin Franklin to Lord Kames), 200.

20. Ibid., 143, 159, 165.

21. Lewis, *Pursuit of Happiness*, xiii, xiv.

22. Ibid., xiii–xiv.

23. Ibid., xiv, xiii, 200.

24. Jan Lewis, "Happiness," 631, 641–45.

25. Lewis, *Pursuit of Happiness*, xiii.

26. Wills, *Inventing America*, 164.

27. Ibid., 365–66, 93, 100.

28. Ibid., 151, 247 (quoting Francis Hutcheson), 217, 254 (quoting Adam Smith).

29. Ibid., 164.

30. Ibid., 247.

31. Hall, Wiecek, and Finkelman, *American Legal History*, 69.

Appendix III

1. Hammond, *"Commentaries,"* vii–viii, xiv–xvi.

2. Ibid., viii; Blackstone, *Commentaries on the Laws of England* (Philadelphia ed.).

3. For information on the first Bell edition and Adams's and Jefferson's ownership of it, see Gold, "Books the Founders Read"; and, for Adams, Prest and Widener, "250 Years of Blackstone's *Commentaries*."

4. Hammond, *"Commentaries,"* viii.

5. Compare Blackstone, *Commentaries*, 1:38–44, with William Blackstone, *Commentaries on the Laws of England* (Philadelphia ed.), 1:38–44.

6. Blackstone, *Commentaries*, 1:41.

7. Hammond, *"Commentaries,"* xv.

8. Ibid., 69.

9. Blackstone, *Commentaries*, 1:41.

10. Hammond shows no changes to Blackstone's use of "real" or "substantial" on vol. 1, p. 41, in the first eight editions of the *Commentaries*. See Hammond, *"Commentaries,"* 69.

11. Blackstone changed "attained" to "obtained" in the eighth edition. Hammond, *"Commentaries,"* 68.

12. Blackstone changed "that man should "pursue his own happiness" to "that man should pursue his own true and substantial happiness" in the eighth edition. Ibid., 69.

13. Hammond claims that this phrase in the first edition was "(primarily speaking)," but the first edition shows the phrase as "(humanly speaking)." Hammond's claim here appears to be a scrivener's error; "(humanly speaking)" makes more sense, given the context.

14. Blackstone changed this sentence in the second edition to read as follows: "Yet undoubtedly the revealed law is of infinitely more authenticity than that moral system, which is framed by ethical writers, and denominated the natural law." Interestingly enough, this change appears in Bell's 1771–72 edition, suggesting that Bell's reprint was from the second, third, or fourth London edition, all of which were printed before 1771; the fifth London edition was published in 1773. Hammond, *"Commentaries,"* xii, xxii.

15. Hammond states that Blackstone replaced "either" with "any" in edits that were published in the posthumous ninth edition. Hammond, *"Commentaries,"* 72.

Appendix IV

1. Becker, *Declaration of Independence*, 160–71.

Appendix V

1. Becker, *Declaration of Independence*, 174–84. Later historians Julian Boyd and Pauline Maier also attempted to reproduce earlier drafts of the Declaration. For Boyd's reconstruction of Jefferson's "original Rough draught," see *The Papers of Thomas Jefferson*, 243–47, which is available through the Library of Congress at "Declaring Independence: Drafting the Documents," "Jefferson's 'original Rough draught' of the Declaration of Independence," https://www.loc.gov/exhibits/declara/ruffdrft.html. For Maier's reconstruction of the Committee of Five's draft with Congress's changes marked, see *American Scripture*, appx. C, pp. 235–41.

BIBLIOGRAPHY

Adair, Douglass. "Fame and the Founding Fathers." In *Fame and the Founding Fathers: Papers and Comments*, edited by Edmund P. Willis, 27–52. Bethlehem, PA: Moravian College, 1967.

Adams, John. "Adams's Resolution Authorizes the Colonies to Establish Legitimate and Independent Governments." In *John Adams and the Massachusetts Constitution*. Government of Massachusetts. http://www.mass.gov/courts/court-info/sjc/edu-res-center/jn-adams/mass-constitution-1-gen.html#TheMassachusettsConstitution.

———. "Autobiography, Part 1, through 1776." Sheet 24 of 53 [electronic edition]. Adams Family Papers: An Electronic Archive. Massachusetts Historical Society. http://www.masshist.org/digitaladams/.

———. *A Defence of the Constitutions of the United States*. 1787–88. Reprint, New York: Da Capo Press, 1971.

———. "Diary 1: 8 November 1755–29 August 1756" [electronic edition]. Adams Family Papers: An Electronic Archive. Massachusetts Historical Society. http://www.masshist.org/digitaladams/.

———. *Inaugural Address in the City of Philadelphia* (March 4, 1797). http://www.gutenberg.org/files/925/925-h/925-h.htm#link2H_4_0003.

———. "The Massachusetts Constitution of 1780." Included in *The Founders' Constitution*, vol. 1, chap. 1, doc. 6. http://press-pubs.uchicago.edu/founders/documents/v1ch1s6.html.

———. "Part XXX: Ancient Republics, and Opinions of Philosophers." In *A Defence of the Constitutions of the United States*. 1787–88. Reprint, New York: Da Capo Press, 1971. http://www.constitution.org/jadams/ja1_00.htm.

———. "Thoughts on Government." In *Papers of John Adams*, edited by Robert J. Taylor et al. Cambridge: Belknap Press of Harvard University Press, 1977–. Included in *The Founders' Constitution*, vol. 1, chap. 4, doc. 5. April 1776. Papers 4: 86–93. http://press-pubs.uchicago.edu/founders/documents/v1ch4s5.html.

———. "'U' to the *Boston Gazette* (Aug. 29, 1763)." In *Papers of John Adams*, edited by Robert Taylor, 1:76–81. Cambridge, MA: Belknap Press of Harvard University Press, 1977.

———. "'U' to the *Boston Gazette* (Sept. 5, 1763)." In *Papers of John Adams*, edited by Robert Taylor, 1:84–90. Cambridge, MA: Belknap Press of

Harvard University Press, 1977. http://founders.archives.gov/documents/Adams/06-01-02-0045-0009.

Alexander, Caleb. *The Columbian Dictionary of the English Language.* Boston: Isaiah Thomas and Ebenezer T. Andrews, 1800. Eighteenth Century Collections Online, EBSCO Industries.

Anderson, Robert. *British Universities Past and Present.* New York: Hambledon Continuum, 2006.

Aristotle. *The Nichomachean Ethics of Aristotle.* Translated by F. H. Peters. 5th ed. London: Kegan Paul, Trench, Truebner, 1893. http://oll.libertyfund.org/titles/903#Aristotle_0328_25.

Atiyah, Michael. "Benjamin Franklin and the Edinburgh Enlightenment." *Proceedings of the American Philosophical Society* 150, no. 4 (2006): 591–606.

Bacon, Francis. "Of Goodness and Goodness of Nature." In *Essays, Civil and Moral*, edited by Henry Morley. London: Cassell, 1907. Accessed through University of Missouri Library ebooks.

Bailyn, Bernard. *The Ideological Origins of the American Revolution.* Cambridge, MA: Belknap Press of Harvard University Press, 1967.

Barker, John W. *Justinian and the Later Roman Empire.* 1966. Reprint, Madison: University of Wisconsin Press, 1977.

Barlow, Frank. *Edward the Confessor.* Berkeley: University of California Press, 1970.

Barzun, Charles L. "Common Sense and Legal Science." *Virginia Law Review* 4 (2004): 1051–92.

Becker, Carl. *The Declaration of Independence: A Study in the History of Political Ideas.* New York: Harcourt Brace, 1922.

Bentham, Jeremy, and John Lind. *An Answer to the Declaration of the American Congress.* London: n.p., 1776.

Bigelow, John, ed. *The Works of Benjamin Franklin.* Vol. 2. New York and London: G. P. Putnam's Sons, 1904. http://oll.libertyfund.org/title/2454/231483.

Bilder, Mary Sarah. *The Transatlantic Constitution: Colonial Legal Culture and the Empire.* Cambridge, MA: Harvard University Press, 2004.

Black, Henry Campbell. *A Dictionary of Law.* St. Paul, MN: West, 1891 digital reprint.

Blackstone, William. *Commentaries on the Laws of England.* Oxford: Clarendon Press, 1765–69. Reprint, Buffalo, NY: William S. Hein, 1992. Citations refer to the reprint edition.

———. *Commentaries on the Laws of England.* Philadelphia: Printed for the subscribers by Robert Bell, 1771–72.

Boorstin, Daniel J. *The Mysterious Science of the Law.* Boston: Beacon Press, 1941.

Boyd, Julian P. *The Declaration of Independence: The Evolution of the Text as Shown in Facsimiles of Various Drafts by Its Author.* Princeton, NJ: Princeton University Press. 1945.

———, ed. *The Papers of Thomas Jefferson.* Vol. 1, *1760–1776.* Princeton, NJ: Princeton University Press, 1950. https://jeffersonpapers.princeton.edu/volumes/volume-1.

Boyer, Allen D., ed. *Law, Liberty, and Parliament: Selected Essays on the Writings of Sir Edward Coke*. Indianapolis: Liberty Fund, 2004.

Breintall, Joseph. "Library Company to John Penn (May 31, 1735)." Papers of Benjamin Franklin. https://franklinpapers.org/framedVolumes.jsp.

Broadie, Alexander. *A History of Scottish Philosophy*. Edinburgh: Edinburgh University Press, 2008.

Buchanan, James. *A New English Dictionary*. London, 1769. Eighteenth Century Collections Online, EBSCO Industries.

Burlamaqui, Jean-Jacques. *The Principles of Natural and Politic Law*. N.p., 1747.

Campbell, James, ed. *The Anglo-Saxons*. London and New York: Penguin Books, 1991.

Cicero, Marcus Tullius. *De Inventione*. Translated by Charles Duke Yonge. London: George Bell & Sons, 1888. http://www.classicpersuasion.org/pw/cicero/dnvindex.htm.

———. "In Defence of Titus Annius Milo." In *Selected Political Speeches of Cicero*, translated by Michael Grant, 215–78. London: Penguin Books, 1969.

———. "On Laws." In *On Government*, translated by Michael Grant. London: Penguin Books, 1993.

———. "On the State." In *On Government*, translated by Michael Grant. London: Penguin Books, 1993.

———. "Pro Archia ('For Archias')." In *Cicero: Defence Speeches*, translated by D. H. Berry. New York: Oxford University Press, 2000.

Cohen, I. Bernard. *Science and the Founding Fathers: Science in the Political Thought of Jefferson, Franklin, Adams and Madison*. New York: W. W. Norton, 1995.

Cohen, I. Bernard, and Richard S. Westfall, eds. *Newton: A Norton Critical Edition*. New York: W. W. Norton, 1995.

Colbourn, Trevor, ed. *Fame and the Founding Fathers: Essays by Douglass Adair*. Indianapolis: Liberty Fund, 1998.

———. *The Lamp of Experience: Whig History and the Intellectual Origins of the American Revolution*. Chapel Hill: University of North Carolina Press, 1998.

"The Constitution of the Commonwealth of Massachusetts (1780)." In *John Adams and the Massachusetts Constitution*. Government of Massachusetts. http://www.mass.gov/courts/court-info/sjc/edu-res-center/jn-adams/mass-constitution-1-gen.html#TheMassachusettsConstitution.

Cooper, Kody W., and Justin Buckley Dyer. "Thomas Jefferson, Nature's God, and the Theological Foundations of Natural-Rights Republicanism." *Politics and Religion* (2017): 1–27.

Coquillette, Daniel R. *The Anglo-American Legal Heritage*. 1999. Reprint, Durham, NC: Carolina Academic Press, 2004.

Crane, Ronald S. "Anglican Apologetics and the Idea of Progress, 1699–1745." *Modern Philology* 31, no. 3 (1934): 273–306.

———. "Anglican Apologetics and the Idea of Progress, 1699–1745 (Concluded)." *Modern Philology* 31, no. 4 (1934): 349–82.

Crowley, John E. *The Invention of Comfort: Sensibilities & Design in Early Modern Britain & Early America*. Baltimore: Johns Hopkins University Press, 2001.

Cunliffe, Christopher, ed. *Joseph Butler's Moral and Religious Thought: Tercentenary Essays*. Oxford: Clarendon Press, 1992.

Declaration and Resolves of the First Continental Congress, October 14, 1774. http://avalon.law.yale.edu/18th_century/resolves.asp.

A Declaration by the Representatives of the United Colonies of North-America, Now Met in Congress at Philadelphia, Setting Forth the Causes and Necessity of Their Taking Up Arms [1775]. http://avalon.law.yale.edu/18th_century/arms.asp.

Declaration of Independence: A Transcription. America's Founding Documents, National Archives. https://www.archives.gov/founding-docs/declaration-transcript.

Devettere, Raymond J. *Introduction to Virtue Ethics: Insights of the Ancient Greeks*. Washington, DC: Georgetown University Press, 2002.

Dierksheide, Christa. *Amelioration and Empire: Progress and Slavery in the Plantation Americas*. Charlottesville: University Press of Virginia, 2014.

Dolnick, Edward. *The Clockwork Universe: Isaac Newton, the Royal Society & the Birth of the Modern World*. New York: Harper Perennial, 2011.

Doolittle, I. G. "Sir William Blackstone and His 'Commentaries on the Laws of England' (1765–1769): A Biographical Approach." *Oxford Journal of Legal Studies* 3 (1983): 99–112.

———. *William Blackstone: A Biography*. N.p.: Ian Doolittle, 2001.

Dreisbach, Daniel. *Reading the Bible with the Founding Fathers*. New York: Oxford University Press, 2017.

Dunne, Gerald T. "American Blackstone." *Washington University Law Quarterly* 3 (1963): 321–37.

Farrell, James M. "'Syren Tully' and the Young John Adams." *Classical Journal* 87 (1992): 373–90.

Finkelman, Paul. "Jefferson and Slavery: 'Treason against the Hopes of the World.'" In *Jeffersonian Legacies*, edited by Peter S. Onuf, 181–224. Charlottesville: University Press of Virginia, 1993.

Franklin, Benjamin. "Articles of Belief and Acts of Religion (Nov. 20, 1728)." Papers of Benjamin Franklin, vol. 1. http://franklinpapers.org/framedVolumes.jsp.

———. "Autobiography, Part 7." Papers of Benjamin Franklin. http://franklinpapers.org/framedVolumes.jsp.

———. "Autobiography, Part 9." Papers of Benjamin Franklin. http://franklinpapers.org/framedVolumes.jsp.

———. "A Man of Sense (February 11, 1735)." Papers of Benjamin Franklin, vol. 2. http://franklinpapers.org/framedVolumes.jsp.

———. "Speech in the Convention on the Constitution (Unpublished) (Sept. 17, 1787)." Papers of Benjamin Franklin. http://franklinpapers.org/framedVolumes.jsp.

Garner, Brian A., ed. *Black's Law Dictionary*. 10th ed. St. Paul, MN: Thomson Reuters, 2014.

Gay, Peter. *The Enlightenment*. Vol. 1, *The Rise of Paganism*. 1969. Reprint, New York: W. W. Norton, 1995.
———. *The Enlightenment*. Vol. 2, *The Science of Freedom*. 1969. Reprint, New York: W. W. Norton, 1996.
Gold, Lisa. "Books the Founders Read: Blackstone's *Commentaries on the Laws of England*" [April 21, 2015]. Bauman Rare Books. https://www.bauman-rarebooks.com/blog/blackstones-commentaries-books-founders-read/.
Hall, Kermit L., William Wiecek, and Paul Finkelman. *American Legal History: Cases and Materials*. 2nd ed. New York: Oxford University Press, 1996.
Hammond, William G., ed. *"Commentaries on the Laws of England" by Sir William Blackstone, KT., One of the Justices of His Majesty's Court of Common Pleas. From the Author's Eighth Edition, 1778. Edited for American Lawyers*. San Francisco: Bancroft-Whitney, 1890.
Harper, Douglas, ed. *Online Etymology Dictionary*. 2001–17. http://www.etymon-line.com.
Hazelton, John. *The Declaration of Independence: Its History*. 1906. Reprint, New York: Da Capo Press, 1970.
Henderson, Christine Dunn, and Mark E. Yellin, eds. *Cato, a Tragedy, and Selected Essays*. Indianapolis: Liberty Fund, 2004.
Herman, Arthur. *The Scottish Enlightenment: The Scots' Invention of the Modern World*. London: Harper Perennial, 2001.
Hofstetter, Michael J. *The Romantic Idea of a University: England and Germany, 1770–1850*. New York: Palgrave, 2001.
Holloway, Carson. *Hamilton versus Jefferson in the Washington Administration: Completing the Founding or Betraying the Founding?* New York: Cambridge University Press, 2016.
Hornblower, Simon, and Anthony Spawforth, eds. *The Oxford Classical Dictionary*. 3rd ed. Oxford: Oxford University Press, 2003.
Horspool, David. *King Alfred: Burnt Cakes and Other Legends*. Cambridge, MA: Harvard University Press, 2006.
Hume, David. "That Politics May Be Reduced to a Science." In *Essays Moral, Political, Literary*, edited by Eugene F. Miller. Indianapolis: Liberty Fund, 1987. http://oll.libertyfund.org/title/704/137482 on 2014-02-02.
Hutcheson, Francis. "Section III: The Senses of Virtue, and the Various Opinions about It, Reducible to One General Foundation. The Manner of Computing the Morality of Actions." In *An Inquiry into the Original of Our Ideas of Beauty and Virtue in Two Treatises*, edited by Wolfgang Leidhold. Indianapolis: Liberty Fund, 2004. http://oll.libertyfund.org/title/2462/244474.
Jacob, James R., and Margaret C. Jacob. "The Anglican Origins of Modern Science: The Metaphysical Foundations of the Whig Constitution." *Isis* 71 (1980): 251.
Jefferson, Thomas. "Autobiography." In *Thomas Jefferson: Writings*, edited by Merrill D. Peterson, 1–102. New York: Library of America, 1984.
———. "Eighth Annual Message to Congress (Nov. 8, 1808)." Jefferson Papers. http://avalon.law.yale.edu/19th_century/jeffmes8.asp.

————. "First Inaugural Address (Mar. 4, 1801)." Jefferson Papers. http://avalon. law.yale.edu/19th_century/jefinau1.asp.

————. "From Thomas Jefferson to Henry Lee, May 8, 1825." In *Thomas Jefferson: Writings*, edited by Merrill D. Peterson, 1500–1501. New York: Library of America, 1984.

————. "From Thomas Jefferson to James Madison, 30 August 1823." Founders Online, National Archives. http://founders.archives.gov/documents/ Jefferson/98-01-02-3728.

————. "Jefferson's 'Original Rough Draught' of the Declaration of Independence." In *Declaring Independence: Drafting the Documents, Library of Congress, Exhibitions*. https://www.loc.gov/exhibits/declara/ruffdrft.html.

————. "Notes on the Doctrine of Epicurus (ca. 1799)." Jefferson Papers. http:// founders.archives.gov/documents/Jefferson/01-31-02-0241.

————. "Notes on the State of Virginia." In *Thomas Jefferson: Writings*, edited by Merrill D. Peterson, 123–326. New York: Library of America, 1984.

————. "Second Annual Message to Congress (Dec. 15, 1802)." Jefferson Papers. http://avalon.law.yale.edu/19th_century/jeffmes2.asp.

————. "Second Inaugural Address (Mar. 4, 1805)." Jefferson Papers. http://avalon.law.yale.edu/19th_century/jefinau2.asp.

————. "A Summary View of the Rights of British America." In *Thomas Jefferson: Writings*, edited by Merrill D. Peterson, 105–22. New York: Library of America, 1984.

————. "Third Annual Message to Congress (Oct. 17, 1803)." Jefferson Papers. http://avalon.law.yale.edu/19th_century/jeffmes3.asp.

————. "Virginia Nonimportation Resolutions (June 22, 1770)." Jefferson Papers. http://founders.archives.gov/documents/Jefferson/01-01-02-0032.

Johnson, Samuel. *A Dictionary of the English Language*. London: W. Strahan, 1755. 2011 digital edition. http://johnsonsdictionaryonline.com/.

Jones, Howard Mumford. *The Pursuit of Happiness*. Cambridge, MA: Harvard University Press, 1953.

Kennedy, Duncan. "The Structure of Blackstone's *Commentaries*." *Buffalo Law Review* 28 (1979): 205–382.

Kersey, John. *A New English Dictionary*. London, 1702. Eighteenth Century Collections Online, EBSCO Industries.

Keynes, Simon, and Michael Lapidge, trans. *Alfred the Great: Asser's Life of King Alfred and Other Contemporary Sources*. London: Penguin Books, 1983.

Koch, Adrienne, and William Peden, eds. *The Life and Selected Writings of Thomas Jefferson*. New York: Random House, 1944.

Kors, Alan Charles. "The Pursuit of Happiness." Address presented at the Lehrman American Studies Institute of Princeton University, Princeton, NJ, June 16, 2010.

Kramnick, Isaac. "Ideological Background." in *The Blackwell Encyclopedia of the American Revolution*, edited by Jack P. Greene and J. R. Pole. Cambridge, MA: Blackwell Reference, 1991.

Kynell, Kurt von S. *Saxon and Medieval Antecedents of the English Common Law.* Lewiston, NY: Edwin Mellen Press, 2000.

Lewis, Jan. "Happiness." In *The Blackwell Encyclopedia of the American Revolution,* edited by Jack P. Greene and J. R. Pole, 641–47. Cambridge, MA: Basil Blackwell, 1991.

———. *The Pursuit of Happiness: Family and Values in Jefferson's Virginia.* Cambridge: Cambridge University Press, 1983.

Library of Congress, Exhibitions. "Declaring Independence: Drafting the Documents." https://www.loc.gov/exhibits/declara/declara2.html.

Lieberman, David. *The Province of Legislation Determined: Legal Theory in Eighteenth-Century Britain.* New York: Cambridge University Press, 1989.

Lobban, Michael. "Blackstone and the Science of the Law." *Historical Journal* 30, no. 2 (1987): 311–35.

Locke, John. *An Essay Concerning Human Understanding.* London: n.p., 1690.

———. *Essays on the Law of Nature.* Edited by Wolfgang von Leyden. London: Oxford University Press, 2002.

———. *Two Treatises of Government.* Edited by Thomas Hollis. London: A. Millar et al., 1764. http://oll.libertyfund.org/title/222/16342/704533.

Lockmiller, David A. *Sir William Blackstone.* Chapel Hill: University of North Carolina Press, 1938.

Maier, Pauline. *American Scripture: Making the Declaration of Independence.* New York: Alfred A. Knopf, 1997.

Matthews, Carol. "A 'Model of the Old House': Architecture in Blackstone's Life and *Commentaries.*" In *Blackstone and His Commentaries: Biography, Law, History,* edited by Wilfrid Prest, 15–34. London: Bloomsbury, 2009.

May, Henry F. *The Enlightenment in America.* Oxford: Oxford University Press, 1978.

McMahon, Darrin M. *Happiness: A History.* New York: Atlantic Monthly Press, 2006.

Meckler, Michael, ed. *Classical Antiquity and the Politics of America: From George Washington to George W. Bush.* Waco, TX: Baylor University Press, 2006.

Meyer, Susan Suavé. *Ancient Ethics: A Critical Introduction.* London: Routledge, 2008.

Miller, Stephen. "The Strange Career of Joseph Addison." *Sewanee Review* 122, no. 4 (2014): 650–60.

Mossner, Ernest Campbell. *Bishop Butler and the Age of Reason: A Study in the History of Thought.* New York: Macmillan, 1971.

Onuf, Peter S. "Ancients, Moderns, and the Progress of Mankind: Thomas Jefferson's Classical World." In *Thomas Jefferson, the Classical World, and Early America,* edited by Peter S. Onuf and Nicholas P. Cole, 35–55. Charlottesville: University of Virginia Press, 2011.

———, ed. *Jeffersonian Legacies.* Charlottesville: University Press of Virginia, 1993.

———. *Jefferson's Empire: The Language of American Nationhood.* Charlottesville: University of Virginia Press, 2000.

Onuf, Peter S., and Nicholas P. Cole, eds. *Thomas Jefferson, the Classical World, and Early America*. Charlottesville: University Press of Virginia, 2011.

Otis, James. *Against Writs of Assistance* [February 1761]. National Humanities Institute. http://www.nhinet.org/ccs/docs/writs.htm.

Paynter, John E. "The Rhetorical Design of John Adams's 'Defence of the Constitutions of . . . America.'" *Review of Politics* 58 (1996): 531–60.

Penelhum, Terrence. *Butler*. Boston: Routledge and Kegan Paul, 1985.

Peterson, Merrill D. *Thomas Jefferson and the New Nation: A Biography*. Oxford: Oxford University Press, 1970.

Plucknett, Theodore F. T. *A Concise History of the Common Law*. 5th ed. Boston: Little, Brown, 1956.

Presser, Stephen B., and Jamil S. Zainaldin. *Law and Jurisprudence in American History*. 5th ed. St. Paul, MN: West Academic, 2003.

Prest, Wilfrid R. "Blackstone and Biography." In *Blackstone and His "Commentaries": Biography, Law, History*, edited by Wilfrid Prest, 3–14. Oxford and Portland, OR: Hart, 2009.

———, ed. *Blackstone and His "Commentaries": Biography, Law, History*. Oxford and Portland, OR: Hart, 2009.

———, ed. *Re-interpreting Blackstone's "Commentaries": A Seminal Text in National and International Contexts*. Oxford and Portland, OR: Hart, 2014.

———. *William Blackstone: Law and Letters*. Oxford: Oxford University Press, 2008.

Prest, Wilfrid R., and Michael Widener. "250 Years of Blackstone's *Commentaries*: An Exhibition/Curated by Wilfrid Prest, Michael Widener" (2015). *British Law*, bk. 3. http://digitalcommons.law.yale.edu/amlaw/10/.

Prior, William J. *Virtue and Knowledge: An Introduction to Ancient Greek Ethics*. London: Routledge, 1991.

"Resolutions of the Continental Congress, October 19, 1765." http://avalon.law.yale.edu/18th_century/resolu65.asp.

Richard, Carl J. *The Founders and the Bible*. Lanham, MD: Rowman & Littlefield, 2016.

———. *The Founders and the Classics: Greece, Rome, and the American Enlightenment*. Cambridge, MA: Harvard University Press, 1994.

Scott, William B. *In Pursuit of Happiness: American Conceptions of Property from the Seventeenth to the Twentieth Century*. Bloomington: Indiana University Press, 1977.

Shain, Barry. *The Declaration of Independence in Historical Context: American State Papers, Petitions, Proclamations & Letters of the Delegates to the First National Congresses*. New Haven, CT: Yale University Press, 2014.

Sigmund, Paul E., ed. *The Selected Political Writings of John Locke*. New York: W. W. Norton, 2005.

Spalding, James C. "Loyalist as Royalist, Patriot as Puritan: The American Revolution as a Repetition of the English Civil Wars." *Church History* 45 (1976): 329–40.

Spooner, William Archibald. *Bishop Butler.* London: Methuen, 1901.

St. Germain, Christopher. *The Doctor and Student* [1518]. Cincinnati: Robert Clarke, 1886. https://archive.org/details/doctorstudentord00sain/page/n5.

Stanton, Lucia C. "'Those Who Labor for My Happiness': Thomas Jefferson and His Slaves." In *Jeffersonian Legacies*, edited by Peter S. Onuf, 147–80. Charlottesville: University Press of Virginia, 1993.

Stein, Peter. *Roman Law in European History.* Cambridge: Cambridge University Press, 1999.

Stern, Craig A. "Justinian: Lieutenant of Christ, Legislator for Christendom." *Regent University Law Review* 11 (1998–99): 151–67.

Tubbs, J. W. *The Common Law Mind: Medieval and Early Modern Conceptions.* Baltimore: Johns Hopkins University Press, 2000.

Tumbleson, Raymond D. "'Reason and Religion': The Science of Anglicanism." *Journal of the History of Ideas* 57 (1996): 131–56.

Ure, P. N. *Justinian and His Age.* 1951. Reprint, Westport, CT: Greenwood Press, 1979.

"Virginia Declaration of Rights (June 12, 1776, Virginia Convention of Delegates, Drafted by George Mason)." http://avalon.law.yale.edu/18th_century/virginia.asp.

Walker, John. *A Critical Pronouncing Dictionary and Expositor of the English Language.* Dublin: P. Wogan, Old-Bridge, 1798. Eighteenth Century Collections Online, EBSCO Industries.

Waterman, Julian S. "Thomas Jefferson and Blackstone's *Commentaries.*" In *Essays in the History of Early American Law*, edited by David H. Flaherty, 451–88. Chapel Hill: University of North Carolina Press, 1969.

Watson, Alan. "The Structure of Blackstone's *Commentaries.*" *Yale Law Journal* 97 (1987–88): 795–821.

Webster, Leslie, and Janet Backhouse, eds. *The Making of England: Anglo-Saxon Art and Culture, AD 600–900.* Toronto: University of Toronto Press, 1991.

Webster's New Universal Unabridged Dictionary. New York: Barnes & Noble, 1996.

Westfall, Richard S. "Newton and Christianity." In *Newton: A Norton Critical Edition*, edited by I. Bernard Cohen and Richard S. Westfall, 365–70. New York: W. W. Norton, 1995.

The Westminster Confession of Faith. In *The Constitution and Standards of the Associate-Reformed Church in North America.* New York: T. & J. Swords, 1799.

White, David E., ed. *The Works of Bishop Butler.* Rochester, NY: University of Rochester Press, 2006.

White, G. Edward. "Recovering the World of the Marshall Court." *John Marshall Law Review* 33 (1999–2000): 781–821.

———. "Volumes III–IV: The Marshall Court and Cultural Change, 1815–35." In *The Oliver Wendell Holmes Devise: History of the Supreme Court of the United States*, edited by G. Edward White et al. New York: Macmillan, 1988.

Wills, Garry. *Inventing America: Jefferson's Declaration of Independence.* Garden City, NY: Doubleday, 1978.

Wood, Gordon. *The Americanization of Benjamin Franklin*. New York: Penguin
    Press, 2004.
————. *The Creation of the American Republic, 1776–1787*. Chapel Hill: University
    of North Carolina Press, 1969.
Zodhiates, Spiros, ed. *Hebrew-Greek Key Word Study Bible: New International Version*.
    Chattanooga, TN: AMG, 1996.

INDEX

Note: page numbers followed by *n* refer to notes, with note number

ABOUT THE AUTHOR

Carli N. Conklin is Associate
Professor at the University of
Missouri School of Law. She
lives in central Missouri.